GEORGIA
100 BEST PLACES TO VISIT
BUCKET LIST

Copyright © 2024

ISBN: 9798344322261

All rights reserved.

No part of this publication may be reproduced, distributed or transmitted in any form or by any means, including photocopying, recording or other electronic or mechanical methods, without the prior written permission of the publisher, except in the case of brief quotations embodied in reviews and certain other non commercial uses permitted by copyright law.

ABOUT GEORGIA

Georgia is a state in the southeastern United States and one of the 13 original colonies. It ranks fourth in total area among U.S. states east of the Mississippi River, and it's the largest in terms of land area in that region. Founded in 1732, Georgia initially included parts of present-day Alabama and Mississippi. The state's diverse landscape stretches from the Appalachian Mountains in the north, bordering Tennessee and North Carolina, to the marshlands along the Atlantic coast and the Okefenokee Swamp in the south, shared with Florida. The Savannah and Chattahoochee rivers form its natural borders with South Carolina and Alabama. Atlanta is the state's capital.

Georgia's early economy was built on the plantation system, heavily dependent on enslaved labor. It was one of the first states to secede from the Union in 1861, supporting the Confederacy during the Civil War. The state endured significant hardship, particularly during General William Tecumseh Sherman's capture of Atlanta in 1864, followed by his devastating "March to the Sea," which destroyed large sections of the state's plantations.

After the Civil War, while many romanticized the old plantation culture, Georgia began shifting toward industrialization. Led by pro-industry figures like Atlanta journalist Henry Grady, the state saw growth in manufacturing, particularly cotton and iron. However, the real catalyst for Georgia's postwar economic expansion was the growth of its rail system, with Atlanta emerging as the key transportation hub.

Atlanta became a symbol of healing from Georgia's turbulent history. It was the birthplace of Martin Luther King, Jr., and a central location for the civil rights movement. During the 1960s, Atlanta's business leaders worked to avoid the racial unrest that plagued other Southern cities, solidifying its progressive image.

By the early 21st century, Georgia's economy was driven primarily by the service sector, particularly in and around Atlanta. The city's strong transportation infrastructure, including rail and air links, has attracted major utilities, financial institutions, and technology companies, making it a prominent center for corporate headquarters. As a result, Georgia had by the late 20th century surpassed other Deep South states in economic development and prosperity, aligning more closely with national socioeconomic standards. Today, it remains a leading state in the southern U.S.

Georgia covers 59,425 square miles (153,911 square km) and had a population of 10,711,908 in 2020, with an estimated 11,029,227 residents by 2023.

The southernmost stretches of the Blue Ridge Mountains cover the northeastern and north-central parts of Georgia. In the northwest, a limestone valley-and-ridge region dominates the area above Rome and the Coosa River. These higher elevations extend about 75 miles (120 km) southward, with notable peaks like Kennesaw and Stone Mountain rising from the upper Piedmont. Georgia's highest point, Brasstown Bald, located in the Blue Ridge, reaches 4,784 feet (1,458 meters) above sea level. Below the mountains, the Piedmont stretches down to the fall line, a boundary marked by cities such as Augusta, Milledgeville, Macon, and Columbus. In this fall line region, which spans nearly 100 miles (160 km) in width, sandy hills form a narrow, uneven belt. Beyond these hills, the landscape flattens out toward the coast, where the coastal plain meets the former pine barrens, much of which is now farmland.

Roughly half of Georgia's rivers flow into the Atlantic Ocean, while the majority of the remaining streams run through Alabama and Florida into the Gulf of Mexico. Some rivers in northern Georgia drain into the Tennessee River and eventually flow into the Gulf via the Ohio and Mississippi rivers. Although the river basins haven't strongly influenced regional divisions, the variations in elevation and soil have played a significant role. Georgia's inland waters include around two dozen man-made lakes, approximately 70,000 small ponds, primarily created by the federal Soil Conservation Service, and natural lakes located in the southwest near the Florida border. These larger lakes have encouraged widespread recreational water activities.

Due to the bedrock foundation of the region, communities and industries in the Piedmont rely on surface runoff for their water supply. In contrast, the coastal plain draws much of its water from underground aquifers, composed of alternating layers of sand, clay, and limestone. However, the growing domestic and industrial demand for groundwater in Savannah, St. Marys, and Brunswick raises concerns about saltwater intrusion into these vital aquifers.

From the coast to the fall line, the dominant soil types are sand and sandy loam, which are gray closer to the coast and become increasingly red at higher elevations. These soil characteristics continue into the Piedmont and Appalachian areas, where more clay is present. Northern Georgia is often referred to as "red land" or "gray land" due to the color of its soils. In the limestone valleys and uplands of the northwest, soils vary between loam, silt, and clay, often appearing brown, gray, or red.

In the summer, the climate is influenced by maritime tropical air masses, while in other seasons, continental polar air masses can also be present. In Atlanta, the average temperature in January is around 42°F (6°C), and in August, it rises to about 79°F (26°C). Further south, January temperatures are generally 10°F (6°C) warmer, though the difference in August is only around 3°F (2°C). Annual precipitation in northern Georgia usually ranges between 50 and 60 inches (1,270 to 1,524 mm), while the east-central part of the state is drier, averaging around 44 inches (1,118 mm). In northern Georgia, precipitation is relatively evenly distributed throughout the year, but the southern and coastal regions experience more rain during the summer months. Snow is rare outside the mountainous northern counties.

Due to its diverse terrain, stretching from the mountains to the coast, Georgia boasts a rich variety of natural vegetation. In the north, near Blairsville, you'll find maples, hemlocks, birches, and beech trees. Moving southward, below the fall line, the stream swamps are home to cypresses, tupelos, and red gums, while marsh grasses dominate the coastal areas and islands. In the Appalachian region, chestnuts, oaks, and yellow poplars are most common, much of which is part of a national forest. The area from the Tennessee border to the fall line features oak and pine trees, with pines more prevalent in the west. South of the fall line, pine forests—including longleaf, loblolly, and slash pines—cover much of the land. These forests are heavily utilized for pulpwood production, a key economic activity. Many areas that were once cleared for farming have since reverted to forest, scrub, and grasslands.

Georgia is also home to abundant wildlife. Alligators are found in the southern parts of the state, while bears inhabit regions near the mountains and the Okefenokee Swamp. Deer are found throughout most counties with controlled hunting seasons, and small game like grouse, quail, opossums, rabbits, raccoons, squirrels, and turkeys can also be found. The state is working to preserve wildlife through stocking programs for game birds and fish. Southern Georgia's coastal waters are home to fish species like snook and bonefish, while freshwater streams and lakes are stocked with most major game fish found across the United States. Unfortunately, over 20 species of plants and more than 20 species of mammals, birds, fish, and reptiles in Georgia are considered endangered.

By the early 21st century, Georgia had become one of the most populous states in the U.S. The majority of its residents were of European descent (white), making up about two-thirds of the population, while African Americans accounted for nearly one-third. Smaller groups included those of Asian, Hispanic, or Native American origin. Many white residents have deep roots in Georgia, though a larger portion of the population was born outside the state compared to other Deep South states like Alabama and South Carolina. The predominant religions are Protestant, with Baptist and Methodist denominations particularly strong among African Americans.

Georgia's settlement patterns are as varied as its landscape. Long before European contact in the early 1500s, Native American tribes had already developed complex, village-based societies. During the 1700s, British colonization led to increasing cultural conflicts with the Creek (Muskogee) people, as white settlers steadily pushed westward into the 1800s. Georgia, one of the original 13 colonies, emerged after the American Revolution as a plantation economy reliant on rice, cotton, and an expanding enslaved African population.

By the 20th century, Georgia's population was shifting from rural to urban as its major cities grew. Throughout the 1980s and 1990s, the old cotton-growing areas in the central and southwestern regions saw population declines, but this was balanced by significant growth in the Atlanta suburbs, which expanded up to 50 miles outward. The coastal areas near Savannah and Brunswick also experienced rapid growth. Since the 1970s, Georgia's population growth has been second only to Florida among Southern states, even surpassing Florida's growth in the 1990s.

In the 20th century, Georgia followed the trend of its Southern neighbors by transitioning from an agriculture-based economy to one centered on manufacturing and services. Today, about four-fifths of the state's jobs are in service industries, including government, finance, real estate, trade, construction, transportation, and public utilities. Manufacturing makes up a significant portion of the remaining jobs, while agriculture now employs only a small fraction of the workforce. By the late 20th century, Georgia's economy outperformed most of the Deep South, and by the early 21st century, it had become one of the strongest in the nation.

As farming operations have consolidated into fewer, larger units and agribusiness has become more prominent, Georgia has seen a nationwide trend of declining agriculture-related jobs. The poultry industry is largely controlled by a few large corporations that contract with small farmers to raise chickens in modern facilities. Livestock, particularly cattle and swine, is important, especially in southern Georgia, and revenue from livestock often surpasses that from crops. While cotton remains a significant crop, its value has declined since its early 20th-century peak. Georgia is a top producer of pecans and peanuts and ranks high in the production of peaches and tobacco. Other important crops include corn, squash, cabbage, and melons.

Despite the depletion of its original forests, Georgia still boasts vast commercial forestland. Lumber, plywood, and paper are significant industries, and the state remains the only one where pine forests are tapped for naval stores like turpentine and rosin. Georgia is also a key producer of building materials such as crushed stone, cement, sand, and gravel. The northern part of the state, particularly Pickens

County, is home to some of the world's richest marble deposits. Additionally, Georgia leads the nation in kaolin production, a clay used in various products, with vast deposits located in the central part of the state.

Georgia primarily generates electricity using fossil fuels, with around two-fifths of its power coming from natural gas and nearly one-third from coal-fired plants. Nuclear power supplies more than a quarter of the state's electricity, and renewable sources, including hydroelectric energy, contribute a small but growing portion of the overall energy supply.

Though manufacturing in Georgia has declined since the early 21st century, in line with national trends, it continues to be an important source of jobs and economic activity. Key industries include food processing, textiles and apparel, paper products, chemicals, plastics, automobiles, machinery, transportation equipment, and electrical goods. Atlanta is famously the birthplace of Coca-Cola, which originated there in the 1880s, and the Coca-Cola Company remains one of the city's major businesses. The cotton textile industry has been a cornerstone of Georgia's economy since the late 19th century, and the northern part of the state is known for its concentration of rug and carpet manufacturing. Although employment in textiles and apparel declined during the 1980s and 1990s, the state experienced growth in sectors like printing, publishing, industrial machinery, and electronic equipment manufacturing.

Atlanta is not only the cultural heart of Georgia but also a major cosmopolitan center in the South. It hosts numerous museums and attractions. The Woodruff Arts Center includes the High Museum of Art, founded in 1905, and offers a school of visual arts along with performance venues for the Atlanta Symphony Orchestra and a professional resident theatre, both known for premiering new works. The Fernbank Museum of Natural History, which opened in 1992, was the first in 2001 to display a specimen of Argentinosaurus, believed to be the largest dinosaur ever discovered. Additionally, the Georgia Aquarium, one of the largest in the world, opened in 2005. Atlanta is also home to various artist-run galleries and an active community of filmmakers.

Throughout the state, there are regional ballet companies and numerous community theaters. Many colleges, such as Georgia Institute of Technology and the University of Georgia, offer education in architecture, environmental design, theater, dance, visual arts, and music. Public museums and galleries across the state display a wide variety of art, including Clark Atlanta University's notable African American art collection. In 1988, Atlanta hosted the inaugural National Black Arts Festival, which has since grown into a significant annual event.

Georgia is also rich in traditional arts and crafts, particularly in the mountainous northern regions. The tufted fabric craft played a role in the development of the carpet industry in Dalton. A mountain arts cooperative operates a store in Tallulah Falls, and several art galleries have adjoining craft shops. Country music conventions are popular in northern Georgia, although there's tension between traditionalists and those who embrace modern electronic equipment. Sacred Harp shape-note singing, an unaccompanied style of hymn singing, remains a strong tradition in the rural churches of northwestern Georgia.

Georgia has produced several influential figures in American popular music. Ray Charles blended rhythm and blues, jazz, and gospel to create soul music, and his famous rendition of "Georgia on My Mind" became the state song. Little Richard was a pioneer of rock and roll, while the Allman Brothers Band helped define the Southern rock genre. In the 1960s and '70s, Gladys Knight and the Pips had numerous hit songs that have since become soul and rhythm-and-blues classics. Since the 1990s, Atlanta has been a major hub for hip-hop, giving rise to artists like OutKast.

The state has also been home to notable literary figures. Alice Walker, best known for her Pulitzer Prize-winning novel The Color Purple, and Margaret Mitchell, author of the American Civil War epic Gone with the Wind, have achieved global recognition. Additionally, Joel Chandler Harris' Uncle Remus tales remain an integral part of American folklore.

Georgia boasts a variety of national historic landmarks, including the Old Governor's Mansion in Milledgeville, a relic from the period when the city was the state capital. Savannah's Historic District preserves much of the original 18th-century town layout and architecture. In the northwestern region, the Etowah Mounds, dating to the 10th-century Mississippian culture, have also been granted landmark status.

Outdoor recreation is plentiful in Georgia. Stone Mountain Park, located near Decatur, is renowned for its natural beauty and the massive Confederate memorial carved into the mountain's granite face. The mountainous north is dominated by the Chattahoochee National Forest, which includes the Cohutta Wilderness Area. On the coast, Cumberland Island National Seashore preserves a large barrier island. Numerous other wildlife areas and refuges are spread across the coastal zone, including the Okefenokee Swamp, which is protected by the Okefenokee National Wildlife Refuge and Wilderness Area, as well as state parks like Stephen C. Foster and Laura S. Walker. Georgia's state parks offer activities ranging from beach visits to mountain hiking and climbing.

Georgia also has a prominent place in competitive sports, both nationally and internationally. Atlanta is home to several professional sports teams, including the Braves (MLB), Falcons (NFL), Hawks (NBA), and Atlanta United FC (MLS). In 1996, Atlanta hosted the Summer Olympic Games, attracting athletes and visitors from around the world. Augusta National Golf Club hosts the prestigious Masters Tournament each year. College football, particularly the University of Georgia's team, is a fall tradition across the state.

Georgia is home to over 100 newspapers, mostly weeklies, with the Atlanta Journal-Constitution being the state's leading publication with a national reputation. The state also has numerous radio and television stations. CNN, the world's first 24-hour news network, was launched in Atlanta in 1980 and remains a leader in international television journalism.

History of Georgia

The first people to settle in what is now Georgia arrived around 10,000 to 12,000 years ago. These early inhabitants of the Paleo-Indian period were nomadic hunters, using finely crafted flint tools to hunt large animals. They set up small, temporary camps as they followed their prey. Between 8000 and 1000 BCE, during the Archaic period, new cultures developed in the region. While these groups relied on a wider variety of food sources, they still followed seasonal migration patterns. Permanent or semi-permanent villages began to emerge during the Woodland period (1000 BCE to 900 CE), when agriculture became more prominent. These Woodland peoples lived in small, dispersed villages and supplemented their farming with wild foods. They left behind significant earthen mounds, some of which were used for burials and contained intricate jewelry, pottery, and figurines, while others were shaped like animals. One notable example is the Rock Eagle effigy in central Georgia, a large bird-shaped structure made of quartz stones.

Following the Woodland culture, the Mississippian culture dominated the region. Known for its mound-building, this society used the mounds for ceremonies and as residences for their chiefs. The Mississippians developed complex social hierarchies with strong, centralized leadership. Their agricultural system, based on crops like corn, beans, squash, pumpkins, and tobacco, was highly efficient and often produced surpluses. This culture was thriving when European explorers arrived in the 1500s.

Around 1540, Spanish explorer Hernando de Soto led the first European expedition into the region now known as Georgia, in search of silver and gold. During his journey, he encountered the organized agricultural society of the Mississippian culture. Unfortunately, this expedition proved devastating for the indigenous population. Besides killing or enslaving many of the locals, the Spanish inadvertently introduced diseases such as measles, smallpox, and whooping cough, which led to widespread deaths and the eventual collapse of Mississippian culture in the area.

In 1565, the Spanish began their occupation of Florida after a French attempt to colonize the southeastern coast. From their stronghold in

St. Augustine, they started to exert influence over the native people of Georgia. They established a network of Roman Catholic missions and military posts on Georgia's barrier islands. The indigenous coastal populations were profoundly affected, converting to Christianity and shifting to more settled village lifestyles. The Spanish referred to the coastal area as Guale, which remained under their mission-presidio system for about a century. However, in the latter half of the 17th century, growing pressure from British settlers in South Carolina led to the withdrawal of Spanish missions from Guale. As Spanish power waned, the region became known as the "Debatable Land," where British traders developed monopolies with the native residents, though permanent settlement south of the Savannah River was slow to begin.

In 1732, King George II granted a charter for the establishment of the Georgia colony, named in his honor. James Edward Oglethorpe, a British soldier and philanthropist, played a leading role in securing the charter. He envisioned Georgia as a place where England's poor could start afresh, and he and other trustees encouraged settlers to produce goods such as wine, silk, and spices, reducing England's reliance on foreign imports. Additionally, the colony was intended to serve as a defensive buffer against Spanish and French territories to the south and west.

The first English settlement in Georgia was founded in Savannah in 1733. While some settlers financed their own journey, others had their expenses covered by the trustees. Oglethorpe oversaw the colony's affairs, focusing primarily on its defense. Central to the trustees' vision was a well-organized settlement structure that promoted small-scale farming communities, with slavery being prohibited to avoid the development of large plantations. Despite these idealistic goals, the colony struggled to meet expectations. However, the city of Savannah was one notable success in terms of planning and development. Faced with growing unrest and emigration, the trustees eventually handed over control of the colony to the British government in 1752, one year before their charter was set to expire. Plantation agriculture, primarily focused on sugar, rice, and indigo, became the backbone of Georgia's economy, heavily reliant on enslaved labor.

Before the American Revolution, significant settlement in Georgia began with a wave of inland migration, forming a region along the Savannah River and extending into the lower Piedmont. The state's response to the tensions of the Revolution was complex, with internal conflict between loyalists and patriots, leading to civil unrest for much of the population. After the Revolution, settlement expanded rapidly, particularly westward from Augusta into what would become central Georgia's "cotton counties."

The westward expansion of British, and later American, settlers in the mid-18th century increasingly encroached on lands belonging to the Cherokee and Muskogee (a branch of the Creek). As settlers moved in, conflicts with these Indigenous groups became common. Within the Muskogee, internal divisions also emerged over how to respond to white encroachment. A series of treaties, often forced upon the Cherokee and Muskogee, led to successive land cessions to Georgia. The land obtained from the Indigenous peoples enabled the development of a commercial agricultural economy, which, after the 1790s, became dominated by cotton. The displacement of the Cherokee and Muskogee continued into the 19th century, culminating in the infamous Trail of Tears in 1838–39, when the Cherokee were forcibly relocated to present-day Oklahoma. By this time, most Muskogee had already been expelled from Georgia.

By the mid-1800s, most white Georgians, like many in the South, saw slavery as essential to their economy. Georgia, with the largest number of large plantations in the South, became emblematic of plantation culture. When the Civil War erupted in 1861, the majority of white southerners, whether slaveholders or not, supported the Confederacy, which Georgia helped to establish.

The Civil War deeply affected Georgians at all levels. Union forces took control of parts of coastal Georgia early on, disrupting the plantation system even before the war's outcome was clear. In 1864, Union General William Tecumseh Sherman invaded Georgia from the north, laying siege to Atlanta, burning much of the city, and then embarking on his infamous March to the Sea, a campaign of total destruction that stretched 50 miles wide from Atlanta to Savannah, covering 200 miles. Savannah, captured in December, was largely spared from destruction.

Following the war, Georgia's agricultural economy was in ruins, and the relationship between landowners and laborers changed dramatically. After experimenting with various labor systems post-emancipation, sharecropping became the dominant model. This system, where tenants paid landowners with a portion of their crops, often resulted in land overuse and depletion of soil fertility. While white landowners retained control of land and capital, most laborers were Black, perpetuating racial and economic inequality until the boll weevil devastated cotton crops in the early 20th century, ending the dominance of "King Cotton."

Reconstruction in Georgia was marked by violence and instability. In 1868, the Republican Party gained power with the election of northern-born Rufus Bullock as governor. However, the Ku Klux Klan and Georgia Democrats, opposing Republican leadership, unleashed terror, killing hundreds of African Americans. Despite Bullock's efforts to promote equality, Democrats regained control in 1871, setting Georgia on a path of white supremacy, low taxes, and minimal government services. Former Confederate officers often held the state's highest offices. In the 1890s, amidst an agricultural depression, a political movement led by Thomas E. Watson and known as the Populists, which included both Black and white farmers, briefly challenged the political elite, advocating for the interests of small farmers over those of the planters and railroads.

By the late 19th century, some Georgians began pushing for industrialization, particularly the development of textile manufacturing. Henry Grady, an influential Atlanta journalist, championed this shift toward a more industrial and commercial economy. During the 1880s and 1890s, textile and iron manufacturing began to grow, and Atlanta emerged as a major commercial hub, fueled largely by railroad transportation.

Racial tensions were a significant part of Georgia's history in the late 19th and early 20th centuries. During the 1890s, Democrats implemented laws that disenfranchised African American voters and enforced segregation across all public spaces in the state. The segregated education system left Black students with inferior schooling. From 1890 to 1920, racial violence was widespread, with numerous lynchings, and in 1906, white mobs in Atlanta rioted, killing several Black residents and destroying many homes. Despite this, Atlanta became a center of African American education and culture during the same period, with the establishment of colleges like Morehouse and Spelman. Many African Americans left Georgia during World War I as part of the Great Migration, seeking better opportunities in the North.

In the 1920s, Georgia's economy continued to rely on cotton, but the boll weevil infestation caused significant crop destruction, leading to an agricultural depression. The Great Depression of the 1930s further worsened conditions, displacing many sharecroppers from farming. Georgia became symbolic of Southern poverty, a fact highlighted by President Franklin D. Roosevelt's frequent visits to Warm Springs, where he witnessed the state's dire conditions firsthand. Although many Georgians supported Roosevelt's policies, Governor Eugene Talmadge and other state leaders often opposed the New Deal's reforms, which threatened the traditional agricultural dominance.

World War II boosted Georgia's economy, with rising agricultural prices and the expansion of military bases, such as Fort Benning. Marietta also became home to a large factory producing B-29 bombers. The war ushered in political changes, notably with Ellis Arnall's election as governor in 1943, marking a shift toward more progressive politics.

After the war, Georgia faced increasing pressure to address its racial issues. African Americans began to challenge segregation more forcefully, though many white Georgians continued to support it. Segregationist Herman Talmadge returned as governor, while writer Lillian Smith publicly called for an end to segregation. Black Georgians launched a major voter registration effort, raising their political influence above that of African Americans in other Southern states. The rise of direct-action protests, such as the Montgomery bus boycott in 1955–56, saw increasing involvement from Georgia's African Americans in the civil rights movement. Atlanta-born Martin Luther King, Jr. became a national leader in this struggle, founding the Southern Christian Leadership Conference (SCLC) in 1957 in Atlanta and leading protests across the country. Other organizations, like the Student Nonviolent Coordinating Committee (SNCC) and the Southern Regional Council, also operated from Atlanta, challenging racial inequality. King remained a central figure in the movement until his assassination in 1968, and he is buried in Atlanta, where his grave is now a national historic site.

Atlanta's business leaders took a more progressive stance on race relations compared to other Southern cities. During the 1960s, Mayor William Hartsfield and major corporations worked with the Black community to avoid the large-scale civil rights protests that occurred in cities like Birmingham and Memphis. While racial discrimination persisted, white leaders in Atlanta were generally more open to dialogue with Black leadership. By the 1970s, as Atlanta's Black population became the majority, African Americans began to achieve significant political victories, including Andrew Young's election to Congress in 1972 and Maynard Jackson becoming Atlanta's first Black mayor in 1973. Since then, African Americans have held numerous political offices in Atlanta and southwestern Georgia.

Statewide political change came more slowly. In 1967, Lester Maddox, a staunch opponent of desegregation, was elected governor. Jimmy Carter followed Maddox as governor, advocating for racial moderation and moving Georgia toward a more progressive image similar to that of Atlanta. Carter's election as U.S. president in 1976, the first Georgian to achieve this, brought national attention to the state. By the 1980s and 1990s, both Democrats and Republicans actively competed for political office, with Republicans gaining several congressional seats. However, Democrats maintained control of the governor's office until 2003, when Sonny Perdue became the first Republican governor since 1868.

Since the 1950s, Georgia's economy and population have grown at a rate well above the national average, largely concentrated in the Atlanta metropolitan area. By the end of the 20th century, Atlanta had gained international recognition, particularly through its hosting of the 1996 Olympic Games.

COUNTIES

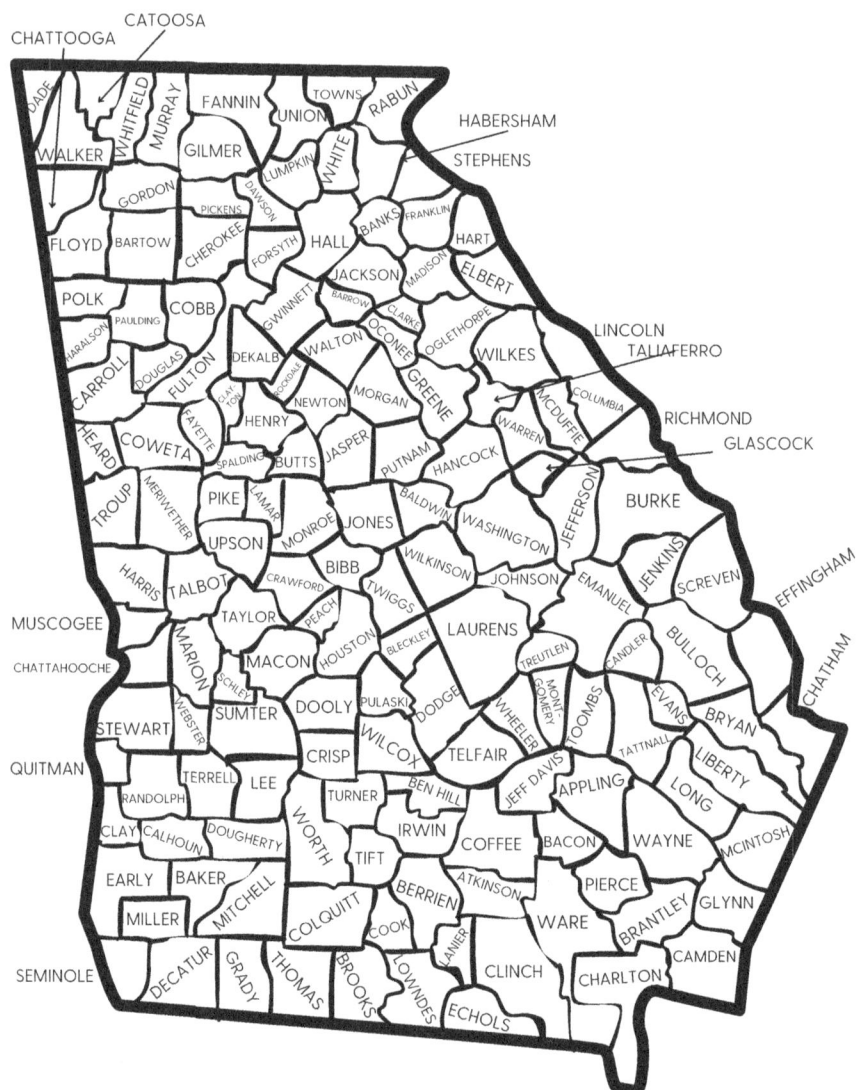

CITIES

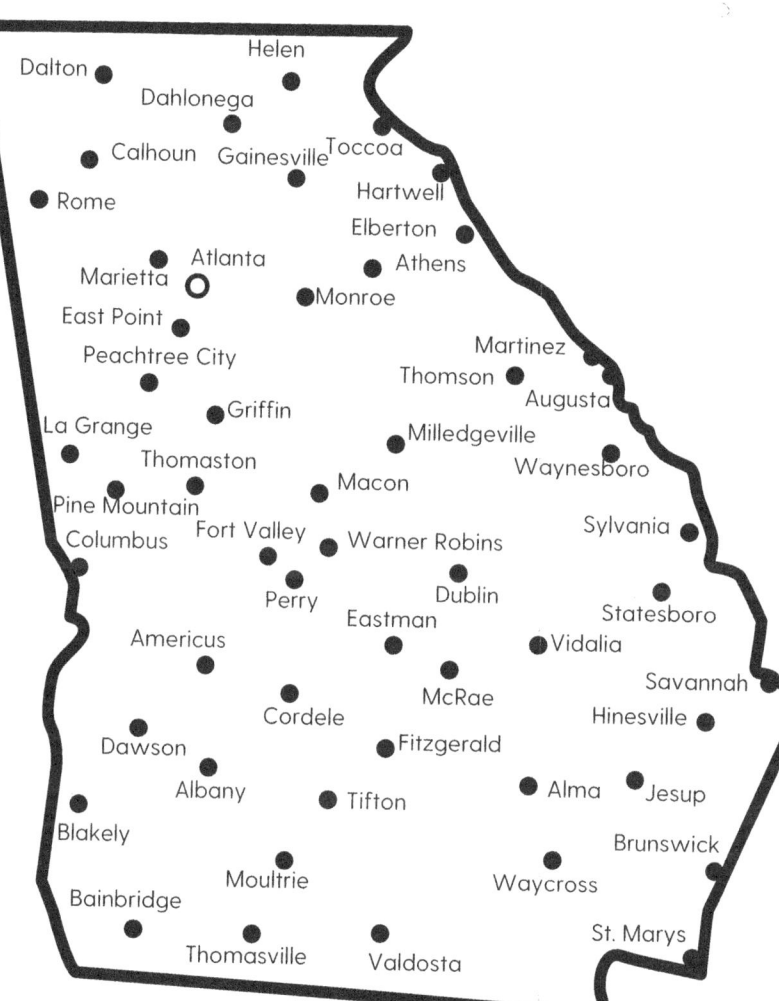

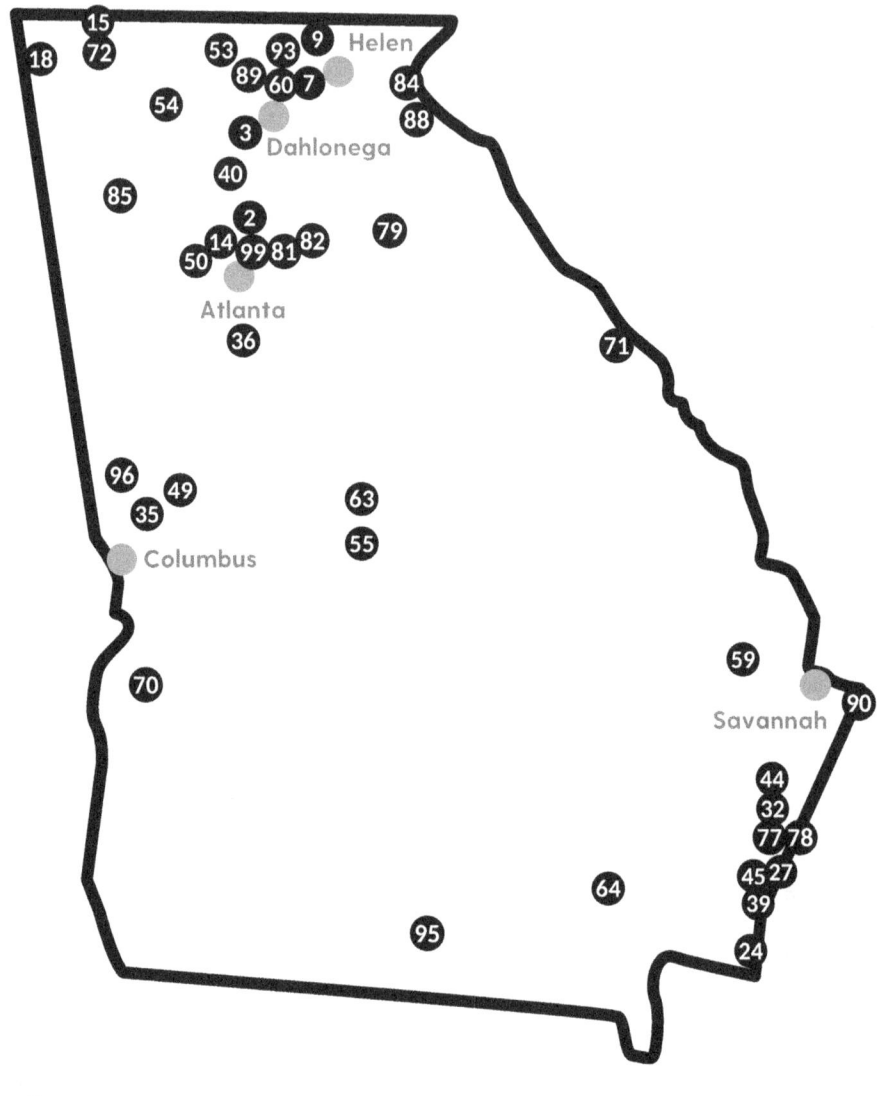

1. American Prohibition Museum
2. Ameris Bank Ampitheatre
3. Amicalola Falls State Park
4. Anna Ruby Falls
5. Atlanta Botanical Garden
6. Atlanta History Center
7. BabyLand General Hospital
8. Bonaventure Cemetery
9. Brasstown Bald Mountain
10. Buckhead
11. Cathedral of St. John the Baptist
12. Centennial Olympic Park
13. Center for Puppetry Arts
14. Chattahoochee River
15. Chickamauga and Chattanooga National Military Park
16. Chippewa Square
17. City Market
18. Cloudland Canyon State Park
19. College Football Hall of Fame
20. Columbus Riverwalk
21. Congregation Mickve Israel
22. Consolidated Gold Mine
23. Crisson Gold Mine
24. Cumberland Island Ferry
25. Davenport House Museum
26. Delta Flight Museum
27. Driftwood Beach
28. Dukes Creek Falls Trail
29. Fernbank Museum
30. First African Baptist Church
31. Forsyth Park
32. Fort Frederica National Monument
33. Fort Pulaski National Monument
34. Fox Theatre
35. Franklin D. Roosevelt State Park
36. Fun Spot America Atlanta
37. Georgia Aquarium
38. Georgia Mountain Coaster
39. Georgia Sea Turtle Center
40. Gibbs Gardens
41. High Museum of Art
42. Historic River Street
43. Historic Savannah Theatre
44. Hofwyl-Broadfield Plantation
45. Jekyll Island Historic District
46. Jimmy Carter Presidential Library & Museum
47. Juliette Gordon Low Birthplace Museum
48. Lenox Square
49. Little White House
50. Marietta Square
51. Martin Luther King Jr. National Historic Site
52. Mercer Williams House Museum
53. Mercier Orchards
54. Mountain Valley Farm
55. Museum of Aviation
56. National Center for Civil and Human Rights
57. National Civil War Naval Museum
58. National Infantry Museum and Soldier Center
59. National Museum of the Mighty Eighth Air Force
60. North Georgia Wildlife Park
61. Oakland Cemetery
62. Oatland Island Wildlife Center
63. Ocmulgee Mounds National Historical Park
64. Okefenokee Swamp Park

- 65 Old Fort Jackson
- 66 Owens-Thomas House & Slave Quarters
- 67 Piedmont Park
- 68 Pin Point Heritage Museum
- 69 Ponce City Market
- 70 Providence Canyon State Park
- 71 Riverwalk
- 72 Rock City Gardens
- 73 Savannah Historic District
- 74 SCADstory
- 75 Ships of the Sea Maritime Museum
- 76 Skidaway Island State Park
- 77 St. Simons Island
- 78 St. Simons Lighthouse Museum
- 79 State Botanical Garden of Georgia
- 80 State Farm Arena
- 81 Stone Mountain Carving
- 82 Summit Skyride
- 83 Swan House
- 84 Tallulah Gorge State Park
- 85 Tellus Science Museum
- 86 The Old Sorrel Weed House Museum & Tours
- 87 The Olde Pink House
- 88 Toccoa Falls
- 89 Toccoa River Swinging Bridge
- 90 Tybee Island Light Station And Museum
- 91 Uhuburg
- 92 Unicoi State Park
- 93 Vogel State Park
- 94 Webb Military Museum
- 95 Wild Adventures Theme Park
- 96 Wild Animal Safari
- 97 Wolf Mountain Vineyards & Winery
- 98 Wormsloe Historic Site
- 99 Your Dekalb Farmers Market
- 100 Zoo Atlanta

PLACE NAME	COUNTY	CITY	✓
American Prohibition Museum	Chatham	Savannah	
Ameris Bank Ampitheatre	Fulton	Alpharetta	
Amicalola Falls State Park	Dawson	Dawsonville	
Anna Ruby Falls	White	Helen	
Atlanta Botanical Garden	Fulton	Atlanta	
Atlanta History Center	Fulton	Atlanta	
BabyLand General Hospital	White	Cleveland	
Bonaventure Cemetery	Chatham	Savannah	
Brasstown Bald Mountain	Towns	Hiawassee	
Buckhead	Fulton	Buckhead	
Cathedral of St. John the Baptist	Chatham	Savannah	
Centennial Olympic Park	Fulton	Atlanta	
Center for Puppetry Arts	Fulton	Atlanta	
Chattahoochee River	multiple	multiple	
Chickamauga and Chattanooga National Military Park	Catoosa	Fort Oglethorpe	
Chippewa Square	Chatham	Savannah	
City Market	Chatham	Savannah	
Cloudland Canyon State Park	Dade	Rising Fawn	
College Football Hall of Fame	Fulton	Atlanta	
Columbus Riverwalk	Muscogee	Columbus	
Congregation Mickve Israel	Chatham	Savannah	
Consolidated Gold Mine	Lumpkin	Dahlonega	
Crisson Gold Mine	Lumpkin	Dahlonega	
Cumberland Island Ferry	Camden	St. Marys	
Davenport House Museum	Chatham	Savannah	
Delta Flight Museum	Fulton	Atlanta	
Driftwood Beach	Glynn	Jekyll Island	
Dukes Creek Falls Trail	White	Helen	

PLACE NAME	COUNTY	CITY	✓
Fernbank Museum	Fulton	Atlanta	
First African Baptist Church	Chatham	Savannah	
Forsyth Park	Chatham	Savannah	
Fort Frederica National Monument	Glynn	St. Simons Island	
Fort Pulaski National Monument	Chatham	Savannah	
Fox Theatre	Fulton	Atlanta	
Franklin D. Roosevelt State Park	Harris	Pine Mountain	
Fun Spot America Atlanta	Fayette	Fayetteville	
Georgia Aquarium	Fulton	Atlanta	
Georgia Mountain Coaster	White	Helen	
Georgia Sea Turtle Center	Glynn	Jekyll Island	
Gibbs Gardens	Cherokee	Ball Ground	
High Museum of Art	Fulton	Atlanta	
Historic River Street	Chatham	Savannah	
Historic Savannah Theatre	Chatham	Savannah	
Hofwyl-Broadfield Plantation	Glynn	Brunswick	
Jekyll Island Historic District	Glynn	Jekyll Island	
Jimmy Carter Presidential Library & Museum	Fulton	Atlanta	
Juliette Gordon Low Birthplace Museum	Chatham	Savannah	
Lenox Square	Fulton	Atlanta	
Little White House	Meriwether	Warm Springs	
Marietta Square	Cobb	Marietta	
Martin Luther King Jr. National Historic Site	Fulton	Atlanta	
Mercer Williams House Museum	Chatham	Savannah	
Mercier Orchards	Fannin	Blue Ridge	
Mountain Valley Farm	Gilmer	Ellijay	
Museum of Aviation	Houston	Warner Robins	
National Center for Civil and Human Rights	Fulton	Atlanta	

PLACE NAME	COUNTY	CITY	✓
National Civil War Naval Museum	Muscogee	Columbus	
National Infantry Museum and Soldier Center	Muscogee	Columbus	
National Museum of the Mighty Eighth Air Force	Chatham	Pooler	
North Georgia Wildlife Park	White	Cleveland	
Oakland Cemetery	Fulton	Atlanta	
Oatland Island Wildlife Center	Chatham	Savannah	
Ocmulgee Mounds National Historical Park	Bibb	Macon	
Okefenokee Swamp Park	Ware	Waycross	
Old Fort Jackson	Chatham	Savannah	
Owens-Thomas House & Slave Quarters	Chatham	Savannah	
Piedmont Park	Fulton	Atlanta	
Pin Point Heritage Museum	Chatham	Savannah	
Ponce City Market	Fulton	Atlanta	
Providence Canyon State Park	Stewart	Lumpkin	
Riverwalk	Richmond	Augusta	
Rock City Gardens	Walker	Lookout Mountain	
Savannah Historic District	Chatham	Savannah	
SCADstory	Chatham	Savannah	
Ships of the Sea Maritime Museum	Chatham	Savannah	
Skidaway Island State Park	Chatham	Savannah	
St. Simons Island	Glynn	St. Simons Island	
St. Simons Lighthouse Museum	Glynn	St. Simons Island	
State Botanical Garden of Georgia	Clarke	Athens	
State Farm Arena	Fulton	Atlanta	
Stone Mountain Carving	DeKalb	Stone Mountain	
Summit Skyride	DeKalb	Stone Mountain	
Swan House	Fulton	Atlanta	
Tallulah Gorge State Park	Rabun	Tallulah Falls	

PLACE NAME	COUNTY	CITY	✓
Tellus Science Museum	Bartow	Cartersville	
The Old Sorrel Weed House Museum & Tours	Chatham	Savannah	
The Olde Pink House	Chatham	Savannah	
Toccoa Falls	Stephens	Toccoa	
Toccoa River Swinging Bridge	Fannin	Blue Ridge	
Tybee Island Light Station And Museum	Chatham	Tybee Island	
Uhuburg	White	Helen	
Unicoi State Park	White	Helen	
Vogel State Park	Union	Blairsville	
Webb Military Museum	Chatham	Savannah	
Wild Adventures Theme Park	Lowndes	Valdosta	
Wild Animal Safari	Harris	Pine Mountain	
Wolf Mountain Vineyards & Winery	Lumpkin	Dahlonega	
Wormsloe Historic Site	Chatham	Savannah	
Your Dekalb Farmers Market	DeKalb	Decatur	
Zoo Atlanta	Fulton	Atlanta	

COUNTY	CITY	PLACE NAME	✓
Bartow	Cartersville	Tellus Science Museum	
Bibb	Macon	Ocmulgee Mounds National Historical Park	
Camden	St. Marys	Cumberland Island Ferry	
Catoosa	Fort Oglethorpe	Chickamauga and Chattanooga National Military Park	
Chatham	Pooler	National Museum of the Mighty Eighth Air Force	
Chatham	Savannah	American Prohibition Museum	
Chatham	Savannah	Bonaventure Cemetery	
Chatham	Savannah	Cathedral of St. John the Baptist	
Chatham	Savannah	Chippewa Square	
Chatham	Savannah	City Market	
Chatham	Savannah	Congregation Mickve Israel	
Chatham	Savannah	Davenport House Museum	
Chatham	Savannah	First African Baptist Church	
Chatham	Savannah	Forsyth Park	
Chatham	Savannah	Fort Pulaski National Monument	
Chatham	Savannah	Historic River Street	
Chatham	Savannah	Historic Savannah Theatre	
Chatham	Savannah	Juliette Gordon Low Birthplace Museum	
Chatham	Savannah	Mercer Williams House Museum	
Chatham	Savannah	Oatland Island Wildlife Center	
Chatham	Savannah	Old Fort Jackson	
Chatham	Savannah	Owens-Thomas House & Slave Quarters	
Chatham	Savannah	Pin Point Heritage Museum	
Chatham	Savannah	Savannah Historic District	
Chatham	Savannah	SCADstory	
Chatham	Savannah	Ships of the Sea Maritime Museum	
Chatham	Savannah	Skidaway Island State Park	
Chatham	Savannah	The Old Sorrel Weed House Museum & Tours	

COUNTY	CITY	PLACE NAME	✓
Chatham	Savannah	The Olde Pink House	
Chatham	Savannah	Webb Military Museum	
Chatham	Savannah	Wormsloe Historic Site	
Chatham	Tybee Island	Tybee Island Light Station And Museum	
Cherokee	Ball Ground	Gibbs Gardens	
Clarke	Athens	State Botanical Garden of Georgia	
Cobb	Marietta	Marietta Square	
Dade	Rising Fawn	Cloudland Canyon State Park	
Dawson	Dawsonville	Amicalola Falls State Park	
DeKalb	Decatur	Your Dekalb Farmers Market	
DeKalb	Stone Mountain	Stone Mountain Carving	
DeKalb	Stone Mountain	Summit Skyride	
Fannin	Blue Ridge	Mercier Orchards	
Fannin	Blue Ridge	Toccoa River Swinging Bridge	
Fayette	Fayetteville	Fun Spot America Atlanta	
Fulton	Alpharetta	Ameris Bank Ampitheatre	
Fulton	Atlanta	Atlanta Botanical Garden	
Fulton	Atlanta	Atlanta History Center	
Fulton	Atlanta	Centennial Olympic Park	
Fulton	Atlanta	Center for Puppetry Arts	
Fulton	Atlanta	College Football Hall of Fame	
Fulton	Atlanta	Delta Flight Museum	
Fulton	Atlanta	Fernbank Museum	
Fulton	Atlanta	Fox Theatre	
Fulton	Atlanta	Georgia Aquarium	
Fulton	Atlanta	High Museum of Art	
Fulton	Atlanta	Jimmy Carter Presidential Library & Museum	
Fulton	Atlanta	Lenox Square	

COUNTY	CITY	PLACE NAME	✓
Fulton	Atlanta	Martin Luther King Jr. National Historic Site	
Fulton	Atlanta	National Center for Civil and Human Rights	
Fulton	Atlanta	Oakland Cemetery	
Fulton	Atlanta	Piedmont Park	
Fulton	Atlanta	Ponce City Market	
Fulton	Atlanta	State Farm Arena	
Fulton	Atlanta	Swan House	
Fulton	Atlanta	Zoo Atlanta	
Fulton	Buckhead	Buckhead	
Gilmer	Ellijay	Mountain Valley Farm	
Glynn	Brunswick	Hofwyl-Broadfield Plantation	
Glynn	Jekyll Island	Driftwood Beach	
Glynn	Jekyll Island	Georgia Sea Turtle Center	
Glynn	Jekyll Island	Jekyll Island Historic District	
Glynn	St. Simons Island	St. Simons Island	
Glynn	St. Simons Island	St. Simons Lighthouse Museum	
Glynn	St. Simons Island	Fort Frederica National Monument	
Harris	Pine Mountain	Franklin D. Roosevelt State Park	
Harris	Pine Mountain	Wild Animal Safari	
Houston	Warner Robins	Museum of Aviation	
Lowndes	Valdosta	Wild Adventures Theme Park	
Lumpkin	Dahlonega	Consolidated Gold Mine	
Lumpkin	Dahlonega	Crisson Gold Mine	
Lumpkin	Dahlonega	Wolf Mountain Vineyards & Winery	
Meriwether	Warm Springs	Little White House	
multiple	multiple	Chattahoochee River	
Muscogee	Columbus	Columbus Riverwalk	
Muscogee	Columbus	National Civil War Naval Museum	

COUNTY	CITY	PLACE NAME	✓
Muscogee	Columbus	National Infantry Museum and Soldier Center	
Rabun	Tallulah Falls	Tallulah Gorge State Park	
Richmond	Augusta	Riverwalk	
Stephens	Toccoa	Toccoa Falls	
Stewart	Lumpkin	Providence Canyon State Park	
Towns	Hiawassee	Brasstown Bald Mountain	
Union	Blairsville	Vogel State Park	
Walker	Lookout Mountain	Rock City Gardens	
Ware	Waycross	Okefenokee Swamp Park	
White	Cleveland	BabyLand General Hospital	
White	Cleveland	North Georgia Wildlife Park	
White	Helen	Anna Ruby Falls	
White	Helen	Dukes Creek Falls Trail	
White	Helen	Georgia Mountain Coaster	
White	Helen	Uhuburg	
White	Helen	Unicoi State Park	

AMERICAN PROHIBITION MUSEUM

COUNTY: CHATHAM	CITY: SAVANNAH
DATE VISITED:	WHO I WENT WITH:
RATING: ☆ ☆ ☆ ☆ ☆	WILL I RETURN? YES / NO

209 W. St. Julian Street
Savannah, GA 31401
912-551-4054

American Prohibition Museum is located in the heart of Savannah, Georgia. This unique museum is dedicated to the era of Prohibition in the United States, a time when the manufacture, sale, and transportation of alcoholic beverages were banned. Through immersive exhibits, fascinating artifacts, and engaging stories, the museum explores the impact of Prohibition on American society and culture. Whether you're a history enthusiast, a lover of the arts, or simply curious about this pivotal moment in American history, the American Prohibition Museum offers a captivating experience that brings the past to life. The American Prohibition Museum features a variety of interactive and educational exhibits that delve into the complexities of the Prohibition era.

Begin your journey with a comprehensive overview of the origins of Prohibition, including the social and political factors that led to its enactment in 1920 and its eventual repeal in 1933. The exhibit covers key figures, organizations, and events that shaped this tumultuous period in American history.

Step into a recreated speakeasy, a secret bar that operated during Prohibition. This immersive environment offers a glimpse into the clandestine world of illegal drinking, complete with period-appropriate decor and ambiance. Discover how patrons navigated the laws of the time and the creative methods used to conceal their activities.

The museum boasts an extensive collection of artifacts from the Prohibition era, providing visitors with a tangible connection to the past.

Explore a variety of artifacts, including vintage liquor bottles, flapper dresses, and original advertisements that showcase the culture of the Roaring Twenties. These items help illustrate the social changes and cultural shifts that occurred during this dynamic period.

Engage with interactive displays that allow you to test your knowledge about Prohibition laws and the impact of alcohol on society. Learn about the role of organized crime, law enforcement, and the social movements that both supported and opposed Prohibition.

The American Prohibition Museum offers educational programs and guided tours that provide deeper insights into the era. Join a guided tour led by knowledgeable staff who will share captivating stories and historical context, enhancing your understanding of Prohibition and its effects on American society.

Keep an eye out for special events, lectures, and film screenings hosted by the museum. These programs often feature guest speakers, historians, and experts who delve deeper into the complexities of the Prohibition era.

Before leaving, be sure to stop by the museum's gift shop, where you can find a variety of Prohibition-themed souvenirs, books, and unique gifts. The shop features: A selection of books on Prohibition history, cocktails, and the Roaring Twenties, perfect for anyone looking to learn more about this fascinating period. Fun memorabilia, including themed glassware, apparel, and decorative items that celebrate the spirit of the 1920s.

Tips

- Plan your time: Allocate at least 1-2 hours to fully explore the museum and engage with the exhibits. Consider joining a guided tour for a more in-depth experience.
- Combine with other attractions: The American Prohibition Museum is located near other historical sites in Savannah, such as the Savannah History Museum and the Juliette Gordon Low Birthplace. Plan a full day of exploration in the historic district.
- Dress comfortably: Wear comfortable shoes and clothing, as you'll be exploring various exhibits and possibly standing for extended periods.
- Stay hydrated: Bring a water bottle to stay hydrated during your visit, especially if you plan to explore the nearby historic district afterward.

Nearby Attractions

- Savannah History Museum: Just a short walk away, this museum provides a comprehensive overview of Savannah's rich history, featuring artifacts and exhibits that date back to the city's founding in 1733.

- Forsyth Park: A beautiful 30-acre park located nearby, Forsyth Park features walking paths, gardens, and the iconic Forsyth Fountain. It's an excellent spot for a leisurely stroll or a picnic.

- River Street: A vibrant waterfront area filled with shops, restaurants, and bars, River Street is perfect for enjoying the local atmosphere, dining, and shopping for unique souvenirs.

AMERIS BANK AMPITHEATRE

COUNTY: FULTON   **CITY:** ALPHARETTA

DATE VISITED: **WHO I WENT WITH:**

RATING: ☆ ☆ ☆ ☆ ☆   **WILL I RETURN?** YES / NO

2200 Encore Parkway
Alpharetta, GA 30009
404-733-5010

Ameris Bank Amphitheatre is one of Georgia's premier outdoor entertainment venues. Located in the vibrant city of Alpharetta, just north of Atlanta, this amphitheater has become a beloved destination for music lovers, hosting some of the biggest names in the music industry. Whether you're attending a summer concert or looking for a relaxing evening under the stars, this guide will help you make the most of your visit.

The Ameris Bank Amphitheatre opened its doors in 2008 and has quickly grown into a popular spot for live performances. It has a seating capacity of around 12,000, offering both reserved seating and general admission lawn areas. The venue's design allows for excellent acoustics, ensuring that every seat in the house offers a great view and sound experience.

The amphitheater is known for hosting a wide range of events, from top-charting pop and rock artists to country, jazz, and classical performances. It is also a popular stop for tours, festivals, and special events, making it a must-visit for anyone who enjoys live music.

Since the Ameris Bank Amphitheatre is an outdoor venue, it's important to come prepared for the weather. In the summer, Georgia can get quite hot, so be sure to bring sunscreen, sunglasses, and a hat for daytime shows. Evenings can cool down significantly, so having a light jacket or blanket is a smart idea if you're sitting in the lawn section.

For lawn seating, visitors often bring blankets or low-profile folding chairs. Be aware that the venue has size restrictions for chairs, so check the guidelines ahead of time to avoid any issues at the entrance.

It's also wise to bring a reusable water bottle. The venue provides free water refill stations, allowing you to stay hydrated throughout the event without having to purchase bottled water.

Ameris Bank Amphitheatre offers a variety of food and drink options for concertgoers. There are several concession stands scattered throughout the venue, serving everything from classic concert fare like burgers, pizza, and hot dogs to more gourmet options like salads and sandwiches. There are also vegetarian and gluten-free choices, ensuring that everyone can find something to enjoy. In terms of beverages, you'll find a wide selection of soft drinks, beer, wine, and cocktails. Keep in mind that alcohol sales typically end about 30 minutes before the conclusion of the show. Outside food and beverages are generally not allowed, but the amphitheater makes exceptions for certain dietary restrictions. Be sure to check the venue's policy if you have any specific needs.

Tips

- Arrive early: Doors usually open about 90 minutes before showtime. Arriving early gives you ample time to find parking, go through security, and settle in before the concert begins. It's also a great opportunity to explore the venue and grab food or drinks without the rush.
- Dress comfortably: Since you'll be outdoors, comfort is key. Wear comfortable shoes, as you might be walking or standing for extended periods. Dress in layers to be prepared for fluctuating temperatures, especially if you're staying for an evening show.
- Stay hydrated: Georgia's heat can be intense during the summer months, so remember to drink plenty of water throughout the day. Take advantage of the free refill stations to stay refreshed.
- Download your tickets: The venue primarily uses mobile tickets, so be sure to download them to your phone before arriving. This helps avoid any last-minute issues with connectivity at the entrance.
- Check the schedule: In addition to main acts, some shows feature opening performances or pre-show events. Checking the schedule ahead of time ensures you won't miss any part of the entertainment.

Nearby Attractions

- Avalon: Avalon is a vibrant mixed-use development that combines shopping, dining, and entertainment. Featuring over 500,000 square feet of retail space, you can find a variety of shops, from high-end boutiques to popular brands. In addition to its great stores, Avalon hosts events throughout the year, including outdoor movie nights and seasonal festivals, making it a perfect spot for a fun day out.

- Wills Park: Wills Park is a spacious community park that offers a variety of recreational activities for all ages. The park features walking trails, sports fields, playgrounds, and a scenic lake, providing plenty of opportunities for outdoor fun. It's also home to the Wills Park Recreation Center, which offers fitness classes, swimming pools, and sports leagues.

- Alpharetta City Center: Alpharetta City Center is a charming area filled with shops, restaurants, and entertainment options, perfect for an afternoon or evening stroll. The center features beautifully landscaped spaces and hosts community events such as farmers' markets and outdoor concerts. Visitors can enjoy a meal at one of the many eateries, ranging from casual cafes to upscale dining establishments.

AMICALOLA FALLS STATE PARK

COUNTY: DAWSON CITY: DAWSONVILLE

DATE VISITED: WHO I WENT WITH:

RATING: ☆ ☆ ☆ ☆ ☆   WILL I RETURN? YES / NO

418 Amicalola Falls Road
Dawsonville, GA 30534
706-344-1500

Amicalola Falls State Park, nestled in the North Georgia Mountains, is one of Georgia's most breathtaking natural attractions. Known for the Amicalola Falls, the tallest cascading waterfall in the southeastern United States at 729 feet, this state park offers a perfect escape for nature lovers, hikers, and outdoor enthusiasts. Located about 70 miles north of Atlanta, it's an ideal destination for a day trip or a weekend getaway. Whether you're seeking scenic views, challenging hikes, or simply a peaceful retreat in nature, Amicalola Falls State Park has something for everyone.

Amicalola Falls – The Star Attraction - The crown jewel of the park is the Amicalola Falls, which means "tumbling waters" in the Cherokee language. This majestic waterfall cascades down a towering cliffside, and there are several ways to experience it. You can hike up the staircase that runs alongside the falls, offering multiple scenic viewpoints, or enjoy a more leisurely walk to the lower observation deck, where you can still admire its full glory. For photographers and nature lovers, it's a perfect spot to capture the beauty of Georgia's rugged wilderness.

The Appalachian Approach Trail - For hiking enthusiasts, one of the park's main draws is the Appalachian Approach Trail, an 8.5-mile trail that leads from Amicalola Falls State Park to Springer Mountain, the southern terminus of the Appalachian Trail. This trail is popular among both long-distance hikers starting their journey on the famous Appalachian Trail and day hikers looking for a challenging adventure. The trail offers stunning views of the surrounding mountains and valleys, and it's a great way to immerse yourself in the pristine beauty of the park's landscape.

The Lodge at Amicalola Falls - For visitors who want to stay overnight, the Lodge at Amicalola Falls offers comfortable accommodations with modern amenities and breathtaking mountain views. The lodge provides the perfect balance of comfort and outdoor adventure, with easy access to hiking trails and the falls. There's also a restaurant on-site offering Southern cuisine and panoramic views of the mountains. For a more rustic experience, the park also has cabins and a campground for those who prefer to be closer to nature.

Zip Line Adventure - For thrill-seekers, the park offers an exciting zip line adventure. With several zip lines running through the forest canopy, visitors can soar through the treetops and enjoy a bird's-eye view of the park's rugged terrain. The zip line courses vary in difficulty, making it a fun activity for both families and adrenaline junkies alike.

At the base of Amicalola Falls, you'll find the Reflection Pool, a tranquil spot where the waters from the falls gather before flowing downstream. This peaceful area is ideal for a quiet picnic or just relaxing by the water while taking in the natural surroundings. The reflection of the surrounding trees and cliffs in the water makes it a favorite spot for photographers and those looking for a moment of serenity.

Start your visit at the Amicalola Falls Visitor Center, where you can gather information about the park, trail maps, and learn about the history and geology of the area. The center also has exhibits on the local flora and fauna, making it an educational stop for families and curious visitors. Staff at the center can provide recommendations on the best trails and activities based on your interests and fitness level.

The park offers a variety of guided hikes and ranger-led programs that give visitors an opportunity to learn more about the ecology, wildlife, and history of the area. From bird-watching tours to survival skills workshops, these programs provide a hands-on experience of the natural environment. Check the park's calendar for special events, such as night hikes and nature photography workshops.

The high elevation of Amicalola Falls State Park makes it a fantastic place to catch stunning sunrises and sunsets. For early risers, watching the sunrise from the top of the falls or from one of the park's scenic overlooks is an unforgettable experience. Likewise, the sunsets over the Blue Ridge Mountains cast a golden glow over the landscape, offering perfect conditions for dramatic photographs.

For more adventurous visitors, the park offers backcountry campsites along some of its longer trails. These secluded spots provide an opportunity to truly connect with nature, offering a peaceful escape from the hustle and bustle of daily life. The park's wilderness areas are teeming with wildlife, and campers often spot deer, wild turkeys, and even black bears in the more remote parts of the park.

Amicalola Falls State Park is a birdwatcher's paradise, with a wide variety of bird species inhabiting the area year-round. The park's diverse habitats, from woodlands to streams, attract birds like the Eastern Bluebird, Red-tailed Hawk, and Pileated Woodpecker. Visitors interested in birdwatching can join ranger-led birding walks or explore on their own using the park's trails.

Tips:

- Wear comfortable footwear: Many of the park's trails, including the steps near the falls, can be steep and uneven, so make sure to wear sturdy hiking shoes.
- Bring water and snacks: While the park has a restaurant at the lodge, it's a good idea to bring your own snacks and water, especially if you plan on hiking the longer trails.
- Check the weather: Weather in the mountains can change quickly, so be sure to check the forecast and pack appropriately, especially if you're camping overnight.
- Stay on the trails: To preserve the park's natural beauty and protect its ecosystems, it's important to stay on marked trails and follow park regulations.

Nearby Attractions

- Dahlonega: A charming nearby town known for its gold mining history and wineries.

- Chattahoochee National Forest: Offering even more hiking trails, waterfalls, and opportunities for outdoor adventures.

- Appalachian Trail: For those seeking more adventure, the Appalachian Trail offers some of the best long-distance hiking in the United States.

ANNA RUBY FALLS

4

COUNTY: WHITE   **CITY:** HELEN

DATE VISITED: **WHO I WENT WITH:**

RATING: ☆ ☆ ☆ ☆ ☆   **WILL I RETURN?** YES / NO

3455 Anna Ruby Falls Rd
Helen, GA 30545
706-878-1448

Nestled within the breathtaking Chattahoochee National Forest near Helen, Georgia, Anna Ruby Falls is one of North Georgia's most scenic and serene natural wonders. Formed by the convergence of two creeks, Curtis and York, these twin waterfalls cascade over moss-covered cliffs, creating a stunning natural spectacle. Just a short drive from the charming Bavarian-style town of Helen, Anna Ruby Falls is a perfect destination for nature lovers, hikers, and anyone looking to escape into the peaceful beauty of the Appalachian Mountains. Managed by the U.S. Forest Service, Anna Ruby Falls is located within the Anna Ruby Falls Scenic Area, adjacent to the Unicoi State Park, making it easily accessible for day trips or weekend getaways.

The falls are named after Anna Ruby Nichols, the daughter of John H. Nichols, a local businessman who owned much of the surrounding land in the late 1800s. According to local legend, Nichols discovered the twin waterfalls during an exploration of the mountains, and he named them in honor of his beloved daughter. Today, Anna Ruby Falls stands as a reminder of the area's rich history, blending natural beauty with local folklore.

The Twin Waterfalls - Anna Ruby Falls is unique for its twin waterfalls. The higher falls, fed by Curtis Creek, drop from an impressive height of 153 feet, while the lower falls, fed by York Creek, descend 50 feet. Together, they create a striking visual, with water crashing over rocky cliffs and into the pools below. The beauty and power of these falls make them the star attraction of the area and a popular spot for photography and quiet contemplation. Visitors can hear the roar of the falls from a distance, and as you approach, the sound of rushing water becomes a peaceful backdrop to the scenic hike.

The journey to Anna Ruby Falls is as much a part of the experience as the falls themselves. A 0.4-mile paved trail leads from the parking area to the falls, winding through lush forest landscapes. The trail follows Smith Creek, offering visitors glimpses of wildflowers, towering hemlocks, and mountain laurel along the way. This gentle hike is accessible for visitors of all ages and abilities, making it perfect for families. Benches are placed along the path, providing spots to rest and take in the surrounding beauty. At the end of the trail, you'll find two wooden viewing platforms that offer stunning, up-close views of the falls.

Anna Ruby Falls is located in the Chattahoochee-Oconee National Forest, an area known for its biodiversity. Visitors might spot a variety of wildlife, including white-tailed deer, raccoons, and an assortment of birds like the Pileated Woodpecker and Eastern Bluebird. The forest is also home to a wide range of plant species, from ferns and wildflowers to towering pines and hardwoods. The pristine natural environment around the falls offers a peaceful and immersive escape into nature, ideal for birdwatchers, photographers, and those simply looking to enjoy the outdoors.

Located near the parking area, the Anna Ruby Falls Visitor Center is a great starting point for your visit. Here, you can find trail maps, brochures, and information about the local flora and fauna. The visitor center also features interpretive exhibits that provide insight into the area's natural history, geology, and the significance of the falls. The helpful staff can answer questions and offer tips for your visit, whether you're planning to hike or simply explore the scenic area around the falls.

For those looking to extend their visit, the scenic area around Anna Ruby Falls offers picnic spots where visitors can relax and enjoy the peaceful surroundings. There are picnic tables near the visitor center, providing a perfect setting for a meal amid the sounds of rushing water and birdsong. Bring along a packed lunch, unwind in the fresh mountain air, and take in the stunning views of the surrounding forest.

One of the standout features of Anna Ruby Falls is its accessibility. The paved trail is well-maintained and manageable, making it suitable for visitors of all ages and fitness levels. The short hike from the parking area to the falls takes about 15-20 minutes at a leisurely pace, making it ideal for families with small children or elderly visitors. The observation platforms at the base of the falls are also easily accessible, allowing everyone to enjoy the views of the cascading waters up close.

Anna Ruby Falls is beautiful year-round, with each season offering a unique perspective of the falls and surrounding forest. In spring, the forest comes alive with blooming wildflowers and fresh greenery. Summer brings cool shade from the towering trees and the refreshing mist of the falls. In autumn, the surrounding trees explode in a kaleidoscope of reds, oranges, and yellows, making it one of the best times to visit for photographers. Winter offers a quieter, more peaceful atmosphere, with the possibility of seeing the falls partially frozen, creating a magical winter wonderland.

Anna Ruby Falls is located just outside Unicoi State Park, one of Georgia's premier state parks. Visitors can extend their trip by exploring the park's many hiking trails, visiting Unicoi Lake, or staying overnight in the park's cabins or campgrounds. The Unicoi to Helen Trail, a 3-mile hike, leads directly from the falls to the Alpine town of Helen, making for a perfect day-long adventure.

Throughout the year, the U.S. Forest Service offers ranger-led programs at Anna Ruby Falls. These educational programs are designed to teach visitors about the area's natural history, wildlife, and conservation efforts. Topics range from guided nature walks to presentations on the history of the Chattahoochee National Forest. Check the visitor center for the schedule of events during your visit.

Tips

- Arrive early: To enjoy a quieter experience, especially during peak tourist seasons, consider arriving early in the day.
- Bring water and snacks: Staying hydrated and having a few snacks on hand will enhance your visit, especially if you plan to hike and explore the surrounding area.
- Check the weather: Before your visit, check the weather forecast. Rain can make trails slippery, so plan accordingly.
- Combine with other attractions: Consider exploring nearby attractions, such as the charming town of Helen or Unicoi State Park, to make the most of your day in the North Georgia mountains.

Nearby Attractions

- Helen, Georgia: Just a short drive away, the charming town of Helen is known for its Bavarian-style architecture and vibrant festivals. After exploring the falls, visitors can enjoy dining, shopping, and seasonal events in this unique mountain town.

- Unicoi State Park: A popular destination for outdoor enthusiasts, Unicoi State Park offers hiking, fishing, boating, and zip-lining adventures.

- Dukes Creek Falls: Another nearby waterfall attraction, Dukes Creek Falls offers a longer but equally scenic hike through the forest, with views of more cascading waters.

5 ATLANTA BOTANICAL GARDEN

COUNTY: FULTON **CITY:** ATLANTA

DATE VISITED: **WHO I WENT WITH:**

RATING: ☆ ☆ ☆ ☆ ☆ **WILL I RETURN?** YES / NO

1345 Piedmont Avenue
Atlanta, GA 30309
404-876-5859

Atlanta Botanical Garden is a stunning 30-acre urban oasis located in the heart of Atlanta, Georgia. This beautifully designed garden features a diverse collection of plants, vibrant floral displays, and innovative exhibits that celebrate the beauty of nature. Whether you're a gardening enthusiast, a family seeking a fun day out, or simply looking to relax in a serene environment, the Atlanta Botanical Garden offers a delightful experience for all ages.

Established in 1976, the Atlanta Botanical Garden has grown into a premier botanical garden known for its commitment to conservation, education, and horticultural excellence. The garden features themed areas, seasonal displays, and a variety of programs that engage and inspire visitors.

The Atlanta Botanical Garden features several themed areas, each showcasing unique plant collections and design.

Orchid Conservatory: Step into the breathtaking Orchid Conservatory, home to one of the largest collections of orchids in the southeastern United States. With vibrant colors and exquisite fragrances, this tropical paradise is a must-see.

Tropical Rainforest: Experience the sights and sounds of a tropical rainforest as you walk through this lush, humid environment. This area features cascading waterfalls, exotic plants, and a variety of butterflies flitting about.

Rose Garden: Explore the stunning Rose Garden, which features over 100 varieties of roses. This beautiful area is perfect for a leisurely stroll and offers fantastic photo opportunities.

Children's Garden: Designed for exploration and play, the Children's Garden includes interactive exhibits, climbing structures, and whimsical sculptures. This area provides a hands-on experience for younger visitors, encouraging them to learn about plants and nature.

The Atlanta Botanical Garden hosts a variety of seasonal exhibits that add to its charm throughout the year.

Scarecrows in the Garden: Every fall, the garden showcases creative scarecrow displays designed by local artists, schools, and community groups. This whimsical event attracts families and photographers alike.

Garden Lights, Holiday Nights: During the holiday season, the garden transforms into a winter wonderland with dazzling light displays. The spectacular illumination creates a magical atmosphere perfect for an evening stroll.

The Atlanta Botanical Garden offers a range of educational programs and workshops for visitors of all ages.

Classes and Workshops: Participate in gardening classes, cooking demonstrations, and art workshops. These programs are designed to inspire and educate, making it easy to deepen your knowledge of plants and gardening.

Guided Tours: Take a guided tour of the garden led by knowledgeable staff who can share insights about the plants and horticultural practices. Group tours and private events can also be arranged.

The visitor center serves as the main entrance and provides information about the garden, upcoming events, and educational opportunities. Friendly staff members are on hand to assist with any questions.

Don't forget to visit the gift shop, where you can find a variety of garden-related items, plants, books, and unique souvenirs to remember your visit.

Tips

- Plan your visit: Check the garden's website for information on special events and exhibits before your visit. This will help you make the most of your experience.
- Bring a camera: The Atlanta Botanical Garden is a photographer's paradise. Don't forget your camera to capture the stunning landscapes and vibrant floral displays.
- Wear comfortable Shoes: The garden covers a large area with various walking paths. Comfortable shoes will enhance your enjoyment as you explore.
- Pack a picnic: While food is not permitted in the garden, nearby parks like Piedmont Park offer lovely spots to enjoy a picnic after your visit.

Nearby Attractions

- Piedmont Park: Adjacent to the garden, Piedmont Park is a spacious urban park offering walking trails, sports fields, and beautiful views of the Atlanta skyline. It's a perfect place to relax or enjoy outdoor activities.

- High Museum of Art: Just a short drive away, the High Museum of Art features an impressive collection of American, European, and African art. The museum also hosts various rotating exhibitions and special events.

- Fox Theatre: An iconic Atlanta landmark, the Fox Theatre hosts a variety of performances, including Broadway shows, concerts, and special events. The stunning architecture and rich history make it a must-visit.

ATLANTA HISTORY CENTER

(6)

COUNTY: FULTON   CITY: ATLANTA

DATE VISITED: WHO I WENT WITH:

RATING: ☆ ☆ ☆ ☆ ☆   WILL I RETURN? YES / NO

130 West Paces Ferry Road NW
Atlanta, GA 30305
404-814-4000

Located in the prestigious Buckhead district of Atlanta, the Atlanta History Center is a comprehensive cultural destination that offers a deep dive into the rich history of the city, the state of Georgia, and the American South. Spanning 33 acres, the center is much more than a museum—it's an immersive experience that includes exhibitions, historic houses, beautiful gardens, and interactive programs. Whether you're a history buff, a garden lover, or just looking for an educational and engaging day out, the Atlanta History Center provides an enriching experience for visitors of all ages.

Founded in 1926, the Atlanta History Center has grown into one of the most significant history institutions in the southeastern United States. From Civil War memorabilia to the stories of the Civil Rights Movement, the center offers insights into both local and national history. Its mission is to preserve and share the diverse stories of the region, making it an essential stop for anyone looking to understand the heart and soul of Atlanta.

At the heart of the Atlanta History Center is the Atlanta History Museum, a vast space that houses a variety of permanent and rotating exhibits. The museum's collections cover a wide range of topics, from the Civil War and Southern folk culture to modern-day Atlanta. Notable exhibits include:

- "Turning Point: The American Civil War": This comprehensive exhibition features one of the largest Civil War collections in the country, with over 1,500 artifacts on display. Visitors can explore the causes, conflicts, and consequences of the war, particularly focusing on Georgia's role. The exhibition includes weapons, uniforms, medical equipment, and personal stories from soldiers and civilians alike.

- "Gatheround: Stories of Atlanta": This exhibit delves into the unique history of Atlanta, from its origins as a railroad hub to its emergence as the capital of the New South. Through personal stories, artifacts, and multimedia presentations, visitors can learn about key figures, events, and movements that shaped the city, including the 1996 Olympics, the Civil Rights Movement, and Atlanta's rise as a business and cultural center.

- "Cyclorama: The Big Picture": One of the museum's standout features is the Cyclorama, a massive 49-foot-tall, 360-degree painting that depicts the Battle of Atlanta during the Civil War. Recently restored, the Cyclorama is one of the largest paintings in the world and offers a dramatic and immersive way to experience this pivotal moment in history. The accompanying film and exhibitions provide context about the war and the painting's creation.

Another jewel of the Atlanta History Center is the Swan House, a stunning 1928 mansion designed in the Classical Revival style. Once the home of the wealthy Inman family, the Swan House is now preserved as a historic house museum. Visitors can tour the beautifully furnished rooms and learn about the lives of the Inmans, their servants, and the social and economic history of Atlanta in the early 20th century.

The Swan House may also look familiar to film buffs, as it was used as a filming location for "The Hunger Games" movies, serving as President Snow's mansion. Visitors can take guided tours to explore both the historical and pop culture significance of this grand home.

Step back in time to the 1860s with a visit to the Smith Family Farm, a fully restored farmhouse that provides a glimpse into rural life in Georgia during the Civil War era. The farm includes a farmhouse, barn, outbuildings, gardens, and animals. Costumed interpreters help bring history to life by demonstrating traditional crafts, farming techniques, and daily tasks, offering visitors a hands-on experience of what life was like for Atlanta's farmers and enslaved people.

The Goizueta Gardens at the Atlanta History Center encompass 22 acres of beautifully maintained gardens and trails, showcasing the region's plant life and landscape history. Highlights of the gardens include:

Mary Howard Gilbert Memorial Quarry Garden: This garden showcases native Georgia plants in a stunning quarry setting, with walking trails, waterfalls, and beautiful wildflowers.

Frank A. Smith Rhododendron Garden: A seasonal favorite, this garden bursts with vibrant blooms of rhododendrons and azaleas in spring.

Swan Woods Trail: This nature trail winds through a peaceful forest, offering a relaxing escape from the city and opportunities for bird watching and wildlife spotting.

Margaret Mitchell House As part of the Atlanta History Center's offerings, visitors can explore the Margaret Mitchell House, located in Midtown Atlanta. This modest apartment was where Mitchell wrote her famous novel, "Gone With the Wind." The house museum offers guided tours that explore Mitchell's life, her writing process, and the impact of her work on American literature and film. The house is an essential stop for fans of the book or movie, as well as anyone interested in Atlanta's literary history.

The Atlanta History Center places a strong emphasis on telling the story of the Civil Rights Movement, with a particular focus on Atlanta's role. Exhibits such as "Black Citizenship in the Age of Jim Crow" provide powerful insights into the struggle for equality and justice. Visitors can learn about the leaders of the movement, including Martin Luther King Jr., and explore artifacts and multimedia presentations that highlight the ongoing fight for civil rights in America.

Throughout the year, the Atlanta History Center hosts living history programs, where actors dressed in period costumes bring historical figures and events to life. These programs offer an engaging way to experience history, whether it's a Civil War re-enactment, a World War I tribute, or a demonstration of 19th-century farming techniques at the Smith Family Farm.

The center also offers a variety of workshops, lectures, and hands-on activities for both adults and children. These range from genealogy workshops and gardening classes to lectures by historians and authors. Seasonal events like the Fall Folklife Festival provide opportunities for visitors to learn traditional crafts, enjoy live music, and participate in family-friendly activities.

The Atlanta History Center hosts several annual events that draw visitors from across the region, including "Haunted Halloween," "Winter Wonderland" holiday events, and seasonal exhibits that showcase unique aspects of Southern culture and history. Temporary exhibits often feature collaborations with local artists, institutions, and community groups, offering fresh perspectives on history and culture.

Tips

- Plan your visit: Check the Atlanta History Center's website for information on current exhibits and upcoming events. This will help you make the most of your time there.

- Wear comfortable shoes: The center covers a large area with various walking paths, so comfortable footwear will enhance your experience.
- Bring a camera: The stunning architecture and beautiful gardens provide excellent photo opportunities. Capture memories of your visit to share with friends and family.
- Consider a guided tour: Take advantage of guided tours to gain deeper insights into the exhibits and historical context. Knowledgeable guides can enhance your experience with engaging stories and facts.

Nearby Attractions

- Buckhead Shopping and Dining: The upscale Buckhead area is known for its shopping and dining options, with destinations like Lenox Square Mall and Phipps Plaza nearby.

- Piedmont Park: If you're looking for more green space, Piedmont Park in Midtown Atlanta offers beautiful walking trails, lakes, and picnic spots.

- Atlanta BeltLine: A multi-use trail that loops through the city, the BeltLine offers additional opportunities to explore Atlanta's parks, art, and neighborhoods.

⑦ BABYLAND GENERAL HOSPITAL

COUNTY: WHITE   CITY: CLEVELAND

DATE VISITED: WHO I WENT WITH:

RATING: ☆ ☆ ☆ ☆ ☆   WILL I RETURN? YES / NO

300 N.O.K. Drive
Cleveland, GA 30528
706-865-2171

Nestled in the charming town of Cleveland, Georgia, lies one of the most unique and whimsical tourist destinations in the United States—BabyLand General Hospital, the birthplace of the world-famous Cabbage Patch Kids. This one-of-a-kind attraction is part museum, part interactive experience, and part toy store, offering visitors of all ages a nostalgic and magical experience. Whether you're a fan of these beloved dolls or just looking for a fun and quirky family outing, BabyLand General Hospital is a must-visit destination that combines playful charm with a dash of imagination.

Since its creation in 1978 by artist Xavier Roberts, the Cabbage Patch Kids phenomenon has enchanted children and adults alike. BabyLand General Hospital is the heart of this magical world, where visitors can witness the "birth" of Cabbage Patch Kids and even adopt their very own doll. Set against the beautiful backdrop of North Georgia's mountains, this enchanting experience brings to life the playful fantasy behind these iconic toys.

BabyLand General Hospital is housed in a stately, southern-style mansion on 650 acres of rolling hills and forests. From the moment you step onto the grand front porch, you're transported into a whimsical world where imagination reigns supreme. The building itself resembles a real hospital, complete with nurses and staff in scrubs, but it's far from a typical medical facility. Inside, every room is dedicated to showcasing and celebrating the magical Cabbage Patch Kid experience.

One of the most delightful experiences at BabyLand General Hospital is witnessing a Cabbage Patch Kid being "born" from a magical cabbage patch. In the central nursery area, known as Mother Cabbage, animatronic cabbages bloom and produce adorable Cabbage Patch babies with the help of dedicated "nurses." These nurses announce each new birth, performing the ritual with great fanfare, and invite visitors to name the newborn doll. The experience is both theatrical and heartwarming, making it a hit with children and nostalgic adults alike.

After seeing how the Cabbage Patch Kids come to life, visitors have the opportunity to adopt one of their own. There are thousands of Cabbage Patch Kids, each with its unique facial features, skin tones, and clothing, displayed throughout the hospital. Whether you're looking for a classic soft-sculptured doll or one of the modern vinyl versions, the selection is vast, ensuring you find the perfect companion to take home.

When you've chosen your Cabbage Patch Kid, you'll go through a formal adoption process. Just like a real adoption, you'll receive adoption papers with your doll's name and details, complete with a personal oath to care for your new "baby." The adoption experience is personalized and makes for a memorable keepsake for both children and adults.

BabyLand General Hospital is designed to be a multi-sensory experience. As you explore the different rooms of the hospital, you'll find displays of vintage Cabbage Patch Kids, historic memorabilia, and themed rooms that highlight the dolls' 40+ year history. One room may take you back to the 1980s, showcasing some of the original soft-sculptured designs by Xavier Roberts, while another room might be themed around holidays or special editions of Cabbage Patch Kids.

Visitors can also view nurseries, where newly "born" Cabbage Patch Kids rest in cribs, waiting to be adopted. There's even a "Premie Ward" for smaller dolls, adding a level of realism and charm to the experience.

Xavier Roberts, the creator of Cabbage Patch Kids, plays a central role in the BabyLand General Hospital experience. Throughout the museum, you'll find tributes to Roberts' vision and creativity, from his original soft-sculptured "Little People" dolls to his development of the Cabbage Patch Kids brand. The story of how Roberts turned a local craft project into a global phenomenon is woven into the fabric of the BabyLand experience, offering an inspiring tale of entrepreneurial success and artistic ingenuity.

BabyLand General Hospital hosts a variety of seasonal events throughout the year, including Cabbage Patch Kid Birthday Parties and themed celebrations during holidays like Christmas and Easter. During these events, the hospital is decked out with festive decorations, and visitors can participate in additional activities, like holiday-themed arts and crafts or photo opportunities with life-sized Cabbage Patch Kid mascots.

The annual Cabbage Patch Kids Birthday Celebration, held each fall, is one of the most popular events. It includes live music, games, food, and a large gathering of

Cabbage Patch Kid enthusiasts from around the country. It's a fun-filled day for families and fans alike, and it's a great opportunity to meet other collectors and share the magic of these beloved dolls.

Throughout the year, BabyLand offers special adoption ceremonies, where visitors can participate in the process of naming and adopting a Cabbage Patch Kid. These ceremonies are designed to make the adoption experience even more memorable, often involving an elaborate naming ritual and personalized attention from the BabyLand "staff."

Tips

- Arrive early: To ensure you have ample time to explore and participate in the "birth" ceremonies, consider arriving early, especially on weekends or during peak seasons.
- Bring a camera: BabyLand is filled with colorful displays and fun moments, making it an excellent location for family photos. Capture the magic of your visit.
- Check for special events: Visit BabyLand's website or call ahead to learn about any special events, themed days, or promotions during your visit.
- Plan for lunch: While there are no on-site dining options, several nearby restaurants and cafes offer family-friendly dining. Consider planning a lunch break to recharge before continuing your adventure.

Nearby Attractions

- Cleveland's Cabbage Patch Kids Store: Located just a short drive away, this store offers an even larger selection of Cabbage Patch Kids and merchandise. It's a great stop for fans looking to expand their collection.

- Unicoi State Park: A scenic park featuring hiking trails, a beautiful lake, and opportunities for outdoor activities such as fishing, picnicking, and camping. It's an ideal spot for families looking to enjoy nature.

- North Georgia Zoo and Farm: Located nearby, this charming zoo features a variety of animals and interactive experiences, including petting zoos and animal encounters. It's a perfect complement to a day at BabyLand.

----

⑧ BONAVENTURE CEMETERY

COUNTY: CHATHAM   **CITY:** SAVANNAH

DATE VISITED: **WHO I WENT WITH:**

RATING: ☆ ☆ ☆ ☆ ☆   **WILL I RETURN?** YES / NO

330 Bonaventure Rd.
Savannah, GA 31404
912-651-6843

Nestled along the picturesque banks of the Ogeechee River in Savannah, Georgia, Bonaventure Cemetery is not just a burial ground; it's a serene sanctuary steeped in history, art, and natural beauty. Established in 1846, the cemetery spans over 100 acres and features a remarkable collection of sculptures, elaborate graves, and lush landscapes. Known for its stunning live oak trees draped in Spanish moss, Bonaventure Cemetery has captivated visitors for generations, making it a must-see destination for anyone exploring Savannah. Whether you are a history enthusiast, an art lover, or simply looking for a peaceful place to reflect, Bonaventure offers a unique and hauntingly beautiful experience.

Bonaventure Cemetery is rich in history, with connections to some of Savannah's most prominent families and historical figures. Originally a plantation known as Bonnie Venture, the land was transformed into a cemetery after the Civil War. Today, it serves as the final resting place for many notable individuals, including:

- Conrad Aiken: The Pulitzer Prize-winning poet and novelist, who drew inspiration from the beauty and tranquility of the cemetery.

- Gracie Watson: The young daughter of a local hotelier whose tragic death in 1889 led to the creation of an iconic angel statue that remains one of the cemetery's most beloved features.

- James H. McAlpin: A prominent Savannah businessman, whose impressive monument is a testament to the architectural grandeur of the cemetery.

The cemetery is also known for its connections to the Civil War, with several soldiers buried within its grounds, adding to its rich historical tapestry.

Bonaventure Cemetery is renowned for its beautiful monuments, sculptures, and mausoleums that tell stories of the people buried there. Visitors can marvel at the intricate details of the gravestones, ranging from simple markers to grand structures adorned with angels, crosses, and elaborate carvings. Some notable monuments include:

- The Gracie Watson Memorial: This poignant statue of a young girl symbolizes love and loss. Gracie's life was tragically cut short at the age of six, and her statue is often decorated with fresh flowers left by visitors.

- The "Bird Girl" Statue: Originally part of the Wright family plot, this statue gained fame as the cover image for the novel Midnight in the Garden of Good and Evil. Today, a replica can be found in the cemetery, drawing fans of the book and movie to pay their respects.

Historic Oak Trees and Natural Beauty

The cemetery's stunning landscape is enhanced by centuries-old live oak trees draped with Spanish moss, creating a hauntingly beautiful atmosphere. The trees provide shade and add to the serene ambiance, making Bonaventure an ideal place for leisurely strolls and quiet reflection. Visitors can explore winding paths that meander through lush gardens, vibrant azaleas, and serene ponds, all contributing to the cemetery's enchanting setting.

Throughout Bonaventure Cemetery, informative markers and signage provide visitors with insights into the history and significance of various plots and monuments. These markers tell the stories of prominent families, local legends, and significant events related to Savannah's past. As you walk through the cemetery, take the time to read these plaques to gain a deeper appreciation for the lives and legacies of those interred here.

For those seeking a more in-depth understanding of Bonaventure's history, guided tours are available. Knowledgeable guides share captivating stories about the cemetery's inhabitants, its architectural features, and the local lore surrounding Savannah. Tours typically cover notable graves, historical context, and the cultural significance of the cemetery.

Additionally, the cemetery often hosts special events, including historical reenactments, art exhibits, and lectures that delve into Savannah's rich history and the lives of those buried at Bonaventure. Check the cemetery's website or local event listings for current programs during your visit.

Tips

- Wear comfortable shoes: The cemetery is expansive, and walking paths can be uneven. Comfortable footwear will enhance your exploration experience.

- Bring water: Staying hydrated is essential, especially during warmer months. Bring a bottle of water to keep you refreshed as you walk through the cemetery.
- Check the weather: Since much of your visit will be outdoors, check the weather forecast before your trip. Dress appropriately for the season and consider bringing sunscreen or a light jacket, depending on the conditions.
- Take your time: Bonaventure Cemetery is a peaceful place meant for contemplation and reflection. Take your time to enjoy the scenery, read the inscriptions on the headstones, and soak in the tranquil atmosphere.

Nearby Attractions

- Savannah's Historic District: Just a short drive from Bonaventure, Savannah's historic district is filled with beautiful squares, antebellum architecture, and charming shops and restaurants. Take time to explore the area and discover the rich history of this Southern gem.

- Forsyth Park: This sprawling park is located in the heart of Savannah and features walking paths, a playground, and the iconic Forsyth Fountain, making it a perfect spot for a leisurely stroll or picnic.

- Savannah Riverfront: The bustling River Street offers shops, restaurants, and stunning views of the Savannah River. Enjoy a meal overlooking the water or take a riverboat cruise for a different perspective of the city.

_____

_____

_____

_____

_____

_____

_____

_____

_____

_____

_____

_____

9   BRASSTOWN BALD MOUNTAIN

COUNTY: TOWNS   **CITY:** HIAWASSEE

DATE VISITED: **WHO I WENT WITH:**

RATING: ☆ ☆ ☆ ☆ ☆   **WILL I RETURN?** YES / NO

2941 Highway Spur 180
Hiawassee, GA 30546
706-896-2556

Nestled in the Blue Ridge Mountains of North Georgia, Brasstown Bald stands proudly as the highest peak in the state, reaching an elevation of 4,784 feet. Part of the Chattahoochee National Forest, Brasstown Bald offers breathtaking views, lush landscapes, and a variety of outdoor activities for visitors of all ages. Whether you're an avid hiker, a nature lover, or simply looking to enjoy stunning panoramic vistas, Brasstown Bald is a must-visit destination that showcases the natural beauty of the region.

Located about 15 miles northeast of Blairsville, Brasstown Bald is easily accessible by car. The main entrance is off Highway 180, with clear signs directing visitors to the Brasstown Bald Visitor Center. The drive to the mountain is scenic, with winding roads that offer glimpses of the beautiful North Georgia countryside. The Brasstown Bald Visitor Center serves as the starting point for your adventure. Open year-round (weather permitting), the center features informative exhibits about the area's natural and cultural history, including the flora and fauna of the region. Here, you can also find:

- Restrooms: Clean facilities are available for visitor convenience.
- Gift Shop: A small gift shop offers souvenirs, educational materials, and local crafts, making it a perfect stop for picking up a memento of your visit.
- Maps and Information: Friendly staff are on hand to provide information about the area, trail conditions, and any special events happening during your visit.

The main trail to the summit is the Brasstown Bald Trail, a 0.6-mile paved path that offers a relatively easy hike suitable for visitors of all ages and abilities. This accessible trail leads you through a beautiful forest setting and culminates at the observation tower at the peak. Along the way, you'll encounter informative signs about the local ecosystem and stunning views.

For those looking for more of a challenge, several longer hiking trails surround Brasstown Bald, including segments of the Appalachian Trail and various backcountry paths that offer a chance to explore the diverse wildlife and natural beauty of the Chattahoochee National Forest. Be sure to check trail maps and conditions at the visitor center before heading out.

At the summit of Brasstown Bald, visitors are rewarded with 360-degree panoramic views of the surrounding mountains and valleys. On clear days, you can see as far as North Carolina, Tennessee, and even South Carolina. The observation tower, completed in 1938, features several viewing platforms, allowing you to take in the stunning landscape from different angles.

Interpretive Signs: The summit is equipped with interpretive signs that identify various mountain ranges, landmarks, and even the cities that can be seen from the peak. These educational displays enhance the experience and provide a deeper appreciation of the geography of the region.

Biodiversity thrives in the Brasstown Bald area, with a variety of plant and animal species inhabiting the lush forests and rocky outcrops. As you explore the area, keep an eye out for:

Depending on the season, vibrant wildflowers bloom along the trails, including rhododendrons, mountain laurels, and various ferns.

The forest is home to diverse wildlife, including deer, black bears, and a variety of bird species. Birdwatchers will particularly enjoy spotting raptors like hawks and eagles soaring overhead.

Brasstown Bald is a year-round destination, offering different activities depending on the season:

- Spring: Witness the explosion of wildflowers and enjoy pleasant hiking weather. Spring is also a great time for birdwatching, as migratory birds return to the area.
- Summer: The cooler temperatures at the summit provide a refreshing escape from the summer heat. This season is perfect for hiking and picnicking in the surrounding areas.
- Fall: Autumn brings stunning fall foliage, transforming the landscape into a colorful tapestry of reds, oranges, and yellows. The breathtaking views of the changing leaves make this a popular time to visit.
- Winter: While access to the summit can be limited due to snow and ice, winter offers a unique beauty, with the possibility of snow-covered landscapes and a quieter atmosphere for those seeking solitude.

Tips

- Dress appropriately: Weather conditions can change rapidly in the mountains, so dress in layers and be prepared for cooler temperatures at the summit.
- Stay hydrated: Bring plenty of water, especially if you plan to hike the trails.
- Pack snacks: While there are no food services at the summit, packing snacks or a picnic can enhance your visit.
- Respect the environment: Follow Leave No Trace principles to help preserve the natural beauty of the area for future visitors.

Nearby Attractions

- Lake Trahlyta: Just a short drive from Brasstown Bald, this beautiful lake is perfect for fishing, kayaking, and picnicking. The area features hiking trails that wind around the lake and provide additional opportunities for exploration.

- Young Harris: Visit the charming town of Young Harris, home to Young Harris College and several local shops and eateries. The town is known for its Southern hospitality and offers a cozy atmosphere.

- Dahlonega: About 30 minutes away, Dahlonega is famous for its gold rush history and charming downtown square. Visitors can explore historic sites, local wineries, and outdoor activities in the surrounding mountains.

🔟 BUCKHEAD

COUNTY: FULTON   **CITY:** BUCKHEAD

DATE VISITED: **WHO I WENT WITH:**

RATING: ☆ ☆ ☆ ☆ ☆   **WILL I RETURN?**   YES / NO

Nestled within Atlanta, Buckhead is a vibrant and affluent neighborhood known for its upscale shopping, fine dining, and stunning architecture. Often referred to as the "Beverly Hills of the South," Buckhead offers a unique blend of urban sophistication and Southern charm. Whether you're interested in luxury shopping, exploring beautiful parks, or enjoying exquisite dining, Buckhead is a must-visit destination for anyone looking to experience the best of Atlanta.

Buckhead is conveniently located just eight miles north of downtown Atlanta and is easily accessible via major highways, including Interstate 85 and Interstate 75. Visitors can also use MARTA, Atlanta's public transportation system, with several train and bus routes connecting Buckhead to the rest of the city. If you're driving, be aware that parking can be limited in some areas, particularly near popular shopping districts and restaurants.

Buckhead is a shopper's paradise, featuring some of the finest retail destinations in the Southeast:

- Phipps Plaza: This upscale shopping mall is home to luxury brands such as Gucci, Louis Vuitton, and Tiffany & Co. In addition to high-end boutiques, Phipps Plaza features a cinema and several dining options.
- Lenox Square: Another premier shopping destination, Lenox Square is one of the largest malls in Georgia, offering a mix of luxury and contemporary brands, including Neiman Marcus and Apple. It also hosts seasonal events, making it a lively spot to explore.

Culinary Delights

Buckhead boasts an impressive culinary scene, with a wide range of dining options to satisfy every palate:

- The Capital Grille: Known for its dry-aged steaks and extensive wine list, this fine dining establishment offers an elegant atmosphere perfect for special occasions.
- Atlanta Fish Market: This seafood restaurant features a menu filled with fresh

catches and a lively ambiance, making it a favorite among locals and visitors alike.
- Bone's: Renowned for its classic steakhouse experience, Bone's is consistently ranked among the best steakhouses in the country, offering top-quality cuisine and impeccable service.

Buckhead Theatre
The Buckhead Theatre, a historic venue dating back to the 1930s, hosts a variety of performances, including concerts, comedy shows, and community events. The beautifully restored art deco design adds to the charm, making it a great place to catch a live show.

Atlanta History Center
Located in the heart of Buckhead, the Atlanta History Center offers a deep dive into the city's past. The center features:

- Permanent Exhibits: Explore the history of Atlanta through interactive displays and artifacts.
- The Swan House: A stunning 1928 mansion that offers guided tours showcasing its beautiful architecture and history.
- Outdoor Gardens: Wander through the Woodland Gardens, featuring beautiful walking paths, seasonal blooms, and tranquil spaces for reflection.

Chastain Park
Chastain Park is one of Atlanta's largest parks, offering a variety of recreational activities. With walking trails, picnic areas, and sports facilities, it's an ideal spot for outdoor enthusiasts. The park also features the Chastain Park Amphitheater, a popular venue for concerts and events during the warmer months.

Buckhead is home to a thriving arts scene, with galleries, theaters, and cultural institutions that showcase local talent:

- The Museum of Contemporary Art of Georgia (MOCA GA): This museum focuses on the work of Georgia artists, featuring rotating exhibitions and educational programs. It's a great place to discover contemporary art and engage with the local creative community.
- Swan House Art Galleries: Located within the Atlanta History Center, these galleries host rotating exhibits showcasing regional artists and historical artifacts.

As the sun sets, Buckhead comes alive with a vibrant nightlife scene. From upscale cocktail bars to lively dance clubs, there's something for everyone:

- The Pink Pony: A renowned local establishment known for its lively atmosphere and live music, The Pink Pony is a Buckhead staple offering a mix of entertainment and delicious food.
- Vortex Bar & Grill: Famous for its burgers and quirky decor, Vortex is a popular spot for casual dining and drinks, often featuring live music and local events.

Tips

- Plan ahead: With its many attractions, dining options, and shopping destinations, it's a good idea to plan your itinerary to make the most of your visit.
- Dress code: Many restaurants and venues in Buckhead have a business casual dress code, so be sure to dress appropriately, especially for fine dining.
- Public transportation: Consider using MARTA to avoid parking hassles, especially during busy weekends or events.
- Stay hydrated: If you plan to spend a lot of time outdoors, especially in the warmer months, be sure to bring water and stay hydrated.

Nearby Attractions

- The High Museum of Art: Located a short drive away in Midtown Atlanta, this renowned art museum features an impressive collection of American and European art, as well as rotating exhibitions.

- The Atlanta Botanical Garden: Just a few miles from Buckhead, this beautiful garden showcases stunning plant collections and seasonal displays, providing a peaceful retreat from the urban hustle.

- Piedmont Park: A large urban park with walking trails, sports facilities, and scenic views, Piedmont Park is a popular destination for both locals and visitors looking to enjoy the outdoors.

----

11. CATHEDRAL OF ST. JOHN THE BAPTIST

COUNTY: CHATHAM   **CITY:** SAVANNAH

DATE VISITED: **WHO I WENT WITH:**

RATING: ☆ ☆ ☆ ☆ ☆   **WILL I RETURN?** YES / NO

222 East Harris Street
Savannah, GA 31401
912-233-4709

Situated in the heart of Savannah, Georgia, the Cathedral of St. John the Baptist stands as a breathtaking testament to architectural beauty and spiritual significance. Founded in the late 18th century, this stunning cathedral is one of the oldest Roman Catholic parishes in the United States and serves as a focal point of the city's rich cultural heritage. With its soaring spires, intricate stained glass, and serene atmosphere, the cathedral attracts both worshippers and visitors, making it a must-see destination in Savannah.

The Cathedral of St. John the Baptist has a storied history that reflects the evolution of the Catholic Church in the region. Originally established in 1799, the first structure was a modest wooden church. The current cathedral, designed in the Gothic Revival style, was completed in 1896 after the original building was destroyed in a fire. Notable features of the cathedral include:

- Architectural Influence: Designed by architect G. H. Wright, the cathedral showcases stunning Gothic elements, including pointed arches, intricate stone carvings, and majestic spires.
- Restoration: The cathedral underwent extensive restoration in the late 20th century, ensuring that its beauty and historical significance are preserved for future generations.

As you approach the cathedral, you'll be struck by its impressive facade, characterized by:

- Twin Spires: Rising 150 feet into the sky, the twin spires are a defining feature of the cathedral's silhouette and can be seen from various points in the city.
- Stonework: The exterior is crafted from tabby, a local material made from oyster shells, combined with bricks and mortar, giving the building a unique texture and character.
- Beautiful Doors: The ornate main entrance features intricately carved wooden doors that invite visitors into this sacred space.

Step inside the cathedral to discover an interior that is equally captivating:

- Stained Glass Windows: The cathedral boasts over 30 stained glass windows, many of which depict biblical scenes and saints. These stunning works of art were crafted in France and add a vibrant play of light to the interior.
- Hand-Carved Altar: The main altar, made from exquisite wood, is adorned with intricate carvings and serves as the focal point of the sanctuary. The altar's design reflects the craftsmanship of skilled artisans.
- Vaulted Ceilings: The soaring vaulted ceilings create a sense of awe, drawing the eye upward and enhancing the spiritual ambiance of the space.
- The Stations of the Cross: Beautifully depicted along the walls, the Stations of the Cross are artistic representations of the events of Christ's Passion, guiding visitors through a visual meditation of the journey to the crucifixion.
- The Baptismal Font: A stunning baptismal font made of marble is located at the entrance, symbolizing the importance of baptism in the Catholic faith.

The Cathedral of St. John the Baptist is open to visitors daily, with specific hours for Mass and prayer. It's recommended to check the official website for the most current schedule, especially if you plan to attend a service.

While self-guided tours are welcome, the cathedral also offers guided tours led by knowledgeable docents. These tours provide insights into the history, architecture, and significance of the cathedral, enhancing your experience. Be sure to check for tour availability and schedule in advance.

Visitors are welcome to take photographs inside the cathedral, but it's important to be respectful of the sacred space. Avoid using flash photography during services and be mindful of other visitors.

The cathedral hosts regular Mass services, which are open to the public. Attending a service allows visitors to experience the spiritual life of the community and enjoy the beauty of the liturgy in this magnificent setting.

The Cathedral of St. John the Baptist often hosts concerts, especially during the holiday season. These performances feature various musical styles, including choral, organ, and classical music, and are a delightful way to experience the acoustics of the cathedral.

Throughout the year, the cathedral organizes community events, including seasonal celebrations and religious festivals. These gatherings provide opportunities for fellowship and deepen the connection between the cathedral and the local community.

Tips

- Dress appropriately: As a place of worship, visitors are encouraged to dress modestly. Comfortable shoes are also recommended, as you may want to explore the surrounding area afterward.
- Plan ahead: If you are interested in attending a Mass or guided tour, - check the schedule in advance to ensure availability.
- Explore the surrounding area: The cathedral is located in Savannah's historic district, surrounded by beautiful squares, parks, and restaurants. Take time to explore the nearby attractions, including Forsyth Park and the Savannah Historic District.

Nearby Attractions

- Forsyth Park: A short walk from the cathedral, Forsyth Park is a sprawling green space known for its iconic fountain, walking paths, and vibrant gardens. It's a perfect spot for a leisurely stroll or a picnic.

- Savannah Historic District: Explore the rich history of Savannah by wandering through its charming streets, lined with historic homes, shops, and eateries. Don't miss the opportunity to visit Chippewa Square and the Savannah History Museum.

- The Owens-Thomas House: This historic home offers guided tours showcasing early 19th-century architecture and the lives of its residents, providing further insight into Savannah's history.

----

⑫ CENTENNIAL OLYMPIC PARK

COUNTY: FULTON   **CITY:** ATLANTA

DATE VISITED: **WHO I WENT WITH:**

RATING: ☆ ☆ ☆ ☆ ☆   **WILL I RETURN?** YES / NO

265 Park Ave W NW
Atlanta, GA 30313
404-223-4412

Centennial Olympic Park, located in the heart of downtown Atlanta, is a vibrant public space that embodies the spirit of the 1996 Summer Olympics held in the city. Spanning 21 acres, this urban park features beautiful green spaces, iconic fountains, and numerous attractions, making it a beloved destination for both locals and visitors. Whether you're looking to relax, enjoy outdoor activities, or learn about Atlanta's history, Centennial Olympic Park offers something for everyone.

Centennial Olympic Park was built as a centerpiece for the 1996 Olympics, serving as a gathering place for athletes and visitors alike. The park was designed to celebrate the Games and the revitalization of downtown Atlanta. Key historical highlights include:

The park was part of the effort to showcase Atlanta's growth and hospitality during the Olympics. It played host to various events and celebrations throughout the games. After the Olympics, the park was transformed into a permanent public space, leading to the redevelopment of surrounding areas and further establishing Atlanta as a thriving metropolis.

One of the park's most iconic features, the Fountain of Rings, is a must-see attraction. This interactive fountain is designed to resemble the Olympic rings. The fountain comes alive with choreographed water shows set to music, creating a mesmerizing experience for visitors, especially children. During warmer months, the fountain provides a fun spot for kids to splash around and cool off.

Located at the park's entrance, the Olympic Cauldron is a symbolic reminder of the Olympic Games. Originally lit during the opening ceremony in 1996, it stands as a tribute to the spirit of the Olympics and is a popular photo spot for visitors.

Centennial Olympic Park features beautifully landscaped gardens and green spaces, perfect for a leisurely stroll or a picnic. Highlights include:

- The Southern Company Amphitheater: This outdoor venue hosts concerts and events throughout the year, offering a lively atmosphere for music lovers.
- Garden Walks: Enjoy the park's walking paths, adorned with seasonal flowers and native plants, providing a peaceful escape from the bustling city.

The park is home to several historic markers and memorials that commemorate the legacy of the Olympics and the city of Atlanta. These include:

- The Georgia Plaza: A tribute to the state of Georgia and its contributions to the Olympics.
- The Memorial to the Victims of the 1996 Olympic Park Bombing: This solemn area pays respect to those affected by the tragic event during the games, reminding visitors of the resilience of the Atlanta community.

Centennial Olympic Park is a hub of activity year-round, hosting a variety of events and festivals. The park often hosts free concerts, particularly during the summer months. Check the park's event calendar for upcoming performances.

Throughout the year, the park hosts seasonal events, including Fourth of July celebrations, holiday festivals, and community gatherings, bringing together locals and visitors alike.

The park offers fitness classes and activities, encouraging visitors to engage in a healthy lifestyle while enjoying the outdoors.

Tips:

- Bring a picnic: Pack a lunch and enjoy a relaxing picnic on the park's green spaces. There are plenty of benches and picnic tables available.
- Plan for the weather: Atlanta's weather can be unpredictable. Be sure to check the forecast and dress accordingly, especially if you plan to attend outdoor events.
- Stay hydrated: If visiting during the warmer months, bring water to stay hydrated as you explore the park and nearby attractions.
- Check the events calendar: Before your visit, check the park's official website for information on upcoming events and activities to make the most of your experience.

Nearby Attractions

- Georgia Aquarium: Just a short walk from the park, the Georgia Aquarium is one of the largest aquariums in the world. Visitors can explore various exhibits featuring marine life from around the globe, including the famous Ocean Voyager exhibit.

- World of Coca-Cola: Located adjacent to the aquarium, the World of Coca-Cola offers an interactive experience showcasing the history and cultural impact of the iconic beverage. Visitors can enjoy tastings, exhibits, and a behind-the-scenes look at Coca-Cola's production.

- SkyView Atlanta: For breathtaking views of the Atlanta skyline, hop on the SkyView Atlanta, a giant Ferris wheel located nearby. Each gondola provides a comfortable ride with panoramic views, making it a perfect way to conclude your day at the park.

CENTER FOR PUPPETRY ARTS

13

COUNTY: FULTON **CITY:** ATLANTA

DATE VISITED:　　　　　　　　　　**WHO I WENT WITH:**

RATING: ☆ ☆ ☆ ☆ ☆　　　　**WILL I RETURN?**　YES / NO

1404 Spring St. NW at 18th
Atlanta, GA 30309
404-873-3391

Nestled in the heart of Atlanta, the Center for Puppetry Arts is a unique cultural institution dedicated to the art of puppetry. Since its founding in 1978, the center has become a beloved destination for families, educators, and art enthusiasts alike. With engaging performances, hands-on workshops, and an impressive museum, the Center for Puppetry Arts offers a magical experience that celebrates the creativity and artistry of puppetry from around the world.

The Center for Puppetry Arts was established by Vincent Anthony, who sought to create a space where the art of puppetry could be preserved and promoted. Over the years, the center has:

- Expanded its mission: From its humble beginnings, the center has grown into one of the largest nonprofit organizations dedicated to puppetry in the United States, offering a diverse range of programs and performances for audiences of all ages.
- Gained national recognition: The center has received numerous awards for its contributions to the arts and education, solidifying its reputation as a leader in puppetry and cultural arts.

The heart of the Center for Puppetry Arts is its live performances. The center features a rotating schedule of shows, including:

- Classic stories: Enjoy puppet adaptations of beloved children's stories, such as "The Very Hungry Caterpillar" and "The Lion, the Witch and the Wardrobe."
- Original productions: The center also creates its own unique puppet performances, showcasing innovative storytelling and artistic talent.
- Adult shows: In addition to family-friendly performances, the center occasionally hosts shows designed for adult audiences, incorporating more sophisticated themes and humor.

The Museum of Puppetry Arts is a treasure trove for puppetry enthusiasts, offering a fascinating glimpse into the world of puppetry:

- Exhibits: The museum features a range of exhibits that showcase the history and art of puppetry from around the globe, including traditional puppets from different cultures and modern innovations.
- Jim Henson collection: One of the museum's highlights is the Jim Henson Collection, which pays tribute to the legendary puppeteer and creator of the Muppets. Visitors can view original puppets, sketches, and memorabilia, gaining insight into Henson's creative process.
- Interactive displays: Engaging interactive exhibits allow visitors to try their hand at puppetry, encouraging creativity and exploration.

The Center for Puppetry Arts offers hands-on workshops for children and adults, providing an opportunity to learn the art of puppetry firsthand:

- Puppet making: Participants can create their own puppets using various materials, learning techniques for construction and performance.
- Performance workshops: These sessions focus on puppetry performance skills, including voice acting, movement, and storytelling, encouraging participants to bring their puppets to life.
- Educational programs: The center offers educational programs for schools and community organizations, teaching the fundamentals of puppetry and storytelling.

The Center for Puppetry Arts hosts a variety of special events and seasonal programs throughout the year:

- Puppet Slam: An exciting event that showcases short performances by local and national puppeteers, providing a platform for emerging artists to present their work.
- Holiday shows: During the holiday season, the center features special performances that capture the festive spirit, making it a perfect destination for family outings.
- Community events: The center frequently hosts community events, such as family festivals and themed celebrations, fostering a sense of community and engagement through the art of puppetry.

Tips

- Arrive early: Plan to arrive at least 30 minutes before your scheduled performance to allow time for parking and exploring the museum exhibits.
- Check the schedule: Visit the center's website for the latest performance schedule and special events to make the most of your visit.
- Bring a camera: Photography is encouraged in the museum, so bring your

camera to capture the colorful displays and unique puppets.
- Consider a workshop: If time allows, sign up for a puppet-making or performance workshop to enhance your experience and learn new skills.

Nearby Attractions

- Piedmont Park: Located just a short drive away, Piedmont Park is Atlanta's largest urban park, featuring walking trails, sports facilities, and beautiful green spaces. It's a great place for a leisurely stroll or a picnic after visiting the center.

- Atlanta Botanical Garden: Adjacent to Piedmont Park, the Atlanta Botanical Garden showcases stunning plant collections, themed gardens, and seasonal exhibits. The garden offers a peaceful retreat and is a wonderful complement to your visit to the Center for Puppetry Arts.

- Fernbank Museum of Natural History: A short drive from the center, the Fernbank Museum offers engaging exhibits on natural history, including dinosaur skeletons and interactive science displays. It's an excellent destination for families and science enthusiasts.

14 CHATTAHOOCHEE RIVER

COUNTY: MULTIPLE **CITY:** MULTIPLE

DATE VISITED: **WHO I WENT WITH:**

RATING: ☆ ☆ ☆ ☆ ☆ **WILL I RETURN?** YES / NO

The Chattahoochee River is a stunning natural resource that flows for 430 miles from the Blue Ridge Mountains in North Georgia to the Gulf of Mexico, serving as a vital source of water, recreation, and beauty for both the state of Georgia and neighboring Alabama and Florida. Known affectionately as the "Hooch," this river offers a wealth of activities for outdoor enthusiasts, picturesque scenery, and a glimpse into the region's rich history. Whether you're interested in hiking, fishing, kayaking, or simply enjoying the natural beauty, the Chattahoochee River is a must-visit destination.

The Chattahoochee River has a rich history that spans thousands of years. Indigenous peoples, including the Creek and Cherokee nations, relied on the river for sustenance and trade long before European settlers arrived. Key historical highlights include:

- Early settlements: In the 18th century, European settlers established communities along the river, utilizing its waters for farming, milling, and transportation.
- Civil War significance: The river played a strategic role during the Civil War, serving as a natural barrier and resource for both Union and Confederate forces.
- Modern conservation: Today, efforts are underway to protect and preserve the river's ecosystems through various conservation initiatives and public awareness campaigns.

The Chattahoochee River is a hub of recreational activities for visitors of all ages. The river's gentle flow makes it an excellent spot for kayaking and canoeing. Rentals and guided tours are available at various locations along the river, including Roswell, Sandy Springs, and Buford Dam.

Anglers will find ample opportunities to catch a variety of fish, including bass, catfish, and trout. Popular fishing spots include Hollis Gardens and the Chattahoochee National Recreation Area.

Stand-up paddleboarding is another popular activity on the river, offering a unique perspective of the surrounding scenery.

The river is bordered by numerous trails, providing scenic routes for hiking and biking:

- The Chattahoochee River National Recreation Area: This area features over 15 miles of trails, allowing visitors to explore the natural beauty of the river and its surrounding ecosystems. Trails range from easy walks to more challenging hikes, suitable for all skill levels.
- The Big Creek Greenway: This paved trail runs alongside the river and connects various parks and communities, making it a popular spot for jogging, biking, and walking.

Numerous parks and picnic areas along the river offer serene spots to relax and enjoy the outdoors.

Facilities like Riverside Park in Roswell and Morgan Falls Park in Sandy Springs provide picnic tables, grills, and scenic views of the river, making them perfect for family outings or a day in nature.
The river is home to diverse wildlife, including herons, otters, and various fish species. Bring your binoculars for a chance to spot these creatures in their natural habitat.

The Chattahoochee River area is rich in cultural and historical significance:

- Historic Roswell: This charming town features historic homes, shops, and restaurants along the river. Explore the Roswell Mill and the Bulloch Hall, which provide insights into the region's history.
- The Chattahoochee Nature Center: Located in Roswell, this center offers educational programs, exhibits, and nature trails, promoting awareness of the local environment and conservation efforts.

Tips

- Plan for the weather: Check the forecast before your visit, as weather conditions can change quickly. Dress in layers and bring sunscreen or rain gear as needed.
- Stay hydrated: Bring plenty of water, especially if you plan to hike or participate in outdoor activities.
- Check for events: Look up local events and festivals happening along the river during your visit to enhance your experience.

Nearby Attractions

- Lake Lanier: A short drive north of the river, Lake Lanier is a popular destination for boating, swimming, and fishing. The lake offers beautiful beaches, picnic areas, and hiking trails, making it an ideal spot for a full day of outdoor fun.

- Stone Mountain Park: Approximately 30 miles east of the Chattahoochee River, Stone Mountain Park features hiking trails, a scenic train ride, and a laser show that lights up the mountain at night. The park is a great place to experience Georgia's natural beauty and history.

- Atlanta History Center: Located a bit further from the river, the Atlanta History Center offers engaging exhibits on the Civil War, Southern history, and local culture. It's a wonderful place to learn more about the region's heritage and enjoy beautiful gardens.

CHICKAMAUGA AND CHATTANOOGA NATIONAL MILITARY PARK

15

COUNTY: CATOOSA **CITY:** FORT OGLETHORPE

DATE VISITED: **WHO I WENT WITH:**

RATING: ☆ ☆ ☆ ☆ ☆ **WILL I RETURN?** YES / NO

3370 LaFayette Road
Fort Oglethorpe, GA 30742
706-866-9241

The Chickamauga and Chattanooga National Military Park is a significant historical site located in northwestern Georgia and southeastern Tennessee. Established in 1890, it was the first national military park in the United States, dedicated to preserving the sites of two major Civil War battles: the Battle of Chickamauga and the Siege of Chattanooga. This park serves not only as a tribute to the brave soldiers who fought here but also as a beautiful natural area for visitors to explore. With over 5,300 acres of preserved land, this park offers rich history, stunning landscapes, and numerous recreational activities.

Fought from September 19 to 20, 1863, this battle marked one of the most significant Confederate victories in the Western Theater of the Civil War. The battle was notable for its intense combat and high casualties.

Following the Battle of Chickamauga, Union forces were besieged in Chattanooga. The subsequent battles, including the Battle of Lookout Mountain and the Battle of Missionary Ridge, resulted in a critical Union victory, boosting morale and changing the course of the war.

The establishment of the park was a pioneering effort to commemorate and preserve the sites of these crucial battles, honoring the sacrifices made by soldiers on both sides.

Start your visit at the Chickamauga Battlefield Visitor Center, where you can:

The center features informative exhibits detailing the history of the battles, the soldiers involved, and the significance of the campaigns. Discover a collection of Civil War artifacts, including uniforms, weapons, and personal items that provide insight into the lives of soldiers. Don't miss the 23-minute orientation film, which provides an overview of the battles and the broader context of the Civil War.

The park offers a variety of ways to explore the historic battlefield:

- Self-Guided Tours: Follow the Chickamauga Battlefield Driving Tour to see key sites and monuments at your own pace. Informational signs along the route provide historical context and narratives.
- Guided Tours: Join a ranger-led tour for an in-depth exploration of the battlefield. These tours often delve into personal stories, strategies, and the impact of the battles.

The park is home to over 1,400 monuments and markers commemorating the soldiers and units that fought in the battles. Highlights include:

- The Illinois State Memorial: A striking monument that honors the soldiers from Illinois who fought in the Battle of Chickamauga.
- The Georgia State Memorial: This impressive memorial honors the soldiers from Georgia who participated in the battle and features intricate sculptures and inscriptions.

Visit Lookout Mountain, a significant site during the Siege of Chattanooga. From the summit, enjoy panoramic views of the surrounding valleys and mountains, a perfect spot for photography and reflection. Hike the trails that lead through the historic landscape, providing insight into the strategic importance of this location during the Civil War.

The park features over 30 miles of trails that cater to hikers and bikers:

Explore the diverse ecosystems of the park, where you can spot local wildlife and enjoy the beautiful scenery. The Chickamauga Battlefield Trail is particularly popular for its scenic views and historical significance. Several paved paths are suitable for cycling, offering a leisurely way to experience the park's natural beauty and history.

The park's waterways offer opportunities for fishing, though a valid fishing license is required. Designated picnic areas provide scenic spots to relax and enjoy lunch surrounded by nature. Bring a picnic and take in the beautiful surroundings.

The park is home to diverse wildlife, including deer, wild turkeys, and various bird species. Bring binoculars to enhance your wildlife watching experience and enjoy the natural habitat.

Tips

- Wear comfortable shoes: With plenty of walking and hiking opportunities,

comfortable footwear is essential for exploring the park and its trails.
- Bring water and snacks: Stay hydrated and energized during your visit, especially if you plan to hike or spend a lot of time outdoors.
- Check the weather: Georgia weather can be unpredictable, so check the forecast and dress accordingly for your visit.
- Plan ahead: Consider joining a ranger-led tour for a more in-depth experience and to learn from knowledgeable staff about the battles and park history.

Nearby Attractions

- Chattanooga, Tennessee: Just a short drive from the park, the vibrant city of Chattanooga offers a wealth of attractions, including the Tennessee Aquarium, Lookout Mountain, and the Chattanooga Riverwalk, a scenic pathway along the Tennessee River.

- Rock City Gardens: Located on Lookout Mountain, Rock City features stunning rock formations, beautiful gardens, and panoramic views. Don't miss the iconic Seven States View, where you can see seven states from one vantage point.

- Ruby Falls: Also on Lookout Mountain, Ruby Falls is an impressive underground waterfall that attracts visitors with its stunning beauty and guided tours. Explore the caverns and learn about the history of this natural wonder.

----

16 CHIPPEWA SQUARE

COUNTY: CHATHAM CITY: SAVANNAH
DATE VISITED: WHO I WENT WITH:
RATING: ☆ ☆ ☆ ☆ ☆   WILL I RETURN? YES / NO

Chippewa Square
Savannah, GA 31401

Nestled in the heart of Savannah, Georgia, Chippewa Square is a picturesque public square that embodies the charm and history of this southern city. Established in 1815, Chippewa Square is one of Savannah's original squares and is renowned for its beautiful oak trees, historic landmarks, and vibrant atmosphere. Whether you're a history buff, a film enthusiast, or simply looking for a relaxing spot to enjoy the outdoors, Chippewa Square has something for everyone.

Chippewa Square is named after the Battle of Chippewa, a conflict fought during the War of 1812. The square reflects Savannah's commitment to honoring its historical roots while providing a space for community gatherings and events. Designed by James Oglethorpe, the founder of Savannah, the city is known for its unique grid layout and abundance of green spaces, with Chippewa Square serving as a centerpiece in this historic planning. Over the years, the square has been a gathering place for locals and visitors alike, hosting public events, celebrations, and demonstrations that reflect the city's rich cultural heritage.

Although not located directly in Chippewa Square, the Forsyth Fountain is just a short stroll away and is one of Savannah's most famous landmarks. This beautiful fountain, completed in 1858, serves as a stunning backdrop for photos and a focal point for visitors.

The square is surrounded by beautifully preserved historic buildings, showcasing Savannah's unique architectural style:

- The Savannah Theatre: Located adjacent to Chippewa Square, this historic theater has been entertaining audiences since 1818. It offers a variety of performances and is a great place to catch a show during your visit.
- The Olde Pink House: A few blocks away, this restaurant is housed in an 18th-century mansion, providing a delightful dining experience in a charming historical setting.

At the center of the square stands a monument dedicated to the Confederate soldiers who fought in the Civil War. The monument serves as a reminder of the complex history of the region and provides a place for reflection.

Chippewa Square is known for its majestic oak trees, draped with Spanish moss, providing ample shade and a serene atmosphere. The square's beautifully landscaped gardens and benches make it an ideal spot to relax and enjoy nature. Take a moment to sit on one of the many benches surrounding the square and soak in the atmosphere. The lush greenery and beautiful surroundings provide a perfect backdrop for relaxation and contemplation.

Chippewa Square is a popular spot for photography, with its historic architecture, beautiful trees, and the iconic fountain nearby. Capture the essence of Savannah by taking photos of the square and its surroundings, especially during golden hour when the light is just right.

Join a guided walking tour to learn more about the history and significance of Chippewa Square and the surrounding areas. Many tours highlight the fascinating stories of Savannah's past, its architecture, and notable figures.

Chippewa Square often hosts community events, including concerts, art shows, and seasonal festivals. Check local listings to see if any events coincide with your visit, providing an opportunity to engage with the local culture.

Tips

- Plan your visit: Consider visiting during the morning or late afternoon when the temperatures are cooler, and the light is ideal for photography.
- Bring a picnic: Pack a picnic to enjoy in the square. The peaceful atmosphere and beautiful scenery make it a lovely spot for a meal outdoors.
- Wear comfortable shoes: Savannah is best explored on foot, so wear comfortable shoes for walking around the square and the nearby historic district.
- Stay hydrated: Especially in warmer months, be sure to drink plenty of water while exploring the area.

Nearby Attractions

- Savannah Historic District: Explore the beautiful Savannah Historic District, which is filled with charming streets, historic homes, and vibrant gardens. This area offers numerous opportunities for shopping, dining, and cultural exploration.

- River Street: Just a short walk away, River Street is a lively waterfront area filled with shops, restaurants, and entertainment options. Enjoy a stroll along the cobblestone streets, sample local cuisine, and take in views of the Savannah River.

- Bonaventure Cemetery: A short drive from the square, Bonaventure Cemetery is known for its stunning sculptures, historic graves, and haunting beauty. This cemetery is a peaceful place to explore and offers a glimpse into Savannah's storied past.

CITY MARKET

(17)

COUNTY: CHATHAM **CITY:** SAVANNAH

DATE VISITED: **WHO I WENT WITH:**

RATING: ☆ ☆ ☆ ☆ ☆ **WILL I RETURN?** YES / NO

219 W Bryan S
Savannah, GA 31401
912-232-4903

City Market is one of Savannah's most beloved destinations, steeped in history and brimming with local charm. Located in the heart of Savannah's historic district, this lively marketplace features a variety of shops, galleries, restaurants, and entertainment options. With its cobblestone streets and vibrant atmosphere, City Market invites visitors to explore, shop, and savor the unique offerings of this enchanting southern city.

Originally developed in the 1730s, City Market served as the center for trade and commerce in Savannah. Merchants sold their goods in open-air markets, establishing a bustling hub of activity. After a decline in the 19th century, the area was revitalized in the 1990s, transforming it into a lively cultural and commercial center that showcases Savannah's rich history and artistry. The market features restored historic buildings that reflect the architectural style of the region, providing a beautiful backdrop for shopping and dining.

City Market is home to an array of shops and galleries that cater to all tastes:

- Local artisans: Discover unique handmade crafts, artwork, and souvenirs at various galleries and boutiques. From paintings to pottery, the local artistry reflects Savannah's creative spirit.
- Fashion and gifts: Explore charming boutiques offering everything from trendy clothing to thoughtful gifts. Look for locally made items that capture the essence of Savannah.

Savor the flavors of Savannah at City Market's diverse dining options:

- Local cuisine: Enjoy traditional Southern dishes and seafood at popular restaurants such as The Shrimp Factory and B&D Burgers. Be sure to try a classic shrimp and grits or a po' boy sandwich.
- Sweet treats: Indulge in delightful desserts at local bakeries and ice cream shops. Savannah's Candy Kitchen is a must-visit for its famous pralines and homemade fudge.

The vibrant atmosphere of City Market often includes live music and entertainment:

- Street performers: Enjoy performances by local musicians and artists, adding to the lively ambiance of the marketplace.
- Seasonal events: City Market hosts various events throughout the year, including art shows, festivals, and holiday celebrations. Check local listings for event schedules during your visit.

As you explore City Market, take note of its historical significance:

- Civil War history: The area played a role during the Civil War, serving as a supply center and gathering place for troops. Historical markers provide insights into the rich history of the marketplace.
- Cultural heritage: City Market reflects the diverse cultural heritage of Savannah, showcasing the city's evolution from its colonial beginnings to its present-day vibrancy.

City Market is a shopper's paradise, offering a wide range of products:

- Art and crafts: Browse through art galleries featuring works by local artists. You can find everything from paintings to handmade jewelry, perfect for souvenirs or gifts.
- Home decor: Explore shops specializing in home decor and furnishings, showcasing southern styles that add charm to any space.

Spend an afternoon or evening savoring delicious food and drinks:

- Outdoor dining: Many restaurants offer outdoor seating, allowing you to enjoy your meal while soaking up the vibrant atmosphere of the market.
- Wine and cocktails: Enjoy a glass of local wine or a creative cocktail at one of the bars or restaurants, perfect for unwinding after a day of exploring.

Join a guided tour or art walk to learn more about the history and artistry of City Market:

- Historical tours: Several companies offer walking tours that delve into Savannah's history, including the significance of City Market and its role in the community.
- Art walks: Participate in art walks that showcase the talents of local artists, giving you the opportunity to meet creators and learn about their work.

Tips

- Plan your time: Allocate enough time to explore the shops, dine, and soak in the atmosphere. A few hours will allow you to enjoy everything City Market has to offer.
- Check for events: Look up local event schedules to see if there are any special activities or festivals happening during your visit.
- Wear comfortable shoes: The cobblestone streets and walking paths are best navigated with comfortable footwear, especially if you plan to explore the surrounding areas.
- Stay hydrated: Keep a bottle of water handy, especially in warmer months, to stay refreshed while enjoying your time in the market.

Nearby Attractions

- River Street: Just a short walk from City Market, River Street is a bustling waterfront area filled with shops, restaurants, and entertainment options. Enjoy views of the Savannah River while exploring this lively district.

- Forsyth Park: A bit further away, Forsyth Park is a beautiful green space that features walking paths, fountains, and gardens. It's a perfect spot for a leisurely stroll or a picnic.

- Savannah Historic District: Explore the historic district, known for its cobblestone streets, historic homes, and picturesque squares. Don't miss Chippewa Square and Monterey Square, which are just a short distance from City Market.

CLOUDLAND CANYON STATE PARK

18

COUNTY: DADE CITY: RISING FAWN

DATE VISITED: WHO I WENT WITH:

RATING: ☆ ☆ ☆ ☆ ☆ WILL I RETURN? YES / NO

122 Cloudland Canyon Park Road
Rising Fawn, GA 30738
706-657-4050

Cloudland Canyon State Park, located in the scenic northwestern corner of Georgia, is a breathtaking natural destination that offers visitors stunning landscapes, outdoor activities, and a peaceful retreat from everyday life. Nestled atop the Appalachian Plateau, the park features deep canyons, cascading waterfalls, lush forests, and panoramic views that make it a must-visit for nature lovers and adventure seekers alike.

Cloudland Canyon State Park was officially established as a state park in 1938, although the area's natural beauty had been appreciated long before then. The park is part of the rich natural heritage of Georgia and reflects the state's commitment to preserving its unique landscapes. During the 1930s, the CCC played a significant role in developing the park's infrastructure, including trails, cabins, and facilities, which are still in use today.

The park is home to diverse ecosystems, including hardwood forests, sandstone cliffs, and lush vegetation, providing a habitat for various wildlife species.

The park's iconic Canyon Overlook provides stunning views of the canyon below, making it a popular spot for photography and contemplation.

Don't miss the picturesque Hemlock Falls and Cherokee Falls, both accessible via well-maintained trails. These cascading waterfalls are perfect for a peaceful retreat or a picnic in nature.

Cloudland Canyon offers a variety of hiking trails catering to all skill levels:

- West Rim Loop Trail: This moderately challenging 4-mile loop offers breathtaking views of the canyon and the surrounding landscape. The trail is well-marked and provides ample opportunities to stop and enjoy the scenery.
- Waterfall Trails: The Waterfall Trail is a 1-mile trek that leads you to Cherokee Falls and Hemlock Falls. The journey is filled with lush foliage and picturesque views, perfect for families and beginners.

For those looking to immerse themselves in nature, Cloudland Canyon offers various accommodation options:

- Campgrounds: The park features a family-friendly campground with tent and RV sites, providing a great opportunity to enjoy the outdoors overnight. Facilities include restrooms, showers, and picnic areas.
- Cottages: If you prefer a more comfortable stay, consider renting one of the park's rustic cabins, which are equipped with modern amenities and offer stunning views of the canyon.

The park is home to diverse wildlife, including deer, wild turkeys, and various bird species. Bring binoculars and a camera to capture the beauty of the park's flora and fauna. Early mornings and late afternoons are the best times for wildlife watching.

Take advantage of the park's extensive trail system. Whether you're looking for a leisurely stroll or a challenging hike, there are trails suited for every fitness level.

With its stunning landscapes, unique geological features, and vibrant plant life, Cloudland Canyon is a photographer's paradise. Capture the beauty of the waterfalls, canyon views, and wildlife, especially during sunrise and sunset.

Pack a picnic to enjoy in one of the park's designated picnic areas. With the sound of flowing water and beautiful surroundings, it's the perfect spot to relax and recharge.

For those who enjoy treasure hunts, Cloudland Canyon offers a geocaching experience where you can search for hidden caches throughout the park. This activity is a fun way to explore the area while engaging in an interactive adventure.

Tips

- Dress appropriately: Wear comfortable clothing and sturdy hiking shoes, as the terrain can be rugged in some areas. Be prepared for changing weather conditions.
- Stay hydrated: Bring plenty of water, especially during warmer months, to stay hydrated while hiking and exploring the park.
- Respect nature: Follow Leave No Trace principles by packing out what you pack in and respecting wildlife and natural habitats.
- Plan your activities: Review trail maps and park brochures available at the visitor

center to plan your day effectively. Check the weather forecast to make the most of your visit.

Nearby Attractions

- Lookout Mountain: Just a short drive from Cloudland Canyon, Lookout Mountain offers additional outdoor activities and attractions, including Rock City Gardens and Ruby Falls, both known for their stunning natural beauty.

- Chickamauga and Chattanooga National Military Park: Located nearby, this national park is rich in Civil War history and features numerous trails, monuments, and historical sites worth exploring.

- Fort Mountain State Park: A bit further away, Fort Mountain State Park is another beautiful destination, featuring hiking trails, a scenic lake, and the mysterious stone fort built by ancient Native Americans.

⑲ COLLEGE FOOTBALL HALL OF FAME

COUNTY: FULTON **CITY:** ATLANTA

DATE VISITED: **WHO I WENT WITH:**

RATING: ☆ ☆ ☆ ☆ ☆ **WILL I RETURN?** YES / NO

250 Marietta St. NW
Atlanta, GA 30313
404-880-4800

Located in the heart of downtown Atlanta, the College Football Hall of Fame is a must-visit destination for sports enthusiasts and college football fans alike. This interactive museum honors the rich history, legendary players, and unforgettable moments of college football. With its engaging exhibits, memorabilia, and immersive experiences, the Hall of Fame offers visitors an opportunity to celebrate the sport's heritage and its impact on American culture.

The College Football Hall of Fame was founded in 1951 in Canton, Ohio, before relocating to Atlanta in 2014. The move to Atlanta allowed for a more prominent location and expanded facilities to showcase the sport's legacy.

The Hall of Fame's mission is to preserve and promote the history of college football while inspiring future generations through education and entertainment.

The building's striking design reflects the excitement and energy of college football. The 94,256-square-foot facility features a modern exterior and a vibrant interior filled with interactive displays and exhibits.

Main Attractions

- The helmet wall: One of the Hall's highlights, this exhibit features over 750 college football helmets from various teams, showcasing the diversity of college football across the nation.
- Field goals and passing challenge: Test your skills with interactive games where you can try to kick a field goal or throw a touchdown pass, experiencing the thrill of the game firsthand.
- Virtual reality experiences: Engage with state-of-the-art virtual reality setups that allow you to feel like a part of the action, from game-winning plays to coaching strategies.

Hall of Fame Gallery

The Hall of Fame Gallery honors the greatest players, coaches, and contributors to college football. Inductees are recognized for their exceptional achievements and contributions to the sport, with:

- Plaques and displays: Each inductee has a dedicated plaque and display detailing their accomplishments, stats, and career highlights, providing visitors with insight into their impact on college football.
- Legends wall: Explore the stories of the sport's legends, including Heisman Trophy winners and coaching greats, and learn about their journeys and achievements.

This exhibit chronicles the evolution of college football, from its origins in the late 19th century to the present day:

- Historical artifacts: View historical memorabilia, including vintage uniforms, trophies, and photographs that tell the story of the sport's development over the decades.
- Multimedia presentations: Enjoy informative videos and displays that highlight key moments and milestones in college football history.

The Fan Zone

The Fan Zone is a vibrant area where visitors can immerse themselves in the spirit of college football:

- Tailgating Experience: Learn about the culture of tailgating, an integral part of college football tradition, through interactive displays and demonstrations.
- Team Pride: Showcase your team spirit by participating in fun activities and games, making it a great place for fans of all ages.

Take advantage of guided tours that provide deeper insights into the exhibits and the history of college football. Knowledgeable guides share stories and anecdotes about the legends and milestones of the sport.

The Hall of Fame hosts various events throughout the year, including:

- Induction ceremonies: Attend the annual induction ceremony, where new members are honored, and their contributions to the sport are celebrated.
- Educational programs: Participate in educational programs designed for students

and young athletes, focusing on leadership, teamwork, and the values of sportsmanship.

Don't forget to visit the Hall of Fame gift shop, where you can find a wide range of college football merchandise, including apparel, memorabilia, and unique gifts. It's the perfect place to pick up a souvenir to remember your visit.

Tips

- Plan ahead: Check the Hall of Fame's official website for special events or exhibits that may be taking place during your visit.
- Arrive early: To make the most of your time, arrive early to enjoy all the exhibits and activities without feeling rushed.
- Stay hydrated: Bring a water bottle or purchase drinks from the on-site café to stay refreshed during your visit.
- Dress comfortably: Wear comfortable clothing and shoes, as you'll likely be walking and participating in interactive activities.

Nearby Attractions

- Centennial Olympic Park: Just a short walk from the Hall of Fame, Centennial Olympic Park is a beautiful green space featuring fountains, walking paths, and the iconic Olympic Ring Fountain. It's an ideal spot for relaxation and enjoying outdoor activities.

- Georgia Aquarium: One of the largest aquariums in the world, the Georgia Aquarium is located nearby and offers a fantastic opportunity to explore marine life. Plan a visit to see stunning exhibits, including the massive Ocean Voyager tank.

- World of Coca-Cola: Explore the history and culture of one of the world's most famous brands at the World of Coca-Cola. This interactive museum features exhibits on the history of Coca-Cola, tastings of beverages from around the globe, and fun photo opportunities.

COLUMBUS RIVERWALK

20

COUNTY: MUSCOGEE	CITY: COLUMBUS
DATE VISITED:	WHO I WENT WITH:
RATING: ☆ ☆ ☆ ☆ ☆	WILL I RETURN? YES / NO

Bay Avenue and 11th Street
Columbus, GA 39701

The Columbus Riverwalk is a picturesque and vibrant pathway along the banks of the Chattahoochee River, offering locals and visitors alike a unique way to experience the beauty of Columbus, Georgia. This scenic walkway stretches for approximately 15 miles, providing a perfect setting for walking, jogging, biking, or simply relaxing while enjoying the stunning views of the river and the surrounding landscape. The Riverwalk is not only a recreational area but also a cultural hub with various attractions, dining options, and events that reflect the city's rich history and community spirit.

The Columbus Riverwalk was developed in the early 1990s as part of a revitalization effort to enhance the riverfront area, turning it into an accessible and enjoyable public space. Since then, it has become a key feature of Columbus, attracting residents and tourists alike. The Riverwalk is steeped in history, with roots tracing back to the early days of Columbus as a bustling cotton trading post. The Chattahoochee River played a crucial role in the city's development, serving as a transportation route and a source of economic growth.

Efforts have been made to preserve the natural beauty of the river and surrounding areas, making the Riverwalk not only a recreational space but also a habitat for local wildlife.

Along the Riverwalk, several parks provide lush green spaces with picnic areas, benches, and beautiful landscaping, perfect for a relaxing afternoon. The Riverwalk features various art installations and sculptures that add a creative touch to the pathway, enhancing the overall experience for visitors.
Recreational Activities

The paved path is ideal for walking, running, and biking, making it a popular spot for fitness enthusiasts and families. Bike rentals are available nearby for those looking to explore on two wheels.

The Chattahoochee River offers opportunities for water sports, including kayaking and paddleboarding. Rentals and guided tours are available for those wishing to explore the river from a different perspective.

Experience the thrill of whitewater rafting on the Chattahoochee River with Whitewater Express. This facility offers guided rafting trips on the river's rapids, providing an exhilarating adventure for both beginners and experienced rafters.

Located near the Riverwalk, the Columbus Museum features exhibits on the city's history and art, providing insight into the cultural heritage of the area.

The Riverwalk is home to several dining options that cater to various tastes:

- Riverside restaurants: Enjoy a meal with a view at one of the riverside restaurants, offering everything from Southern cuisine to international dishes. Outdoor seating allows you to soak in the scenic surroundings while enjoying your food.
- Live music and events: Throughout the year, the Riverwalk hosts various events, including concerts, festivals, and seasonal celebrations. Check the local calendar for upcoming happenings that may coincide with your visit.

Join a guided walking tour along the Riverwalk to learn about the history, architecture, and cultural significance of the area. Knowledgeable guides share stories and insights about the landmarks you'll encounter along the way.

Pack a picnic and find a peaceful spot along the Riverwalk to enjoy your meal while taking in the beautiful views. Several parks along the way have picnic tables and grills available for public use.

The Riverwalk provides a habitat for various bird species and wildlife. Bring binoculars for a chance to spot local birds and other animals along the riverbanks, especially in the early morning or late afternoon.

Participate in seasonal events hosted along the Riverwalk, such as summer concerts, holiday celebrations, and outdoor movie nights. These events create a lively atmosphere and provide opportunities to connect with the local community.

Tips

- Plan your route: The Riverwalk spans several miles, so plan your route in advance based on the attractions you want to see. You can easily spend a few hours exploring different sections of the pathway.

- Dress comfortably: Wear comfortable shoes and clothing suitable for outdoor activities, especially if you plan to walk or bike along the Riverwalk.
- Stay hydrated: Bring water with you, particularly during warmer months, to stay refreshed while enjoying your time outdoors.
- Check the weather: Before heading out, check the weather forecast to ensure you dress appropriately and enjoy your visit to the fullest.

Nearby Attractions

- National Civil War Naval Museum: A short drive from the Riverwalk, this museum features exhibits on naval history during the Civil War, including ship models and artifacts. It offers an informative glimpse into a significant period of American history.

- Port Columbus Civil War Naval Museum: This museum, dedicated to the history of naval warfare during the Civil War, showcases artifacts, exhibits, and a variety of naval vessels. It's an engaging experience for history buffs and families alike.

- Fort Benning: Located just south of the Riverwalk, Fort Benning is a military base with a rich history. The National Infantry Museum and Soldier Center at Fort Benning is worth a visit, offering insights into the history of the U.S. Army Infantry.

㉑ CONGREGATION MICKVE ISRAEL

COUNTY: CHATHAM **CITY:** SAVANNAH

DATE VISITED: **WHO I WENT WITH:**

RATING: ☆ ☆ ☆ ☆ ☆ **WILL I RETURN?** YES / NO

20 East Gordon St.
Savannah, GA 3140
912-233-1547

Congregation Mickve Israel is one of the oldest synagogues in the United States, located in the heart of Savannah, Georgia. Established in 1733, this historic congregation is a vibrant community steeped in rich traditions, history, and culture. Known for its stunning architecture and engaging programs, Mickve Israel is not only a place of worship but also a cultural landmark that tells the story of Jewish life in America. Whether you are a visitor interested in Jewish heritage or a local looking to connect with the community, Congregation Mickve Israel offers a warm welcome and a glimpse into its fascinating past.

Founded by a group of Jewish settlers who arrived in Savannah in the early 18th century, Mickve Israel has a long and storied history. The congregation has played a significant role in the Jewish community of Savannah and has been an active participant in the broader social fabric of the city. The current synagogue building, constructed in 1891, features a beautiful blend of Gothic and Moorish architectural styles, making it a true gem in Savannah's architectural landscape.

The exterior of Congregation Mickve Israel showcases intricate brickwork and stunning stained-glass windows. The main entrance is marked by an elegant archway that invites visitors to explore the interior. Inside, visitors will find a beautiful sanctuary adorned with historic artifacts, including a magnificent Ark that houses the Torah scrolls. The sanctuary features high ceilings, wooden pews, and beautiful artwork that reflects the congregation's heritage and faith.

Congregation Mickve Israel offers guided tours that provide insight into the history, architecture, and traditions of the synagogue. These tours are led by knowledgeable staff and volunteers who share fascinating stories and details about the congregation's past and present.

Discover the rich history of the synagogue and the Jewish community in Savannah, including notable figures who have been part of its story. Learn about the challenges and triumphs of the congregation throughout the centuries.

The synagogue hosts various cultural and educational programs throughout the year, including lectures, art exhibits, and holiday celebrations. These events offer an opportunity to engage with the community and learn more about Jewish traditions and practices.

Congregation Mickve Israel holds regular worship services, including Shabbat services and holiday celebrations. Visitors are welcome to attend and experience the beauty of Jewish worship. The services often include traditional prayers, music, and readings from the Torah, creating a spiritually enriching environment.

The congregation is committed to community service and outreach, providing various programs to support those in need. Visitors can learn about the synagogue's initiatives, including educational programs for children and adults, social justice efforts, and interfaith dialogue initiatives.

Tips

- Plan ahead: Consider checking the calendar of events on the synagogue's website to coincide your visit with special programs or services that may interest you.
- Take your time: Allow yourself plenty of time to explore the synagogue and soak in the history and beauty of the space.
- Ask questions: Don't hesitate to ask staff or volunteers questions during your visit. They are passionate about the synagogue and its history and are happy to share their knowledge.

Nearby Attractions

- Forsyth Park: Just a short walk from the synagogue, Forsyth Park is a beautiful 30-acre public park that features walking paths, gardens, and a famous fountain. It's a perfect spot for a leisurely stroll, a picnic, or simply to enjoy the outdoors. The park often hosts local events and farmers' markets, making it a lively gathering place for the community.

- Savannah History Museum: Located in the historic Central of Georgia Railway depot, the Savannah History Museum offers a fascinating look at the city's past. Exhibits cover various aspects of Savannah's history, from its founding in 1733 to its role in the Civil War and beyond. The museum also houses artifacts, including items related to James Oglethorpe and Juliette Gordon Low, the founder of the Girl Scouts.

- Bonaventure Cemetery: A bit further away but worth the visit, Bonaventure Cemetery is renowned for its hauntingly beautiful landscapes, historic monuments, and impressive oak trees draped with Spanish moss. The cemetery is the final resting place of many notable figures, and guided tours are available to learn about its history and the stories of those buried there.

㉒ CONSOLIDATED GOLD MINE

COUNTY: LUMPKIN   **CITY:** DAHLONEGA

DATE VISITED: **WHO I WENT WITH:**

RATING: ☆ ☆ ☆ ☆ ☆   **WILL I RETURN?** YES / NO

185 Consolidated Gold Mine Road
Dahlonega, GA 30533
706-864-8473

Consolidated Gold Mine is a fascinating destination located in Dahlonega, Georgia, where history and adventure come together! As the site of the first major gold rush in the United States, this mine offers visitors a unique opportunity to learn about the gold mining industry while experiencing the thrill of panning for gold themselves. Whether you're a history buff, a nature enthusiast, or just looking for a fun family outing, the Consolidated Gold Mine provides a memorable experience in the heart of the beautiful North Georgia mountains.

The Consolidated Gold Mine began operations in the late 19th century and played a significant role in the Dahlonega gold rush of 1828. The mine produced a substantial amount of gold and contributed to the area's economic development. After its closure in the early 20th century, the site was preserved as a historical landmark, allowing visitors to step back in time and discover the rich history of gold mining in Georgia.

Visitors can take guided tours of the underground mine, which last approximately 40 minutes. Led by knowledgeable guides, these tours provide insight into the history of gold mining and the techniques used by miners in the past. During the tour, you'll learn about the tools and methods used to extract gold and see how the mine operated during its peak production years.

The tour takes you deep into the mine, where you can see the original tunnels and learn about the challenges faced by miners. The atmosphere inside the mine is both educational and exciting, making it a memorable experience.

Throughout the tour, visitors will encounter various historical artifacts and exhibits that showcase the life and work of miners during the gold rush era. This immersive experience brings history to life and helps visitors appreciate the hard work and determination of those who sought their fortunes underground.

One of the highlights of a visit to the Consolidated Gold Mine is the chance to try your hand at gold panning. This hands-on experience allows visitors to learn the techniques used by miners to find gold while enjoying the thrill of discovering real treasures.

After your tour, head to the panning station, where you'll be provided with all the necessary equipment and instruction to start panning for gold. The friendly staff will guide you through the process, ensuring you have a fun and successful experience.

Any gold or gemstones you discover while panning are yours to keep! It's an exciting way to engage with the history of the area and take home a unique souvenir from your visit.

Tips

- Arrive early: To make the most of your visit, arrive early to allow time for the tour and gold panning experience. This is especially important during peak tourist seasons when crowds may be larger.
- Bring water and snacks: Although the mine has a gift shop and snack bar, it's a good idea to bring water and some snacks, especially if you plan to spend the day exploring Dahlonega.
- Explore dahlonega: After your visit to the Consolidated Gold Mine, take some time to explore the charming town of Dahlonega. Known for its historic downtown, unique shops, and local wineries, it's a great place to continue your adventure.
- Plan for weather: Check the weather forecast before your visit, especially if you plan to do outdoor activities or panning for gold, as conditions can change quickly in the mountains.

Nearby Attractions

- Dahlonega Gold Museum: Located in the historic courthouse, the Gold Museum features exhibits about the history of gold mining in the area, including artifacts and information about the 19th-century gold rush.

- Cannon Falls: A short hike from downtown Dahlonega, Cannon Falls offers beautiful views and a scenic waterfall. It's a lovely spot for a picnic or a leisurely nature walk.

- Wolf Mountain Vineyards & Winery: Just a short drive away, this beautiful winery offers tastings and tours, allowing you to relax and enjoy the stunning views of the North Georgia mountains while sampling delicious wines.

CRISSON GOLD MINE

(23)

COUNTY: LUMPKIN **CITY:** DAHLONEGA

DATE VISITED: **WHO I WENT WITH:**

RATING: ☆ ☆ ☆ ☆ ☆   **WILL I RETURN?** YES / NO

2736 Morrison Moore Pkwy E
Dahlonega, GA 30533
706-864-6363

Crisson Gold Mine is a captivating destination located in Dahlonega, Georgia, that immerses visitors in the rich history of gold mining in the region. Established in 1969, Crisson Gold Mine is one of the oldest gold mines in the state and offers a unique blend of historical education and hands-on experiences. Whether you're a history enthusiast, a nature lover, or just looking for a fun family outing, Crisson Gold Mine promises an unforgettable adventure where you can pan for gold, explore the mine, and learn about the fascinating story of Georgia's gold rush.

The gold rush in Dahlonega began in 1828 and played a pivotal role in the area's development. Crisson Gold Mine has been in operation since the late 19th century, allowing visitors to explore the same grounds where miners once sought their fortunes. The mine features original equipment and artifacts that highlight the mining process, making it a living museum of gold mining history.

Visitors can take guided tours of the historic gold mine, where knowledgeable staff share the fascinating history of gold mining in Dahlonega. During the tour, you'll have the chance to see how gold was extracted from the earth, including a demonstration of the mining equipment used. You'll also learn about the various methods miners employed to locate and extract gold. The tour includes various historic artifacts and exhibits that provide insight into the daily lives of miners and the gold mining industry. You'll get a sense of the challenges and triumphs faced by those who sought their fortunes in the hills of Georgia.

One of the most exciting aspects of visiting Crisson Gold Mine is the opportunity to try your hand at gold panning. This hands-on activity allows visitors to experience the thrill of discovering real gold. Equipped with a gold pan and guidance from staff, you can search for gold and gemstones in the designated panning area. The staff are friendly and knowledgeable, ensuring you have an enjoyable experience. Any gold or gemstones you discover while panning are yours to keep! This interactive experience adds an extra layer of excitement to your visit, as you might just uncover a little treasure.

Crisson Gold Mine features a small museum showcasing mining history, including displays of gold nuggets, mining tools, and historical photographs. The museum offers educational displays that explain the gold mining process, the significance of gold in Georgia's history, and the impact of the gold rush on the local community.

Don't forget to stop by the gift shop, where you can find unique souvenirs, gemstones, and gold-related items. It's a great place to pick up a memento from your visit or find a special gift.

Tips

- Arrive early: To maximize your experience, arrive early to enjoy the full range of activities, including the mine tour and gold panning.
- Bring water and snacks: Although there are snacks available for purchase, bringing your own water and snacks is a good idea, especially if you plan to spend the day.
- Explore dahlonega: After your visit to Crisson Gold Mine, take some time to explore Dahlonega's charming downtown area, which features unique shops, restaurants, and local wineries.
- Check eeather: Be sure to check the weather forecast before your visit, as conditions can change quickly in the mountains, especially if you plan on spending time outdoors.

Nearby Attractions

- Dahlonega Gold Museum: Located in the historic courthouse, this museum offers a deeper dive into the area's gold mining history with exhibits featuring artifacts and information about the gold rush era.

- Wolf Mountain Vineyards & Winery: Enjoy a scenic drive to this beautiful winery, where you can sample a variety of local wines, enjoy breathtaking mountain views, and relax in the picturesque surroundings.

- Amicalola Falls State Park: A short drive from Dahlonega, this state park features stunning waterfalls, hiking trails, and beautiful picnic areas. The falls are among the tallest in Georgia and provide excellent photo opportunities.

----

24 CUMBERLAND ISLAND FERRY

COUNTY: CAMDEN CITY: ST. MARYS

DATE VISITED: WHO I WENT WITH:

RATING: ☆ ☆ ☆ ☆ ☆ WILL I RETURN? YES / NO

113 St. Marys Street
St. Marys, GA 31558
877-860-6787

Cumberland Island Ferry is your ticket to one of Georgia's most breathtaking and untouched natural treasures. Located just off the coast of St. Marys, Georgia, Cumberland Island is a serene escape known for its stunning landscapes, pristine beaches, wild horses, and rich history. The ferry service provides an essential link to this idyllic island, allowing visitors to explore its beauty, wildlife, and historical landmarks. Whether you're looking for a day trip, a family outing, or a peaceful retreat, the Cumberland Island Ferry is the perfect way to begin your adventure.

The ferry operates several trips daily, but it's essential to check the current schedule on the ferry's website or contact the terminal for up-to-date information. The ferry ride itself takes approximately 30 minutes, offering beautiful views of the marshlands and coastal scenery.

As you embark on your ferry journey, prepare to be mesmerized by the stunning vistas of the Georgia coastline. Look out for dolphins playing in the water and seabirds soaring overhead, making for an unforgettable start to your visit. The ferry ride offers excellent opportunities to spot local wildlife, including various bird species, turtles, and even the occasional manatee.

Once you arrive on the island, you'll be greeted by the sights and sounds of nature. The island is home to diverse ecosystems, including maritime forests, salt marshes, and pristine beaches.

Cumberland Island boasts over 50 miles of trails, making it perfect for hiking and biking. Explore the lush forests, coastal dunes, and serene beaches at your own pace.

One of the island's most famous inhabitants is the herd of wild horses that roam freely. Keep an eye out for these majestic creatures as you explore the island's landscape.

Don't miss the opportunity to visit the ruins of the Dungeness Mansion, a once-grand estate that tells the story of the island's past. Guided tours are available to provide insight into the history of the mansion and the families that once called it home.

Cumberland Island is renowned for its beautiful, undeveloped beaches. Take a leisurely stroll along the shore, relax in the sun, or enjoy a picnic while listening to the sound of the waves. The natural beauty of the island offers a perfect backdrop for unwinding and reconnecting with nature. The island's beaches are ideal for swimming and shelling. Search for unique seashells along the shore or take a refreshing dip in the Atlantic Ocean.

Tips

- Plan your day: With so much to see and do, consider planning your itinerary in advance. Prioritize the sights you want to visit, such as the Dungeness Ruins and the beaches, to make the most of your time on the island.
- Bring essentials: Pack plenty of water, snacks, sunscreen, and insect repellent. There are no stores or restaurants on the island, so it's essential to bring everything you'll need for the day.
- Dress for adventure: Wear comfortable clothing and sturdy shoes suitable for hiking and beach walking. Consider bringing a hat and sunglasses to protect yourself from the sun.
- Check weather conditions: Before your trip, check the weather forecast, as conditions can change quickly in coastal areas. Be prepared for both sun and rain.

Nearby Attractions

- St. Marys Submarine Museum: Located in downtown St. Marys, this museum offers a fascinating look at the history of submarines and the role they have played in naval history. It features exhibits, artifacts, and displays that are sure to interest history buffs.

- Crooked River State Park: Just a short drive from St. Marys, this state park offers hiking trails, picnicking areas, and opportunities for kayaking and fishing. The park is known for its beautiful views of the Crooked River and its diverse wildlife.

- Fort Clinch State Park: Located on Amelia Island, just across the state line in Florida, this historic park features a well-preserved Civil War-era fort, hiking trails, and beautiful beaches. It's a great place for history enthusiasts and outdoor lovers alike.

25 DAVENPORT HOUSE MUSEUM

COUNTY: CHATHAM **CITY:** SAVANNAH

DATE VISITED: **WHO I WENT WITH:**

RATING: ☆ ☆ ☆ ☆ ☆ **WILL I RETURN?** YES / NO

323 E. Broughton Street
Savannah, GA 31401
912-236-8097

The Davenport House Museum, located in the heart of historic Savannah, Georgia, is a beautifully restored Federal-style home that offers visitors an authentic look into the city's early 19th-century history. Built in 1820 by master builder Isaiah Davenport, the house is a testament to the craftsmanship and elegance of the era. Today, the museum stands as one of Savannah's most important historic landmarks, offering guided tours, special events, and educational programs. Visiting the Davenport House Museum is an opportunity to step back in time and experience the architectural splendor, domestic life, and cultural significance of Savannah during the early 1800s.

Isaiah Davenport was a skilled carpenter and builder who settled in Savannah in the early 19th century. He built the Davenport House for his family, showcasing his mastery of Federal-style architecture. After his death in 1827, the house went through various uses, including a boarding house, before its historical significance was fully recognized.

In the 1950s, the house was at risk of demolition. However, a group of concerned citizens, led by the Historic Savannah Foundation, saved it from destruction. This effort marked the beginning of the city's historic preservation movement, and the Davenport House became the foundation's first major project. Today, it stands as a symbol of Savannah's commitment to preserving its rich architectural and cultural heritage.

The Davenport House is a fine example of Federal-style architecture, characterized by its symmetry, elegant proportions, and restrained decorative elements. As you approach the house, you'll notice its classic brick façade, fanlight above the door, and tall, narrow windows.

Inside, the house has been meticulously restored to reflect the style and furnishings of the 1820s. The rooms are furnished with period-appropriate pieces, including elegant mahogany furniture, decorative wallpapers, and fine silverware. Visitors can explore various rooms, including the parlor, dining room, and bedrooms, each offering a glimpse into the daily life of an affluent family in early 19th-century Savannah.

The museum offers guided tours led by knowledgeable docents who provide fascinating insights into the history of the house, the Davenport family, and Savannah's broader social and economic landscape during the antebellum period.
Garden and Grounds

Behind the house, visitors can explore a charming historic garden, which has been designed to reflect the types of plants and landscaping that would have been popular in the early 19th century. The garden provides a peaceful retreat and offers a lovely backdrop for photos or quiet reflection.

The garden is also a popular venue for special events, including weddings, seasonal celebrations, and educational programs. It's a beautiful space to experience Savannah's mild climate and Southern charm.

The museum features a collection of artifacts that provide a deeper understanding of life in the 1820s. From everyday household items to decorative arts, these objects help paint a vivid picture of the lifestyle of Savannah's wealthy residents during this period.

The Davenport House Museum often hosts temporary exhibits that highlight different aspects of life in early Savannah. These exhibits cover topics such as slavery, women's roles in the 19th century, and the city's architectural evolution.

The museum frequently hosts living history demonstrations, where costumed interpreters reenact daily activities from the 1820s. These events bring the house to life and allow visitors to experience the sights, sounds, and smells of the past.
Educational Programs

The Davenport House Museum offers a variety of educational programs, including workshops, lectures, and tours focused on Savannah's history, architecture, and preservation. These programs are perfect for history buffs and students looking to deepen their knowledge of the region's past.

The museum is a popular destination for school groups, offering tailored educational tours that align with curriculum standards and provide a hands-on learning experience about Savannah's rich history.

During the holiday season, the Davenport House is beautifully decorated in period style, offering special candlelight tours that transport visitors back in time. These tours are a magical way to experience the house's festive ambiance.

The museum hosts annual Valentine's Day wedding ceremonies in its garden, making it a unique and romantic venue for couples looking to tie the knot in a historic setting.

Tips

- Arrive early: Tours of the Davenport House Museum are limited to small groups, so arriving early ensures you get a spot on the next available tour.
- Photography: Photography is allowed in certain areas of the museum, but be sure to check with your guide before snapping photos.
- Plan for weather: Savannah's weather can be hot and humid, especially in the summer months, so dress appropriately and bring water if you plan to walk around the historic district.

Nearby Attractions

- Owens-Thomas House & Slave Quarters: Another excellent example of Federal-style architecture, the Owens-Thomas House offers insights into both the lives of Savannah's elite and the enslaved people who worked in their homes.

- Forsyth Park: Just a short walk from the Davenport House, Forsyth Park is Savannah's largest green space, featuring the iconic Forsyth Fountain, tree-lined paths, and beautiful gardens. It's a great place to relax after your museum visit.

- Cathedral of St. John the Baptist: This stunning cathedral, located near the Davenport House, is one of the most impressive examples of Gothic Revival architecture in the South. It's worth a visit for its beautiful stained-glass windows and intricate interior details.

----

26 DELTA FLIGHT MUSEUM

COUNTY: FULTON   CITY: ATLANTA

DATE VISITED: WHO I WENT WITH:

RATING: ☆ ☆ ☆ ☆ ☆   WILL I RETURN? YES / NO

1060 Delta Blvd. Bldg. B, Dept. 914
Atlanta, GA 30354
404-715-7886

The Delta Flight Museum, located in Atlanta, Georgia, is a must-visit destination for aviation enthusiasts and those curious about the history of flight. Situated at the headquarters of Delta Air Lines, this unique museum is housed in two original 1940s aircraft hangars and showcases over 90 years of Delta's storied history. From vintage aircraft to interactive exhibits, the Delta Flight Museum offers a fascinating journey through the evolution of aviation, making it a fantastic attraction for all ages. Whether you're a frequent flyer or someone with a casual interest in aviation, this museum offers a deep dive into the technological advancements and human stories that have shaped air travel.

Delta Air Lines started as a small crop-dusting operation called Huff Daland Dusters in 1924. By 1929, it had transitioned into passenger services, evolving over the decades into one of the world's largest and most respected airlines. The museum was created to preserve and celebrate Delta's rich history and aviation achievements.

Opened in 1995, the Delta Flight Museum became a significant part of Delta's heritage, offering a place where visitors can explore historic planes, learn about the airline's milestones, and engage with the history of commercial flight in the U.S.

Vintage Aircraft Collection

Douglas DC-3: The jewel of the Delta Flight Museum is its restored Douglas DC-3, one of the most important aircraft in aviation history. The DC-3 revolutionized air travel by making it more affordable and comfortable, and Delta's "Ship 41" is the oldest surviving DC-3 in existence, restored to its original 1940 livery.

Boeing 767-200: One of the highlights of the museum is the Spirit of Delta, a Boeing 767 purchased by Delta employees in 1982 as a gift to the company. This iconic aircraft now serves as a central exhibit where visitors can tour its interior and see firsthand the advancements in air travel technology.

Travel Back in Time: The museum features other rare and historic aircraft, including a Boeing 747-400 that allows visitors to explore the inside of the jumbo jet. These aircraft are displayed in the museum's massive hangars, providing an impressive backdrop for learning about aviation history.

Interactive Exhibits and Simulators

Flight Simulator Experience: One of the most thrilling experiences at the Delta Flight Museum is the Boeing 737 flight simulator, the same type used to train Delta pilots. This hands-on exhibit allows visitors to test their flying skills and experience the challenge of piloting a commercial airliner.

Interactive Exhibits: Throughout the museum, interactive exhibits engage visitors with topics ranging from aerodynamics to the mechanics of modern aircraft. The museum offers a fun and educational experience for families and school groups, with activities designed to inspire curiosity about the science of flight.

Historic Memorabilia

Delta Archives: The museum showcases an extensive collection of Delta-related memorabilia, including vintage uniforms, historic airline posters, and original equipment. From the golden age of air travel to the present, the artifacts on display offer a window into how flying and Delta Air Lines have changed over time.

Cockpit and Cabin Displays: Visitors can step inside recreated cockpits and cabin interiors from different eras of aviation, giving them a chance to see how flight experiences have evolved. These displays include early airline seats, flight attendant uniforms, and in-flight service items.

The History of Commercial Aviation

Delta's Timeline: One of the key exhibits traces Delta's growth from its humble beginnings as a crop-dusting service to its current status as a global airline leader. The timeline showcases important milestones in Delta's history, including its mergers with other airlines and its role in advancing commercial aviation.

Commercial Aviation Pioneers: Learn about the pioneers of aviation who helped shape the commercial airline industry. From early aircraft engineers to trailblazing pilots, the museum celebrates the individuals who pushed the boundaries of flight.

The Delta Flight Museum offers special behind-the-scenes tours that provide an in-depth look at Delta's history and its impact on aviation. These tours often include access to areas of the museum not available on the standard tour, offering aviation enthusiasts an even closer look at rare aircraft and artifacts.

The museum offers a range of STEM-based educational programs designed to engage students and visitors of all ages. These programs explore the science behind flight, engineering principles, and the history of aviation, making it a popular destination for school field trips and youth programs.

Special Events

Throughout the year, the Delta Flight Museum hosts a variety of special events, including aviation-themed lectures, book signings, and family days. These events often feature guest speakers from the aviation industry, allowing visitors to learn from professionals and aviation experts.

The museum's hangars provide a unique venue for corporate events, weddings, and other private functions. With the backdrop of historic aircraft, the Delta Flight Museum offers an extraordinary setting for special occasions.

Tips

- Plan your visit: If you want to experience the flight simulator, it's recommended to book in advance, as slots fill up quickly.
- Comfortable shoes: The museum covers a large area, and you'll be doing a lot of walking, so be sure to wear comfortable shoes.
- Photography: Photography is allowed in most areas of the museum, so don't forget your camera to capture your visit.
- Allow enough time: To fully explore the exhibits, plan to spend at least 2-3 hours at the museum, especially if you want to take advantage of the interactive experiences.

Nearby Attractions

- Hartsfield-Jackson Atlanta International Airport: Being so close to one of the world's busiest airports, visitors can take advantage of plane-spotting opportunities and even visit the ATL SkyTrain for a view of the airport's operations.

- Porsche Experience Center Atlanta: Just a short drive from the museum, the Porsche Experience Center offers an exciting and interactive driving experience.

Visitors can take a spin in a high-performance Porsche or explore the company's history through their extensive collection of cars.

- Zoo Atlanta: If you're visiting with family, consider making a stop at Zoo Atlanta, located about 15 minutes away from the museum. It's home to a wide variety of animals and is a favorite attraction for visitors of all ages.

DRIFTWOOD BEACH

(27)

COUNTY: GLYNN **CITY:** JEKYLL ISLAND

DATE VISITED: **WHO I WENT WITH:**

RATING: ☆ ☆ ☆ ☆ ☆ **WILL I RETURN?** YES / NO

Beachview Drive
Jekyll Island, GA 31527

Located on the northern tip of Jekyll Island off the coast of Georgia, Driftwood Beach is a place where nature's artistry is on full display. Famous for its hauntingly beautiful landscape of weathered driftwood trees scattered along the shoreline, Driftwood Beach offers a serene and surreal escape for nature lovers, photographers, and beachgoers alike. The beach's unique beauty, sculpted by years of erosion and natural forces, creates an otherworldly atmosphere that has made it one of Georgia's most iconic natural attractions. Whether you're seeking a quiet place to relax, take stunning photographs, or simply enjoy the marvels of nature, Driftwood Beach is an ideal destination.

Driftwood Beach wasn't created overnight. Over the years, natural coastal erosion has gradually reshaped the shoreline of Jekyll Island, leaving behind a forest of bleached and weather-beaten trees. These trees, once part of a thriving forest, now stand as magnificent sculptures, providing a picturesque and almost eerie landscape that is constantly evolving due to the shifting tides and coastal winds.

Jekyll Island is a protected state park, and the natural beauty of Driftwood Beach is carefully preserved to ensure that future generations can enjoy its unique charm. The island is managed by the Jekyll Island Authority, which focuses on maintaining a balance between conservation and recreation.

The most striking feature of Driftwood Beach is, of course, the towering skeletons of trees that have been shaped by wind, saltwater, and time. These natural sculptures create an unforgettable visual experience, making it a popular spot for photographers looking to capture the raw beauty of nature. Each tree, bleached by the sun and sea, tells a story of resilience, as they stand or lie in dramatic poses along the beach.

Whether you're a professional photographer or simply someone with a smartphone, Driftwood Beach provides endless opportunities for breathtaking shots. The contrasts of weathered wood against the sky, sand, and ocean make for stunning compositions, especially at sunrise or sunset when the light enhances the textures and colors of the driftwood.

Driftwood Beach offers an ideal setting for peaceful, reflective walks along the coast. The beach stretches for miles, providing ample space to explore the landscape and appreciate the ever-changing shoreline. Walking among the twisted trunks and branches, you'll feel as though you've stepped into a dreamlike world far removed from the hustle and bustle of everyday life.

While walking along the beach, you may also encounter some of the local wildlife. Jekyll Island is home to a variety of bird species, including herons, egrets, and ospreys. It's a prime spot for birdwatching, especially during migratory seasons. Occasionally, you might even see dolphins playing in the waters just off the coast.

Due to its natural beauty and serene atmosphere, Driftwood Beach has become a popular spot for weddings and special events. The breathtaking backdrop of ancient driftwood, combined with the soft waves and golden sands, creates a romantic setting that is perfect for couples looking to exchange vows in a truly unforgettable location.
Wedding permits are required and can be arranged through the Jekyll Island Authority, ensuring that the beach remains protected even as it hosts such meaningful events.

Driftwood Beach is also a great place for a family outing or a casual picnic. The wide, open spaces and peaceful environment make it an ideal spot for families to spend time together, relax on the sand, or enjoy a picnic amidst the unique landscape.

During low tide, small tide pools form along the beach, which can be fascinating for children to explore. They often contain tiny marine creatures like crabs and small fish, offering an educational and fun experience for the whole family.

Driftwood Beach is perfect for beachcombers. As you stroll along the shore, you'll find small shells, interesting rocks, and fragments of driftwood. While taking large pieces of driftwood is not allowed, as it's part of the natural landscape, you can still collect small keepsakes from your visit.

Driftwood Beach is a photographer's paradise. If you're a budding photographer, be sure to visit during the golden hours (early morning or late afternoon), when the sunlight casts soft, warm tones across the landscape. The play of light and shadow across the driftwood creates mesmerizing photo opportunities. Many couples and families come here specifically for professional photo shoots, whether it's for engagement photos, family portraits, or simply to capture the natural beauty of the beach.

Jekyll Island has an extensive network of biking trails, many of which connect directly to Driftwood Beach. Renting a bike and exploring the island is a fantastic way to experience not only Driftwood Beach but also the other natural attractions on Jekyll Island. The trails are mostly flat and well-maintained, making them suitable for all ages and fitness levels.

Fishing enthusiasts will find that Driftwood Beach provides great opportunities for surf fishing. The area's rich marine environment offers the chance to catch species such as redfish, trout, and flounder. Just be sure to follow local regulations and obtain the necessary fishing permits if required.

Nearby Attractions

- Jekyll Island Historic District: Just a short drive from Driftwood Beach, the Jekyll Island Historic District offers a step back in time with its grand Gilded Age cottages and the iconic Jekyll Island Club Hotel, once a retreat for some of America's wealthiest families.

- Georgia Sea Turtle Center: Located on Jekyll Island, the Georgia Sea Turtle Center is an excellent place to learn about the island's efforts to rehabilitate and conserve sea turtles. The center provides educational exhibits, and visitors can observe turtles being cared for in the hospital.

- Great Dunes Park: If you're looking for a more traditional beach day, Great Dunes Park, located on the island's eastern shore, offers miles of sandy beach for sunbathing, swimming, and beach activities.

----

28 DUKES CREEK FALLS TRAIL

COUNTY: WHITE **CITY:** HELEN

DATE VISITED: **WHO I WENT WITH:**

RATING: ☆ ☆ ☆ ☆ ☆ **WILL I RETURN?** YES / NO

Russell Scenic Highway
Helen, GA 30545

Tucked away in the heart of the Chattahoochee National Forest, the Dukes Creek Falls Trail offers one of the most picturesque hiking experiences in northern Georgia. Located just a short drive from the charming town of Helen, Georgia, this 2-mile round trip trail leads you through a lush forest, eventually rewarding you with breathtaking views of the Dukes Creek Falls, a majestic waterfall that cascades over 150 feet down a rugged rock face. The hike is perfect for adventurers of all skill levels, offering both natural beauty and tranquility along the way. Whether you're a seasoned hiker, a family with children, or a nature lover looking to relax in the outdoors, Dukes Creek Falls Trail is a must-see destination when exploring the North Georgia Mountains.

The highlight of the trail is undoubtedly Dukes Creek Falls itself, a multi-tiered waterfall that plunges into a serene gorge below. The waterfall is fed by Dukes Creek, which flows from the scenic Yonah Mountain and eventually joins the Chattahoochee River. Surrounded by dense greenery and towering trees, the waterfall offers a peaceful escape into nature, where the sound of rushing water creates a calming atmosphere.

The rock formations around the falls are equally captivating, showcasing the ancient geology of the Blue Ridge Mountains. The granite cliffs and rock faces along the trail offer a dramatic backdrop for photographs and add to the sense of adventure as you make your way to the falls.

The Dukes Creek Falls Trail is a moderate, well-maintained trail that covers approximately 2 miles round trip. It's a relatively easy hike with an elevation change of about 300 feet, making it suitable for most fitness levels. The trail is primarily downhill to the falls, with a gentle ascent on the way back.

The trail begins at the Dukes Creek Falls parking area, where you'll find ample parking and restroom facilities. From the trailhead, the path leads through a dense forest of hardwood trees, including oak, hickory, and poplar. During the fall, the foliage transforms into a vibrant display of reds, oranges, and yellows, making it one of the best times to visit. In spring and summer, wildflowers and ferns line the trail, adding to the beauty of the hike.

Along the way, there are several observation platforms that provide stunning views of both the upper and lower sections of Dukes Creek Falls. These decks are great for taking photos, resting, or simply soaking in the beauty of the surrounding wilderness.

As you hike along the trail, you'll encounter Davis Creek, which runs parallel to the path and eventually joins Dukes Creek. The soothing sound of the flowing water is a constant companion, adding to the peaceful ambiance of the trail. Small cascades and pools along the creek offer scenic spots to pause and appreciate the natural surroundings.

The Chattahoochee National Forest is home to a diverse array of plant and animal life, and the Dukes Creek Falls Trail is no exception. Hikers may spot deer, squirrels, and a variety of birds along the way. In spring, wildflowers such as mountain laurel and rhododendron bloom along the trail, while in autumn, the colorful leaves create a magical canopy overhead. The mix of evergreen and deciduous trees ensures that the trail is beautiful year-round.

The combination of waterfalls, streams, and lush forest makes the Dukes Creek Falls Trail a dream location for photographers. The observation decks provide perfect vantage points for capturing the grandeur of the falls, while the forest itself offers a variety of photo opportunities. Be sure to bring a camera or smartphone to document your hike, as the scenery is both dramatic and peaceful.

One of the most popular times to hike the Dukes Creek Falls Trail is in the fall, when the surrounding forest transforms into a brilliant display of autumn colors. The trail provides panoramic views of the changing leaves, and the crisp mountain air makes for ideal hiking conditions.
Spring and Summer

Spring and early summer are also excellent times to visit, as the trail comes alive with blooming wildflowers and vibrant greenery. The waterfalls are typically at their most powerful during these months, thanks to the seasonal rainfall. The trail remains shaded for much of the hike, offering a cool and pleasant retreat from the heat of summer.
Winter

In the winter, the trail takes on a quieter, more tranquil atmosphere. While the trees may be bare, the waterfall is often still flowing, and the lack of crowds makes it a peaceful escape into nature. Winter hikes offer clear, crisp views of the surrounding mountains and valleys, making it a unique experience for those who enjoy hiking in cooler weather.

The Dukes Creek Falls trailhead is easily accessible by car, located just off Richard B. Russell Scenic Highway (GA-348). There is a paved parking lot at the trailhead with space for several vehicles, and the lot often fills up during weekends, especially in the fall. It's recommended to arrive early to secure a parking spot, particularly if you plan to visit during peak foliage season.

Restrooms are available at the parking area, making it convenient for visitors to prepare before heading out on the trail. There are also picnic tables nearby, perfect for enjoying a post-hike snack or meal with views of the surrounding forest. However, there are no facilities along the trail itself, so be sure to carry water and any necessary supplies with you.

The Dukes Creek Falls Trail is pet-friendly, making it a great option for those looking to bring their furry friends along. Dogs are welcome on the trail, as long as they are kept on a leash.

Tips

- Footwear: Though the trail is well-maintained, certain sections can be rocky or muddy, especially after rain. It's advisable to wear sturdy hiking shoes with good traction to ensure a comfortable and safe hike.
- Stay on the trail: While it may be tempting to venture closer to the water or explore off the main path, it's important to stay on the marked trail for your safety and to help preserve the natural environment.
- Hydration and snacks: The hike is moderate but still requires energy, especially on the uphill return trip. Be sure to bring plenty of water and light snacks, particularly during warmer months.
- Wildlife awareness: While wildlife sightings are common, always remember that the animals in the Chattahoochee National Forest are wild. Keep a safe distance and avoid feeding any animals you may encounter.

Nearby Attractions

- Helen, Georgia: Just a short drive from Dukes Creek Falls is the quaint alpine village of Helen, known for its Bavarian-style architecture and charming shops. After your hike, consider exploring Helen's restaurants, boutiques, or enjoy tubing along the Chattahoochee River.

- Anna Ruby Falls: For those seeking more waterfall adventures, Anna Ruby Falls is located nearby in Unicoi State Park. This short and accessible trail leads to twin waterfalls and is a perfect complement to your visit to Dukes Creek Falls.

- Smithgall Woods State Park: Another nearby destination, Smithgall Woods State Park, offers additional hiking trails, fishing opportunities, and serene natural settings. It's a great place to extend your outdoor adventure after visiting Dukes Creek Falls.

29 FERNBANK MUSEUM

COUNTY: FULTON **CITY:** ATLANTA

DATE VISITED: **WHO I WENT WITH:**

RATING: ☆ ☆ ☆ ☆ ☆ **WILL I RETURN?** YES / NO

767 Clifton Road
Atlanta, GA 30307
404-929-6300

Located in the heart of Atlanta, Georgia, the Fernbank Museum of Natural History is a must-visit destination for anyone fascinated by science, nature, and history. With its captivating exhibits, immersive theaters, and lush outdoor spaces, Fernbank offers a unique blend of learning and adventure for visitors of all ages. Opened in 1992, the museum has become one of the leading cultural institutions in the Southeast, showcasing a range of topics from the prehistoric world of dinosaurs to the intricate ecosystems of the modern-day Georgia landscape. Whether you're visiting with family, friends, or as a solo explorer, Fernbank promises an educational and exciting experience that connects you to the wonders of the natural world.

One of Fernbank's most popular and striking displays is the Giants of the Mesozoic exhibit, where life-sized dinosaur skeletons are arranged in a dramatic prehistoric tableau. The exhibit is housed in the museum's grand atrium and features the towering skeletons of the Argentinosaurus, the largest dinosaur ever discovered, and the fearsome predator Giganotosaurus, a rival to the more famous Tyrannosaurus Rex. These giants are set within a representation of a Cretaceous landscape, complete with fossil plants and prehistoric creatures. For dinosaur enthusiasts, this exhibit is an unmissable experience and offers insight into the scale and grandeur of life on Earth millions of years ago.

For families and young visitors, Fernbank NatureQuest is an interactive playground where kids can become scientists and explorers. This hands-on exhibit allows children to learn through play as they discover ecosystems, animals, and natural phenomena. The exhibit features immersive environments, such as a coastal wetlands zone, where children can interact with lifelike models of animals, follow footprints, or even climb through tunnels representing an underground cave system. It's a fun and educational space where young minds can engage with nature and science through discovery and imagination.

A Walk Through Time in Georgia is a signature exhibit that takes visitors on a journey through the natural history of Georgia, spanning over 500 million years.

This permanent display highlights the state's diverse ecosystems and geological history, from the prehistoric seas that once covered the region to the ancient forests that still thrive today. Visitors can explore dioramas depicting various habitats, including coastal plains, mountain ranges, and wetlands, while learning about the plants, animals, and geological changes that shaped Georgia's natural environment. The exhibit is perfect for anyone interested in understanding the local ecology and how the landscape has evolved over time.

Beyond the indoor exhibits, Fernbank Museum offers a remarkable outdoor experience with its WildWoods and Fernbank Forest. These areas provide visitors with a chance to explore nature firsthand, right in the middle of Atlanta.

WildWoods features elevated walkways that wind through the trees, interactive nature stations, and outdoor exhibits that teach about Georgia's natural ecosystems. It's a great spot for a relaxing nature walk, family adventure, or birdwatching.

Fernbank Forest, a 65-acre old-growth forest, is a true urban oasis. Visitors can hike through this serene natural space, filled with towering trees, native plants, and wildlife. This rare glimpse into Georgia's primeval forests provides a contrast to the urban environment of Atlanta, offering peace and a connection to nature.

One of the standout features of the Fernbank Museum is its Giant Screen Theater, where visitors can enjoy stunning nature documentaries and science films on a massive screen. These films, often shown in 3D, take viewers on global journeys, exploring natural wonders, wildlife, and human achievements. Popular films in rotation include stories about space exploration, marine life, and deep jungle ecosystems. The theater's immersive experience enhances learning by placing viewers right in the middle of the action, whether they're flying over mountain ranges, diving into coral reefs, or exploring distant planets.

In addition to its permanent collections, Fernbank regularly hosts special temporary exhibits, often in partnership with other renowned museums and scientific institutions. These exhibits cover a wide range of topics, from ancient civilizations and world cultures to cutting-edge scientific discoveries. These temporary exhibits offer something new with each visit, ensuring that even repeat visitors find fresh and exciting things to explore.

For adults looking for a unique and fun night out, Fernbank After Dark is a monthly event that blends science with socializing. Held on select Friday nights, the event includes after-hours access to the museum's exhibits, special presentations, and hands-on science activities, all paired with live music and cocktails. It's a great way to experience Fernbank's offerings in a more relaxed and vibrant atmosphere.

Throughout the year, Fernbank also hosts live science demonstrations and presentations, providing interactive learning experiences for visitors of all ages. These shows range from hands-on experiments in chemistry and physics to live animal encounters that bring visitors up close to fascinating creatures. These events are perfect for children and families, sparking curiosity and deepening understanding of the natural world.

Nearby Attractions

- Atlanta Botanical Garden: Just a short drive from Fernbank, the Atlanta Botanical Garden is an enchanting place to explore vibrant plant displays, themed gardens, and seasonal exhibitions, making it an excellent complement to a day at Fernbank.

- Piedmont Park: A beautiful urban park located near the museum, Piedmont Park is perfect for a relaxing stroll, a picnic, or outdoor sports. It's one of Atlanta's most beloved green spaces and offers great views of the city skyline.

③ FIRST AFRICAN BAPTIST CHURCH

COUNTY: CHATHAM	CITY: SAVANNAH
DATE VISITED:	WHO I WENT WITH:
RATING: ☆ ☆ ☆ ☆ ☆	WILL I RETURN? YES / NO

23 Montgomery Street
Savannah, GA 31401
912-233-6597

First African Baptist Church, located in Savannah, Georgia, is one of the most historically significant churches in the United States. Established in 1773, it is the oldest African American congregation in North America, with a rich history deeply intertwined with the struggles and triumphs of African Americans. As a cornerstone of Savannah's history, the church played a pivotal role in the lives of the local Black community, serving as a spiritual home, a beacon of hope during slavery, and even a stop on the Underground Railroad. Today, visitors from all over the world come to explore its profound legacy, admire its beautiful architecture, and learn about its role in shaping the history of civil rights and faith in America.

First African Baptist Church was organized under the leadership of Rev. George Leile, a formerly enslaved man who became the first ordained African American Baptist minister in the U.S. It began as a small congregation of enslaved and free African Americans who met in secret. The church's rich history spans over two centuries, making it one of the most enduring symbols of African American perseverance and faith in the South.

During the era of slavery, the church was a place where the enslaved could gather for worship and spiritual strength. It provided not only religious guidance but also a sense of community and solidarity for those oppressed by the system of slavery. The congregation's commitment to faith amidst adversity has made First African Baptist Church a powerful symbol of resilience.

The church was also a secretive yet critical part of the Underground Railroad. Its basement contained unique holes drilled into the floorboards in the shape of an African prayer symbol, believed to have been used for ventilation, allowing enslaved individuals to hide while on their journey to freedom. This courageous history is memorialized in the church today, where visitors can see these hidden spaces firsthand.

The church also played a prominent role during the Civil Rights Movement, hosting many important meetings and gatherings. Leaders like Dr. Martin Luther King Jr. visited the church, and it became a hub for organizing peaceful protests and advocating for social justice in Savannah. Its legacy as a center for civil rights activism continues to inspire visitors.

The First African Baptist Church is not just significant for its history but also for its architecture. Built by both enslaved and free African Americans, the church showcases unique features that reflect both African and Christian traditions.

Original Pew Benches: The church's original pews, made by hand by enslaved members of the congregation in the 1800s, still remain. The benches have distinctive African tribal symbols carved into their sides, symbolizing the congregation's strong cultural ties to their African heritage. Visitors can sit in these very pews, connecting with the powerful history of those who worshipped here.

Stained Glass Windows: The beautiful stained glass windows that line the sanctuary are another feature that captivates visitors. These windows depict biblical stories and scenes, while also honoring key figures in the church's history. The vibrant colors and intricate designs bring a sense of peace and reflection to the space.

The Underground Railroad Holes: Perhaps the most famous architectural feature of the church is its connection to the Underground Railroad. As mentioned earlier, visitors can still see the holes drilled into the church floorboards that once provided ventilation for those hidden beneath. This unique feature is a powerful reminder of the church's role in the fight for freedom and its connection to African American history.

Pulpit and Balcony: The hand-carved pulpit and high balcony in the sanctuary are also notable for their historical significance. The pulpit has been used by many prominent ministers and civil rights leaders over the centuries, while the balcony was traditionally where enslaved individuals sat during services.

The First African Baptist Church offers guided tours for those interested in learning more about its history, architecture, and role in the African American experience. These tours provide a detailed look into the church's past, including its role during slavery, its architectural features, and its involvement in the Underground Railroad and civil rights activism.

Tours are typically available throughout the week, and it is recommended to check the church's official website or call ahead for current tour times and availability.

The tours last about an hour and are led by knowledgeable guides who bring the church's history to life through storytelling and historical insight.

On these tours, visitors can explore the sanctuary, sit in the historic pews, and visit the basement area connected to the Underground Railroad. Guides will share detailed accounts of the church's founding, the challenges faced by its early members, and its role in the fight for freedom. The experience is both educational and deeply moving, giving visitors a greater appreciation for the church's legacy.

Visitors are typically allowed to take photos during their visit, though it is always a good idea to confirm photography rules with your guide.

First African Baptist Church remains a vibrant, active congregation today. It continues to serve as a spiritual home for the people of Savannah, hosting regular services, community events, and cultural programs.

Sunday services are open to the public, and visitors are welcome to attend. These services are a great way to experience the lively and soulful worship style that is a hallmark of the African American church tradition. The gospel music, heartfelt prayers, and powerful sermons offer a unique and uplifting experience for attendees.

The church also hosts events that celebrate African American culture and history, such as Black History Month programs, choir performances, and community outreach initiatives. These events help foster a sense of unity and reflect the church's ongoing commitment to social justice and education.

Nearby Attractions: As part of Savannah's historic district, First African Baptist Church is close to other notable landmarks such as Chippewa Square, Forsyth Park, and River Street. Visitors can easily make the church a stop on a broader tour of Savannah's rich history and vibrant culture.

FORSYTH PARK

COUNTY: CHATHAM **CITY:** SAVANNAH

DATE VISITED: **WHO I WENT WITH:**

RATING: ☆ ☆ ☆ ☆ ☆ **WILL I RETURN?** YES / NO

10 Whitaker St.
Savannah, GA 31401
912-351-3841

Nestled in the heart of Savannah, Georgia, Forsyth Park is a 30-acre public park that serves as the crown jewel of the city's historic district. Known for its scenic beauty, iconic fountain, and rich history, Forsyth Park is a must-visit destination for tourists and locals alike. Whether you're looking to enjoy a peaceful walk under moss-draped oak trees, explore historical monuments, or engage in vibrant community events, Forsyth Park offers something for everyone. Its lush green lawns, walking paths, and cultural significance make it one of the most cherished landmarks in Savannah.

Named after John Forsyth, a former governor of Georgia, Forsyth Park was created in the mid-19th century as a large public space where the people of Savannah could gather, relax, and enjoy outdoor activities. The park's design was influenced by European garden styles, making it a grand and inviting space in the heart of the city.

The park holds significant historical importance, especially during and after the American Civil War. It was used as a campground for Confederate soldiers and later for Union forces after Savannah was captured. Several memorials within the park honor soldiers from various conflicts, adding to its cultural and historical value.

Over the years, Forsyth Park has become a symbol of Savannah's charm and beauty. The park remains a gathering place for the community and visitors, offering a peaceful retreat and an opportunity to immerse in the city's Southern elegance.

At the heart of Forsyth Park lies its most recognizable feature: the Forsyth Fountain. Built in 1858, this stunning white fountain was modeled after the fountains in Paris and is one of the most photographed spots in Savannah. The grand two-tiered structure sprays water into the air from multiple spouts, creating a serene and beautiful scene. Visitors can often find the fountain illuminated with different colors for special events or holidays, making it a constantly changing attraction. The fountain is surrounded by pathways, benches, and manicured gardens, making it the perfect spot to sit, relax, and people-watch.

Forsyth Park is crisscrossed by several wide, shaded paths that make it ideal for walking, jogging, and biking. Lined with magnificent live oak trees draped in Spanish moss, the park's trails provide a peaceful escape from the bustle of the city. The park's walking loop is about a mile long, making it a favorite for morning or afternoon strolls. Whether you're an avid runner or just looking to enjoy a leisurely walk, Forsyth Park's trails are a beautiful way to experience the natural beauty of Savannah.

Forsyth Park is home to several important historical monuments. The most notable is the Confederate Memorial, a towering monument dedicated to the soldiers who fought for the Confederacy during the American Civil War. Erected in 1879, this monument stands near the northern end of the park and offers a glimpse into Savannah's complex history. Other monuments in the park include tributes to Spanish-American War veterans and World War I soldiers, as well as a striking Holocaust Memorial. These monuments give visitors an opportunity to reflect on the historical significance of the area and the sacrifices made by previous generations.

Tucked away in Forsyth Park is a charming and sensory-rich garden known as the Fragrant Garden for the Blind. This specialized garden features plants and flowers chosen for their strong fragrances and textures, allowing visually impaired visitors to enjoy the park through scent and touch. It's a peaceful corner of the park, filled with lavender, rosemary, jasmine, and other aromatic plants, creating an immersive sensory experience for all visitors.

The wide, open green spaces of Forsyth Park are perfect for a picnic or simply relaxing under the shade of a towering oak tree. Whether you bring a blanket and a book or enjoy a meal from one of Savannah's many food trucks or cafés, Forsyth Park offers plenty of spots to unwind and enjoy the outdoors. The park's sprawling lawns also host impromptu soccer games, Frisbee tossing, and yoga classes, making it a hub of activity and leisure.

Forsyth Park is a popular venue for local festivals, concerts, and cultural events throughout the year. Some of the most famous events held here include the Savannah Music Festival, Savannah Jazz Festival, and Sidewalk Arts Festival. On Saturdays, Forsyth Park also hosts a Farmer's Market, where visitors can purchase fresh local produce, baked goods, flowers, and artisanal products. This lively market brings together farmers and artisans from across the region and is a favorite weekend activity for both tourists and locals.

Families visiting Forsyth Park will appreciate the Children's Playground, located near the southern end of the park. The playground features swings, slides, and climbing structures, offering a safe and fun space for kids to burn off energy. During the summer months, the splash pad provides a refreshing way for children to cool off. The interactive water features and fountains make it a popular spot for families visiting the park on hot Savannah days.

Nearby Attractions

Forsyth Park is surrounded by other noteworthy Savannah landmarks and attractions, making it easy to explore more of the city after a visit to the park. Nearby attractions include:

- The Mercer-Williams House: Located just off Forsyth Park, this historic home was made famous by the novel Midnight in the Garden of Good and Evil. It offers guided tours and insight into Savannah's architectural and social history.

- The Armstrong House: Another historic mansion located near the park, the Armstrong House is a beautiful example of Savannah's grand antebellum architecture.

- Savannah College of Art and Design (SCAD): SCAD has several buildings located near Forsyth Park, and visitors can often see students sketching or working on projects in the park.

32) FORT FREDERICA NATIONAL MONUMENT

COUNTY: GLYNN	CITY: ST. SIMONS ISLAND
DATE VISITED:	WHO I WENT WITH:
RATING: ☆ ☆ ☆ ☆ ☆	WILL I RETURN? YES / NO

6515 Frederica Rd.
St. Simons Island, GA 31522
912-638-3639

Located on St. Simons Island, Georgia, Fort Frederica National Monument is a fascinating historical site that offers visitors a glimpse into colonial America and the early struggles between European powers for control of the southeastern coast. Established in 1736 by General James Oglethorpe, the fort and its surrounding town played a critical role in protecting the southernmost British colonies from Spanish invasion. Today, the ruins of Fort Frederica are preserved as a national monument, providing an immersive experience into Georgia's colonial past. With its scenic views, archaeological remains, and educational exhibits, Fort Frederica is a must-see destination for history enthusiasts and anyone looking to explore one of the most significant early settlements in the United States.

General James Oglethorpe, founder of the colony of Georgia, established Fort Frederica as a military outpost to defend the British colonies from Spanish forces based in Florida. The fort was named after Frederick, Prince of Wales, and was strategically positioned along the Frederica River to protect Georgia's southern frontier.

One of the most significant events in the fort's history occurred in 1742 during the War of Jenkins' Ear, a conflict between Britain and Spain. The Spanish launched an invasion from their base in St. Augustine, but Oglethorpe's troops, along with local militia, successfully repelled them during the Battle of Bloody Marsh. This decisive victory ensured British control of Georgia and cemented Fort Frederica's place in American history.

After the threat of Spanish invasion diminished, the fort and its town slowly declined. By the mid-18th century, Frederica had largely been abandoned, and the fort fell into ruin. However, its historical importance remained, and the site was designated a national monument in 1945, preserving it for future generations.

The primary attraction at Fort Frederica is the well-preserved ruins of the original fort and the surrounding colonial town. Visitors can explore the remains of the fort's walls, bastions, and earthen defenses, which have been carefully preserved by the National Park Service. Walking through these remnants gives you a sense of the strategic importance of the site and the challenges faced by the early settlers. The nearby town ruins are equally intriguing. Stone foundations and tabby (a type of colonial-era concrete) structures mark the locations of homes, shops, and public buildings from the 18th century. Interpretive signs throughout the site provide information about the lives of the settlers and the layout of the once-thriving town.

Begin your visit at the Fort Frederica Visitor Center, where you can watch a short introductory film that provides an overview of the site's history and its significance in the broader context of colonial America. The visitor center also features a museum with fascinating exhibits, including artifacts unearthed during archaeological digs at the site. These items, such as pottery, tools, and weapons, offer valuable insights into the daily life of the settlers. The museum also showcases maps, documents, and models that help visitors understand the fort's strategic importance and the military tactics used during the conflicts with Spanish forces.

Fort Frederica is an active archaeological site, and visitors have the chance to see ongoing excavations that continue to reveal new information about the settlement. Archaeological markers throughout the park indicate the locations of important discoveries, and archaeological tours are sometimes available, offering a deeper look into the methods and findings of the excavations.

Throughout the year, living history demonstrations and reenactments are held at Fort Frederica. These events bring the colonial period to life, with actors dressed in period attire demonstrating colonial crafts, military drills, and cooking techniques. During special events, you might witness reenactments of the Battle of Bloody Marsh, allowing you to see firsthand how the British forces defended the fort from the Spanish. These programs are especially popular with families and school groups, as they provide a dynamic and engaging way to learn about the fort's history.

Fort Frederica is perfect for those who prefer to explore at their own pace. The site offers self-guided tour booklets, available at the visitor center, that provide detailed information about the fort's history and key locations throughout the grounds. This allows visitors to take their time while exploring the ruins and imagining life in the 18th century. For a more in-depth experience, you can join one of the ranger-led tours that are offered at various times throughout the week.

These tours are led by knowledgeable National Park Service rangers who share stories about the fort's construction, its role in the colonial era, and the people who lived there.

One of the most beautiful aspects of Fort Frederica National Monument is its location along the Frederica River. The park offers stunning views of the river and the surrounding marshlands, providing a peaceful backdrop to the historical ruins. Visitors can enjoy a leisurely stroll along the riverbank or take advantage of the many picnic areas to relax and take in the scenery. The river played a crucial role in the defense of the fort, as it provided both a transportation route and a natural barrier against potential invaders. Today, it remains one of the most picturesque spots in the park.

In addition to its historical significance, Fort Frederica is home to a variety of wildlife, including birds, deer, and reptiles. Nature lovers will appreciate the opportunity to see local flora and fauna while walking through the park's trails. Keep an eye out for egrets, herons, and other native bird species that frequent the area. The combination of history and nature makes Fort Frederica a perfect destination for those interested in outdoor exploration as well as cultural heritage.

Tips

- Wear comfortable shoes: The site requires some walking, especially if you plan to explore the full extent of the ruins and trails.
- Bring water: While shaded areas are plentiful, the Georgia heat can be intense, especially during the summer months. It's a good idea to stay hydrated.
- Allow plenty of time: To fully appreciate the site, plan on spending at least 2-3 hours at Fort Frederica. This will give you time to explore the ruins, visit the museum, and participate in a ranger-led tour if available.
- Combine with other local attractions: St. Simons Island offers plenty of other historical and natural attractions, such as the nearby Christ Church and St. Simons Lighthouse. A visit to Fort Frederica can easily be combined with these for a full day of exploration.

Nearby Attractions

- St. Simons Island Lighthouse Museum: Located just a short drive from Fort Frederica, the St. Simons Island Lighthouse is one of only five remaining lighthouses in Georgia. Visitors can climb the 129 steps to the top for breathtaking views of the Atlantic Ocean and the surrounding island. The adjacent museum, housed in the former keeper's residence, provides insights into the lighthouse's history and the lives of its keepers.

- Christ Church, Frederica: Founded in 1736, Christ Church, Frederica is one of the oldest churches in Georgia and is located near Fort Frederica. The current structure, built in 1884, stands amid towering oak trees and serene gardens. Visitors can tour the beautiful grounds, explore the historic cemetery, and appreciate the church's stained-glass windows and peaceful atmosphere.

- Cannon's Point Preserve: Cannon's Point Preserve is a nature conservation area on the northern end of St. Simons Island, just a few miles from Fort Frederica. This 600-acre preserve offers hiking, birdwatching, and the chance to explore the island's coastal ecosystems, including marshes and forests. The site also includes archaeological remnants of prehistoric Native American settlements, adding a layer of historical interest to the natural beauty.

㉝ FORT PULASKI NATIONAL MONUMENT

COUNTY: CHATHAM   CITY: SAVANNAH

DATE VISITED: WHO I WENT WITH:

RATING: ☆ ☆ ☆ ☆ ☆   WILL I RETURN? YES / NO

101 Fort Pulaski Road
Savannah, GA 31410
912-219-4233

Located on Cockspur Island, near Savannah, Georgia, Fort Pulaski National Monument is a fascinating destination steeped in American Civil War history. This coastal fortress, constructed in the early 19th century, was the site of a pivotal battle during the war, marking the first significant use of rifled cannon technology in combat. Today, Fort Pulaski is preserved as a national monument, offering visitors a chance to explore its massive brick walls, moats, drawbridges, and scenic views of the surrounding marshlands. A visit to Fort Pulaski is an opportunity to step back in time and learn about military engineering, Civil War strategies, and the everyday life of soldiers stationed at the fort.

Fort Pulaski was built between 1829 and 1847 as part of a coastal defense system designed to protect the United States from foreign invasion. Named after Count Casimir Pulaski, a Polish hero of the American Revolution, the fort was considered state-of-the-art for its time. With walls made of 25 million bricks and surrounded by a deep moat, Fort Pulaski was regarded as impenetrable by conventional artillery.

During the American Civil War, the Confederate Army took control of the fort early in the conflict to protect the vital port of Savannah. In 1862, however, Union forces began a siege of the fort, using newly developed rifled cannons that could penetrate the thick brick walls from over a mile away. After only 30 hours of bombardment, a breach was opened in Fort Pulaski's walls, forcing the Confederate garrison to surrender. This battle is significant because it marked the end of traditional masonry fortifications in military design.

After the Civil War, Fort Pulaski was used briefly as a prison for Confederate soldiers but was eventually abandoned. In 1924, it was designated as a national monument, and today it is maintained by the National Park Service, offering visitors a well-preserved glimpse into 19th-century military life.

A tour of Fort Pulaski's massive brick fortifications is the highlight of any visit. Visitors can explore the various rooms and quarters where soldiers lived, including barracks, storerooms, and officers' quarters. As you walk through these spaces, you'll see original features like brick arches, iron doors, and even cannonball damage from the 1862 siege. One of the most impressive aspects of the fort is its moat, which encircles the entire structure. You can walk across the drawbridge to enter the fort and explore its intricate design, including gun platforms where cannons are still mounted. The fort's parade ground, located in the center of the structure, is a wide open space where military drills were once conducted.

Fort Pulaski's Southeast Bastion is where the Union rifled cannon fire made the decisive breach in the walls during the Civil War. This part of the fort still bears the scars of the bombardment, with visible damage in the brickwork. Standing in this area gives visitors a real sense of the intensity of the battle and the revolutionary impact of rifled artillery on warfare. Several original and replica cannons are on display throughout the fort, providing insight into the firepower available to both Union and Confederate forces. You can learn about the different types of artillery used and how they were loaded, aimed, and fired during the siege.

One of the best ways to experience Fort Pulaski is through the ranger-led tours that are offered daily. These tours provide an in-depth look at the fort's history, the technology used during its construction, and the significance of the 1862 siege. Rangers share fascinating stories about the soldiers who lived and fought here, bringing the fort's history to life. Throughout the year, living history programs and reenactments are held at Fort Pulaski, featuring costumed interpreters who demonstrate 19th-century military drills, musket firings, and cannon firings. These events allow visitors to experience what life was like for soldiers stationed at the fort and offer a hands-on way to engage with the history of the Civil War.

For a stunning panoramic view of the surrounding landscape, climb to the top of Fort Pulaski's walls. From this vantage point, you can see the Savannah River, the Cockspur Island Lighthouse, and the marshlands that stretch toward the Atlantic Ocean. The top of the fort also provides a closer look at the gun emplacements and offers a better understanding of the fort's defensive design.

In addition to exploring the fort, Fort Pulaski National Monument offers several scenic walking trails that showcase the natural beauty of the area. The North Pier Trail takes visitors along the old fort pier and through coastal marshes, offering the chance to see native wildlife such as egrets, herons, and even alligators. The Lighthouse Overlook Trail is another popular route, leading to a viewpoint where you can see the historic Cockspur Island Lighthouse, which dates back to 1856. The lighthouse, standing at the mouth of the Savannah River, is a symbol of the area's maritime history.

Before or after your tour of the fort, be sure to stop by the Fort Pulaski Visitor Center. The museum inside the visitor center features exhibits on the fort's construction, the Siege of Fort Pulaski, and the soldiers who served there. Artifacts from the period, including military uniforms, weapons, and personal items, are on display, helping to paint a vivid picture of life at the fort. A short orientation film provides a helpful overview of the fort's history, and interactive displays offer additional information about the technological advancements that made the siege possible.

Fort Pulaski is a great place for a picnic, with several picnic areas located near the visitor center and along the scenic trails. Visitors can enjoy a meal surrounded by the beauty of coastal Georgia, with views of the fort and its surrounding marshlands. Whether you bring your own food or visit during one of the park's special events that feature local vendors, the park offers a peaceful setting to relax and enjoy the outdoors.

Tips

- Wear comfortable shoes: Much of the park is best explored on foot, and the trails around the fort can be uneven.
- Bring binoculars: The park is a haven for birdwatchers, so having binoculars handy will help you get a closer look at the diverse wildlife in the marshes.
- Plan for weather: Georgia's coastal weather can be unpredictable, so bring sunscreen and plenty of water if visiting during warmer months. In cooler seasons, a light jacket may be needed, especially in the windy areas along the water.

Nearby Attractions

- Tybee Island: Just a few miles from Fort Pulaski, Tybee Island is a popular beach destination known for its laid-back atmosphere and beautiful coastline. Visitors can relax on the beach, explore the Tybee Island Lighthouse, or enjoy water sports such as kayaking and paddleboarding.

- Savannah Historic District: A short drive west will bring you to the Savannah Historic District, famous for its cobblestone streets, oak trees draped in Spanish moss, and well-preserved antebellum architecture. Take a guided tour, stroll through Forsyth Park, or visit the many museums and galleries that showcase Savannah's rich history.

- Skidaway Island State Park: For outdoor enthusiasts, Skidaway Island State Park offers miles of scenic trails through maritime forests and salt marshes. The park is perfect for hiking, birdwatching, and camping, providing a peaceful retreat not far from Fort Pulaski.

34 FOX THEATRE

COUNTY: FULTON　　　　　　　　　　　　　　　　**CITY:** ATLANTA

DATE VISITED:　　　　　　**WHO I WENT WITH:**

RATING: ☆ ☆ ☆ ☆ ☆　　**WILL I RETURN?** YES / NO

660 Peachtree Street NE
Atlanta, Georgia 30308
404-881-2100

Nestled in the heart of Midtown Atlanta, the Fox Theatre is one of Georgia's most beloved cultural landmarks and an iconic symbol of the city's rich architectural and entertainment history. Originally built as a movie palace in 1929, the Fox Theatre now hosts a wide range of performances, including Broadway shows, concerts, and special events. With its stunning Moorish Revival architecture, rich history, and vibrant programming, the Fox Theatre offers visitors an unforgettable experience, whether they are attending a performance or simply touring the majestic building. A visit to the Fox Theatre is a must for anyone looking to explore Atlanta's cultural heritage.

The Fox Theatre began its life in the late 1920s as part of a larger project by the Shriners to build a lavish meeting place, known as the Yaarab Temple Shrine Mosque. However, the project's cost exceeded their budget, and it was taken over by film mogul William Fox, who transformed the building into one of the grandest movie palaces in the United States. When it opened in 1929, the Fox Theatre was celebrated for its stunning design and cutting-edge technology, including an impressive Mighty Mo pipe organ, one of the largest theater organs in the world.

The Fox Theatre's design is a blend of Moorish, Egyptian, and Islamic styles, reflecting the architectural exuberance of the 1920s. The exterior features domes, minarets, and intricate tile work, while the interior is even more opulent. The main auditorium is designed to resemble an open-air courtyard, complete with twinkling stars and drifting clouds projected onto the ceiling. Other spaces, such as the Egyptian Ballroom and the Grand Salon, showcase lavish details and craftsmanship that have been meticulously preserved over the decades.

By the 1970s, the Fox Theatre had fallen into disrepair and was in danger of being demolished. However, thanks to a passionate public campaign known as "Save the Fox," the building was spared and restored to its former glory. The Fox Theatre was listed on the National Register of Historic Places in 1974, and today it stands as one of the most iconic landmarks in the Southeast, continuing to attract visitors from around the world.

One of the best ways to appreciate the grandeur of the Fox Theatre is to take a guided tour. These tours provide a behind-the-scenes look at the theatre's stunning interiors, including areas not typically accessible to the public. You'll learn about the theater's fascinating history, its architectural features, and the famous performers who have graced its stage. Highlights of the tour include a visit to the Mighty Mo organ, the Orchestra Pit, and a closer look at the starry sky ceiling in the main auditorium. The tour also offers insight into the restoration efforts that saved the theatre from destruction and how it has maintained its position as a cultural hub in Atlanta.

The Fox Theatre is renowned for its world-class entertainment, hosting a wide variety of performances throughout the year. Whether you're a fan of Broadway musicals, concerts by top artists, or ballet and opera, the Fox's diverse programming has something for everyone. The theatre is known for its exceptional acoustics and intimate seating, ensuring that every performance is a memorable experience. Some of the most popular shows at the Fox include long-running Broadway productions like "The Lion King", "Hamilton", and "Wicked". In addition, the theatre regularly hosts performances by the Atlanta Ballet, Atlanta Opera, and internationally acclaimed musicians and comedians.

The architecture of the Fox Theatre is a sight to behold. The Moorish-inspired design features intricate tilework, sweeping arches, and exotic motifs that transport visitors to another world. The main auditorium, modeled after an Arabian courtyard, is one of the most visually stunning spaces in any American theater, with its twinkling ceiling, ornate balconies, and plush seating. Visitors can also explore the theatre's other lavish spaces, such as the Egyptian Ballroom, which features intricate hieroglyphics and luxurious decor, and the Spanish Room, with its colorful murals and Old World charm. These rooms are often used for special events and weddings, adding a layer of glamour to private occasions.

One of the unique features of the Fox Theatre is the famous Mighty Mo organ, one of the largest theater organs still in operation. Originally designed to accompany silent films, the Mighty Mo is a marvel of engineering and craftsmanship, with over 3,600 pipes that produce a rich, powerful sound. During select performances, including special screenings of classic films and silent movies, the Mighty Mo is played live, offering visitors a rare chance to hear this legendary instrument in action. The organ is also showcased during guided tours, where visitors can learn about its history and unique design.

In addition to live performances, the Fox Theatre hosts a variety of special events throughout the year. One of the most popular traditions is the Fox Theatre's Summer Film Series, where classic movies are shown on the big screen, often accompanied by live performances on the Mighty Mo organ. Watching a film at the Fox is a nostalgic experience that harkens back to the theater's origins as a grand movie palace. The Fox also hosts seasonal events, such as holiday concerts, New Year's Eve celebrations, and themed galas that allow guests to experience the theatre in a festive and immersive atmosphere.

While the Fox Theatre does not have a full-service restaurant on site, there are concession stands offering a variety of snacks, drinks, and alcoholic beverages during performances. For those looking to enjoy a meal before or after a show, the theatre is surrounded by excellent dining options in Midtown Atlanta, including fine dining, casual eateries, and vibrant bars. Visitors can also make an evening of their trip to the Fox by exploring the nearby Midtown Arts District, which is home to other cultural institutions like the High Museum of Art and the Woodruff Arts Center.

Tips

- Book early: Many of the Fox Theatre's performances, especially popular Broadway shows and concerts, sell out quickly. It's recommended to book tickets well in advance to secure the best seats.
- Arrive early: Arriving early allows you to take in the theater's stunning architecture, enjoy a drink at the Fabulous Fox Marquee Club, and get settled before the show begins.
- Dress for the occasion: While there is no strict dress code, many attendees choose to dress up for the occasion, especially for evening performances. Dressing up adds to the elegant, timeless atmosphere of the Fox Theatre experience.

Nearby Attractions

- The High Museum of Art: Located just a short distance from the Fox Theatre, the High Museum of Art is Atlanta's premier art museum. With an extensive collection of modern and classical works, rotating exhibitions, and family-friendly events, it's a fantastic cultural destination to combine with your visit to the Fox.

- Piedmont Park: Just a few blocks from the Fox Theatre, Piedmont Park is Atlanta's most famous green space, offering walking trails, picnic areas, and scenic views of the city skyline. It's a great place to relax before or after a show, and the park regularly hosts events such as music festivals and farmers markets.

- The Atlanta Botanical Garden: Located adjacent to Piedmont Park, the Atlanta Botanical Garden features beautiful gardens, conservatories, and art installations. Visitors can explore themed gardens, including the Japanese Garden and the Orchid House, making it a peaceful and visually striking addition to your Fox Theatre trip.

35 FRANKLIN D. ROOSEVELT STATE PARK

COUNTY: HARRIS **CITY:** PINE MOUNTAIN

DATE VISITED: **WHO I WENT WITH:**

RATING: ☆ ☆ ☆ ☆ ☆ **WILL I RETURN?** YES / NO

2970 Georgia Highway 190
Pine Mountain, GA 31822
706-663-4858

Franklin D. Roosevelt State Park, located in the picturesque mountains of Pine Mountain, Georgia, is a stunning destination that offers visitors a perfect blend of outdoor adventure and natural beauty. Established in 1932, this park was dedicated to President Franklin D. Roosevelt, who frequently visited the area during his presidency for its therapeutic benefits. Spanning over 9,000 acres, the park features serene landscapes, diverse wildlife, and a variety of recreational activities, making it an ideal spot for families, nature enthusiasts, and history buffs alike.

The park is named after President Franklin D. Roosevelt, who visited the area for polio treatment at the nearby Warm Springs. His connection to the region helped spur interest in its development as a state park. In the 1930s, the Civilian Conservation Corps (CCC) played a significant role in constructing many of the park's facilities and trails, ensuring its preservation for future generations.

The park's rich history is evident in its well-maintained structures, including stone bridges, cabins, and picnic areas. The CCC's contributions have left a lasting legacy, and many of their original features are still in use today, providing a glimpse into the past.

With over 40 miles of hiking trails, Franklin D. Roosevelt State Park is a hiker's paradise. The trails range from easy to challenging, accommodating all skill levels. Notable hikes include the Pine Mountain Trail, which offers breathtaking views of the surrounding mountains and valleys. The Loop Trail is a popular choice for families, providing a scenic route that showcases the park's natural beauty and wildlife. Keep an eye out for the diverse flora and fauna, including deer, wild turkeys, and various bird species.

Lake Delanor, a centerpiece of the park, is perfect for fishing, kayaking, and picnicking. The lake is stocked with a variety of fish, including bass and catfish, making it a popular spot for anglers. There are designated areas for canoe and kayak rentals, offering a serene way to explore the tranquil waters. Visitors can enjoy a leisurely day by the lake, surrounded by the beauty of nature.

The park features several picnic areas equipped with tables and grills, making it an excellent spot for family gatherings or a quiet lunch in nature. The serene surroundings provide a peaceful atmosphere for relaxation. For a more rustic experience, visitors can also reserve one of the campsites available within the park. Camping under the stars is a wonderful way to connect with nature and enjoy the sounds of the forest.

Franklin D. Roosevelt State Park is home to a rich diversity of wildlife, making it an excellent destination for wildlife enthusiasts and photographers. The park's varied habitats, including forests, meadows, and wetlands, attract numerous species. Be sure to bring your binoculars and camera to catch a glimpse of deer, rabbits, and an array of bird species. The park is particularly beautiful in the early morning and late afternoon when wildlife is most active.

History buffs will appreciate the park's historical significance, as it was a favorite retreat for FDR. Visit the Little White House in nearby Warm Springs, where the president spent time and worked on his New Deal programs. The site includes a museum and exhibits detailing FDR's life and legacy. While in the area, consider taking a short trip to explore the Warm Springs Historic District, which features historic buildings, shops, and the famous springs that attracted visitors seeking healing.

In addition to hiking and fishing, the park offers a variety of recreational activities. Visitors can enjoy biking on designated trails or engage in birdwatching throughout the park. Geocaching is another fun activity, with several caches hidden throughout the park for adventurers to find. This modern-day treasure hunt adds an exciting twist to exploring the natural surroundings.

Franklin D. Roosevelt State Park hosts a variety of events and educational programs throughout the year, including guided nature walks, campfire programs, and seasonal festivals. These events provide an opportunity to learn more about the park's ecology and history while connecting with fellow nature enthusiasts. Check the park's official website or visitor center for information on upcoming events and activities during your visit.

The park offers campsites for tent and RV camping, as well as primitive camping for those looking for a more rugged experience. Reservations are recommended, especially during peak seasons, to secure a spot. For visitors seeking more comfort, nearby towns such as Pine Mountain and Warm Springs offer a variety of lodging options, including cabins, hotels, and bed-and-breakfast establishments.

Tips

- Check trail conditions: Before heading out on a hike, stop by the park office or check the park's website for current trail conditions, especially after rainy weather.
- Pack for the weather: Georgia's weather can be unpredictable, so pack sunscreen, hats, and plenty of water for summer visits, and dress in layers if visiting in cooler months.
- Leave No Trace: Help preserve the park's natural beauty by following Leave No Trace principles. Always clean up after yourself and respect wildlife by keeping a safe distance.

Nearby Attractions

- The Little White House: Just a short drive from the park, the Little White House in Warm Springs was Franklin D. Roosevelt's personal retreat and the place where he passed away in 1945. Today, it's a museum open to the public, showcasing Roosevelt's life and legacy with exhibits, photographs, and memorabilia.

- Callaway Gardens: Located just a few miles from the park, Callaway Gardens is a premier destination for nature lovers. The expansive gardens feature walking and biking trails, a butterfly conservatory, golf courses, and beautiful seasonal displays, making it a perfect complement to a visit to the state park.

- Wild Animal Safari: For a family-friendly adventure, the Wild Animal Safari in Pine Mountain offers a drive-through experience where visitors can see exotic animals such as giraffes, zebras, and bison up close. The park also features a petting zoo and walking area for interactive wildlife encounters.

36 FUN SPOT AMERICA ATLANTA

COUNTY: FAYETTE   CITY: FAYETTEVILLE

DATE VISITED: WHO I WENT WITH:

RATING: ☆ ☆ ☆ ☆ ☆   WILL I RETURN?   YES / NO

1675 Hwy 85N
Fayetteville, GA 30214
407-363-3867

Fun Spot America Atlanta is a thrilling amusement park located just a short drive from downtown Atlanta. Opened in 2017, this family-friendly destination offers a wide array of rides, attractions, and entertainment options that cater to visitors of all ages. With its vibrant atmosphere, exciting rides, and focus on fun, Fun Spot America is the perfect place to spend a day filled with laughter and adventure. Whether you're a thrill-seeker or looking for a relaxed family outing, Fun Spot America has something for everyone.

SkyCoaster: Experience the ultimate adrenaline rush on the SkyCoaster, where you'll soar 100 feet above the ground at speeds of up to 60 miles per hour. This breathtaking ride combines the thrill of skydiving with the excitement of roller coasters for an unforgettable experience.

Mine Bender Coaster: Take a ride on the Mine Bender Coaster, a classic wooden roller coaster that features sharp turns and exhilarating drops. This ride is perfect for those who enjoy the thrill of roller coasters without being too intense for younger riders.

Giant Swing: Get ready to swing high into the sky on the Giant Swing! This ride takes you on a pendulum-like journey, providing panoramic views of the park as you swing back and forth.

Fun Spot America offers a variety of rides specifically designed for younger children, ensuring that everyone can join in on the fun. Attractions like the Mini Ferris Wheel and Bumper Cars allow kids to experience the thrill of the amusement park in a safe and enjoyable environment.

Don't miss the chance to visit the Gator Spot, where you can see live alligators and learn about these fascinating reptiles. The attraction features various species, including the impressive American alligator, and provides educational opportunities for the whole family.

One of the main highlights of Fun Spot America is its exciting go-kart tracks. With multiple tracks to choose from, including the Grand Prix track and the Family track, visitors can compete against each other for the best lap times. The go-karts are suitable for both kids and adults, making it a perfect activity for family bonding.

Step into the arcade, where you'll find a vast selection of games ranging from classic pinball machines to modern video games. Whether you prefer racing games, shooting games, or skill-based challenges, there's something for everyone in the arcade. Earn tickets as you play and redeem them for fun prizes at the prize counter. The arcade is an excellent way to take a break from the rides and enjoy some friendly competition.

Fun Spot America hosts a variety of special events throughout the year, including seasonal celebrations, holiday-themed events, and live entertainment. Check the park's schedule for information on upcoming events, concerts, and promotions. The park also features themed nights and activities, such as karaoke competitions and family game nights, ensuring there's always something new and exciting happening.

Fun Spot America offers a range of dining options to keep you fueled throughout your day of fun. Stop by the Fun Spot Cafe for delicious snacks, burgers, and refreshing beverages. The cafe provides a variety of choices to cater to all taste buds, ensuring you can recharge before heading back to the rides. For a quick snack, you can find food carts throughout the park serving popular treats like cotton candy, popcorn, and funnel cakes.

If you're looking to enjoy a sit-down meal, the area surrounding Fun Spot America has a variety of restaurants to choose from. Popular options include Buffalo Wild Wings, Chick-fil-A, and Mellow Mushroom, offering a range of cuisines to satisfy your cravings.

Tips

- Arrive early: To make the most of your day, arrive early when the park opens. This helps you avoid long lines for popular rides and ensures you have plenty of time to explore all the attractions.
- Purchase tickets online: Save time and money by purchasing your unlimited ride armbands or tickets online before your visit. The park sometimes offers discounts for online purchases, making it a great way to save a few dollars.
- Wear comfortable clothing: With so many rides and attractions to enjoy, make

sure to wear comfortable clothing and shoes that are suitable for walking and riding. Closed-toe shoes are recommended, especially for go-kart racing and thrill rides.

- Stay hydrated: Georgia's weather can be hot, especially during the summer. Be sure to bring a water bottle, and take advantage of the park's water fountains to stay hydrated throughout the day. Many rides have shade, but sunscreen is also a must to protect against the sun.

Nearby Attractions

- Atlanta Motor Speedway: Located just a short drive from Fun Spot America Atlanta, the Atlanta Motor Speedway is a must-see for racing fans. The track hosts major NASCAR events and offers tours that give visitors a behind-the-scenes look at one of the country's premier racing facilities.

- Pinewood Forest: For a more relaxed experience, take a trip to Pinewood Forest, a nearby community known for its beautiful architecture, restaurants, and art galleries. It's a great spot to unwind and explore after a day of excitement at the park.

- Starr's Mill: Nature enthusiasts will enjoy visiting Starr's Mill, a historic mill located on the banks of Whitewater Creek. This picturesque spot is perfect for photography, picnicking, and enjoying a peaceful afternoon surrounded by natural beauty.

GEORGIA AQUARIUM

COUNTY: FULTON **CITY:** ATLANTA

DATE VISITED: **WHO I WENT WITH:**

RATING: ☆ ☆ ☆ ☆ ☆   **WILL I RETURN?** YES / NO

225 Baker St
Atlanta, GA 30313
404-581-4000

Georgia Aquarium is one of the largest and most impressive aquariums in the world. Located in downtown Atlanta, Georgia, this incredible facility is home to more than 100,000 aquatic animals and features thousands of species from around the globe. With its stunning exhibits, interactive experiences, and commitment to conservation, the Georgia Aquarium offers visitors a unique opportunity to explore the wonders of the ocean and its inhabitants. Whether you're a marine life enthusiast or looking for a fun family outing, the Georgia Aquarium promises an unforgettable experience.

Opened in 2005, the Georgia Aquarium was founded by businessman and philanthropist Bernard Marcus, who envisioned a world-class facility dedicated to marine conservation and education. The aquarium has grown rapidly since its inception and now features one of the largest aquatic collections in the world, with over 10 million gallons of fresh and saltwater.

The Georgia Aquarium features a wide range of exhibits that showcase the incredible diversity of marine life. Some of the most popular exhibits include:

Ocean Voyager: This signature exhibit is home to a stunning array of marine animals, including whale sharks, manta rays, and various species of fish. The exhibit features a massive underwater tunnel that allows visitors to walk through and experience the breathtaking beauty of these majestic creatures up close.

Tropical Diver: Dive into the vibrant world of tropical coral reefs in this immersive exhibit, which showcases colorful fish, sea turtles, and coral species from the Caribbean and Indo-Pacific regions. The exhibit is designed to replicate the natural habitat of these animals, providing visitors with a true sense of the underwater ecosystem.

Cold Water Quest: Explore the fascinating creatures that thrive in colder waters, such as beluga whales, sea otters, and various species of penguins. This exhibit highlights the unique adaptations these animals have developed to survive in their chilly environments.

River Scout: Discover the diverse ecosystems of rivers and freshwater habitats in this engaging exhibit, featuring animals like alligators, otters, and piranhas. The River Scout exhibit showcases the importance of freshwater conservation and the challenges faced by these ecosystems.

The Georgia Aquarium offers numerous interactive experiences designed to engage visitors and enhance their understanding of marine life:

Dolphin Celebration: This popular show features trained dolphins showcasing their intelligence and agility. Visitors can watch these incredible animals perform tricks and learn about their behaviors and habitats.

Behind-the-Scenes Tours: For those seeking a more in-depth experience, the aquarium offers behind-the-scenes tours that provide insight into the daily operations of the facility, including animal care and husbandry practices.

Touch Pools: Visitors can get hands-on at the touch pools, where they can gently touch and learn about various marine animals, including stingrays and sea stars, under the supervision of knowledgeable staff.

Aquarium Sleepovers: For a truly unique experience, consider booking an overnight adventure at the aquarium. Participants can sleep near the exhibits, enjoy special activities, and learn about marine conservation in a fun and interactive environment.

The Georgia Aquarium is committed to marine conservation and education. The aquarium actively participates in global conservation initiatives and research projects aimed at protecting marine habitats and species. Through educational programs, visitor experiences, and community outreach, the aquarium seeks to inspire visitors to become stewards of the ocean.

The aquarium features several dining options, including cafes and a full-service restaurant. Visitors can enjoy a variety of meals, from casual snacks to more substantial entrees. The Aquarium Café offers a range of options, including sandwiches, salads, and kid-friendly meals, all with views of the exhibits.

Be sure to visit the aquarium's gift shop, where you can find a wide selection of souvenirs, educational materials, and unique gifts related to marine life. Proceeds from the gift shop support the aquarium's conservation efforts.

Tips

- Arrive early: To make the most of your day and avoid crowds, try to arrive early, especially on weekends and holidays.
- Plan your visit: The aquarium is large, so consider reviewing the map and planning your route to prioritize the exhibits you want to see.
- Bring a camera: With so many incredible exhibits and photo opportunities, be sure to bring your camera or smartphone to capture your memories.
- Stay hydrated: There are several water fountains throughout the aquarium, but consider bringing a reusable water bottle to stay hydrated during your visit.

Nearby Attractions

- World of Coca-Cola: Just a short walk away, this interactive museum showcases the history of the Coca-Cola brand. Visitors can learn about the beverage's origins, see the bottling process, and taste different Coca-Cola products from around the world.

- Centennial Olympic Park: Located adjacent to the aquarium, this beautiful park features walking paths, fountains, and green spaces. It's a great place to relax and enjoy the outdoors after your aquarium visit.

- Atlanta Botanical Garden: A short drive away, the Atlanta Botanical Garden features stunning plant collections, seasonal displays, and beautiful landscapes. The garden offers educational programs and events throughout the year.

----

38 GEORGIA MOUNTAIN COASTER

COUNTY: WHITE **CITY:** HELEN

DATE VISITED: **WHO I WENT WITH:**

RATING: ☆ ☆ ☆ ☆ ☆ **WILL I RETURN?** YES / NO

8409 S Main Street
Helen, GA 30545
706-878-1347

Georgia Mountain Coaster is an exhilarating attraction located in the scenic Blue Ridge Mountains of Georgia. Opened in 2017, this alpine coaster offers visitors a unique opportunity to experience the beauty of the mountains while enjoying an adrenaline-pumping ride. With its stunning views, twists, and turns, the Georgia Mountain Coaster promises an unforgettable adventure for thrill-seekers and families alike.

The Georgia Mountain Coaster is one of the longest coasters of its kind in the United States, stretching over 3,200 feet through the beautiful forested landscape. Riders can control their speed as they navigate the coaster's thrilling drops, sharp turns, and breathtaking views of the surrounding mountains. Whether you're looking to zoom down the track or take it slow to enjoy the scenery, the choice is yours!

The coaster is designed to accommodate guests of all ages. Children as young as 3 years old can ride with an adult, making it a perfect family-friendly attraction. The coaster's safety features ensure a secure ride while still allowing for a fun and exciting experience.

As you ascend the mountain on the coaster, prepare to be mesmerized by the stunning views of the Blue Ridge Mountains. The ride takes you through lush forests, past scenic overlooks, and even alongside serene streams. The natural beauty of the area is a highlight of the experience, especially during the fall when the leaves change colors. Keep your camera handy to capture the picturesque landscapes, as there are several spots along the ride that offer breathtaking photo opportunities.

The coaster features an uphill climb that allows riders to take in the views before the thrilling descent begins. The ride reaches speeds of up to 25 miles per hour, with plenty of twists and turns to keep your adrenaline pumping. Riders can control their speed using hand brakes, allowing for a customized experience. Whether you prefer to race down the track or savor a leisurely ride, the choice is yours.

Safety is a top priority at the Georgia Mountain Coaster. The ride is equipped with state-of-the-art safety features, including a dual-rail system and individual sleds with secure harnesses. Trained staff members are on hand to provide instructions and ensure all safety protocols are followed. Riders are required to meet specific height and weight restrictions to ensure a safe and enjoyable experience. Children under 3 years old cannot ride, and those between 3 and 7 years must ride with an adult.

For those seeking even more excitement, consider trying the zip line tours offered in the same area. Soar through the trees and experience the thrill of flying high above the forest canopy. The zip line tours provide another opportunity to enjoy the stunning views of the mountains while adding to your adventure.

The surrounding area features a variety of hiking trails for those who want to explore the natural beauty of the Blue Ridge Mountains further. Trails range from easy walks to challenging hikes, providing options for all skill levels. Be sure to bring water and wear appropriate footwear for your hiking adventures.

After your ride, grab a bite to eat at the on-site snack bar, where you'll find a variety of quick snacks and refreshments to refuel after your exciting adventure. Enjoy classic favorites like hot dogs, pretzels, and ice-cold beverages.

If you're looking for a more substantial meal, the nearby towns of Blue Ridge and Ellijay offer a wide range of dining options. From cozy cafes to family-friendly restaurants, you'll find something to satisfy every palate. Don't miss the chance to try local specialties, including Southern comfort food and farm-fresh produce.

Tips

- Arrive early: To avoid long wait times, consider arriving early, especially during weekends and peak tourist seasons.
- Check the weather: Weather can affect ride operations, so be sure to check the forecast and dress accordingly.
- Bring sunscreen: If visiting during sunny days, apply sunscreen to protect your skin while enjoying the outdoors.
- Stay hydrated: Bring a water bottle to stay hydrated throughout your visit, especially if you plan to hike or spend extended time outdoors.

Nearby Attractions

- Mercier Orchards: Just a short drive away, Mercier Orchards is a family-owned apple orchard offering pick-your-own fruit experiences, a farm market, and a café with delicious baked goods. Visit during the fall for apple picking, or stop by in the summer for fresh peaches and berries.

- Blue Ridge Scenic Railway: Experience the beauty of the mountains from a different perspective on the Blue Ridge Scenic Railway. This picturesque train ride takes you along the Toccoa River, through charming towns, and offers stunning views of the surrounding landscapes. It's a great way to relax and take in the sights, especially for families with younger children.

- Lake Blue Ridge: Located just a few miles from the coaster, Lake Blue Ridge offers opportunities for outdoor activities such as boating, fishing, and swimming. Rent a kayak or paddleboard to explore the crystal-clear waters, or simply relax by the shore with a picnic. The lake is a perfect spot for a day of fun in the sun.

GEORGIA SEA TURTLE CENTER

39

COUNTY: GLYNN	CITY: JEKYLL ISLAND
DATE VISITED:	WHO I WENT WITH:
RATING: ☆ ☆ ☆ ☆ ☆	WILL I RETURN? YES / NO

214 Stable Rd
Jekyll Island, GA 31527
912-635-4444

Georgia Sea Turtle Center is a vital marine conservation facility located on Jekyll Island, Georgia. Established in 2007, this center plays a crucial role in the rehabilitation of injured sea turtles, education about marine ecosystems, and promoting the conservation of these remarkable creatures. With its engaging exhibits and hands-on learning experiences, the Georgia Sea Turtle Center offers a unique opportunity for visitors to learn about sea turtles and their habitats while supporting vital conservation efforts.

The Georgia Sea Turtle Center is dedicated to the rescue, rehabilitation, and release of sea turtles, as well as conducting research and educating the public about the threats these animals face. The center aims to inspire conservation and protect sea turtles through community engagement and education programs.

Situated on Jekyll Island, the center is conveniently located near the island's beautiful beaches, making it easy for visitors to explore the natural beauty of the area while learning about marine life.

The center features a variety of interactive exhibits that educate visitors about sea turtle biology, ecology, and conservation efforts. Explore the lifecycle of sea turtles through informative displays, touch tanks, and engaging multimedia presentations. Don't miss the chance to view the "Turtle Hospital", where you can observe the rehabilitation process and learn about the various injuries that sea turtles encounter, such as entanglement in fishing gear and plastic ingestion.

The Georgia Sea Turtle Center is home to several resident turtles undergoing rehabilitation. Guests can see these incredible animals up close and learn about their stories, including the challenges they faced and the efforts being made to help them recover. The center regularly hosts public feedings where visitors can watch as staff members feed the turtles and discuss their dietary needs and behaviors. This unique experience offers insight into the care and rehabilitation of these majestic creatures.

The center offers guided tours led by knowledgeable staff who share valuable insights about sea turtles and their habitats. These tours provide an in-depth look at the rehabilitation process and the importance of conservation efforts. Special programs, such as turtle walks during nesting season, allow visitors to witness nesting sea turtles and learn about the nesting process. Be sure to check the schedule for availability and reservations, as spots can fill up quickly.

Throughout the year, the center hosts a variety of educational workshops and events aimed at different age groups, including school field trips, family activities, and community outreach programs. These programs promote awareness of marine conservation and encourage participants to take action in protecting marine environments.

The Georgia Sea Turtle Center features an on-site café where visitors can grab a bite to eat. Enjoy a selection of sandwiches, salads, snacks, and refreshing beverages. This convenient option allows you to refuel without leaving the center.

Jekyll Island offers a variety of dining options for all tastes and budgets. Enjoy seafood at local favorites like The Crab Trap or Cameron's Coastal Kitchen. For a casual atmosphere, check out Zachry's Riverhouse, which offers waterfront dining and a laid-back vibe.

Tips

- Arrive early: To maximize your experience, consider arriving early to enjoy the exhibits before they become crowded.
- Bring water: Stay hydrated, especially if you plan to explore the outdoor areas and nearby attractions.
- Dress comfortably: Wear comfortable clothing and shoes suitable for walking, as you'll want to explore both the center and the beautiful Jekyll Island surroundings.
- Check for events: Keep an eye on the calendar for special events, workshops, and seasonal activities that may enhance your visit.

Nearby Attractions

- Jekyll Island Historic District: Just a short distance away, the Historic District offers a glimpse into the island's rich history with beautifully preserved buildings, guided tours, and scenic walking paths. Explore the former Jekyll Island Club, a winter retreat for America's wealthiest families in the late 19th century.

- Driftwood Beach: This picturesque beach, known for its stunning driftwood formations and beautiful sunsets, is a must-visit. It's an excellent spot for photography, beachcombing, and enjoying a relaxing day by the ocean. Look for nesting turtles during the summer months!

- Jekyll Island State Park: The park offers a variety of outdoor activities, including hiking, biking, and wildlife viewing. Explore the trails, picnic areas, and pristine beaches, all while enjoying the island's natural beauty. The park is also home to the Jekyll Island Museum, which provides further insight into the island's history and ecology.

GIBBS GARDENS

40

COUNTY: CHEROKEE　　　　　　　　　　　　　　　　CITY: BALL GROUND

DATE VISITED:　　　　　　　　WHO I WENT WITH:

RATING: ☆ ☆ ☆ ☆ ☆　　　　WILL I RETURN?　YES / NO

1987 Gibbs Drive
Ball Ground, GA 30107
770-893-1880

Gibbs Gardens is an enchanting 300-acre botanical garden located in the scenic North Georgia mountains, just a short drive from Ball Ground. Established by the renowned landscape designer Jim Gibbs, this garden showcases an extraordinary collection of flora, breathtaking landscapes, and themed gardens that celebrate the beauty of nature throughout the seasons. With its stunning displays, walking trails, and serene atmosphere, Gibbs Gardens is a must-visit destination for nature lovers, families, and anyone looking to escape into a floral paradise.

Founded in 2012, Gibbs Gardens is the culmination of Jim Gibbs' lifelong dream to create a world-class botanical garden. The gardens were designed to harmonize with the natural landscape, featuring a mix of native and exotic plants arranged in a way that emphasizes seasonal beauty and tranquility.

Located at 1987 Gibbs Drive, Ball Ground, GA 30107, Gibbs Gardens is easily accessible from major highways and offers ample parking for visitors.

Water Lily Garden: One of the highlights of Gibbs Gardens is the stunning Water Lily Garden, home to over 140 varieties of water lilies and lotuses. Visitors can stroll along the paths, admire the vibrant blooms, and enjoy the peaceful ambiance of the ponds.

Japanese Garden: Inspired by traditional Japanese landscaping, this serene area features koi ponds, stone lanterns, and meticulously pruned trees. It's a perfect spot for reflection and photography, especially during the cherry blossom season.

Perennial Garden: This colorful garden showcases a diverse array of perennials that bloom throughout the spring and summer. From vibrant daisies to delicate foxgloves, the Perennial Garden is a feast for the senses.

Gibbs Gardens offers a network of walking trails that meander through the gardens, allowing visitors to explore at their own pace. The trails are well-maintained and suitable for all ages, making it easy for families to enjoy the outdoors together. Along the trails, you'll encounter charming bridges, sculptures, and tranquil seating areas where you can rest and soak in the beauty of your surroundings.

Throughout the year, Gibbs Gardens hosts a variety of seasonal events and activities. From spring bloom festivals featuring flower shows to autumn color celebrations, there's always something happening at the gardens. Be sure to check the event calendar on the Gibbs Gardens website to plan your visit around special events. During the holiday season, the gardens come alive with festive lights and decorations, creating a magical atmosphere perfect for families and friends.

Gibbs Gardens is committed to education and conservation. The gardens offer various educational programs for visitors of all ages, including guided tours, workshops, and classes focused on gardening, horticulture, and sustainable practices. Special programs for school groups and families are designed to inspire a love for nature and gardening in young visitors.

On-site dining is available at The Gardens Restaurant, which offers a delightful selection of seasonal dishes made with locally sourced ingredients. Enjoy a meal with stunning views of the gardens and a menu that highlights the flavors of the region.

If you prefer to explore dining options in the area, the nearby towns of Ball Ground and Dahlonega offer a variety of cafés and restaurants. Enjoy southern cuisine, farm-to-table dining, or casual eateries to refuel after a day of exploration.

Tips

- Arrive early: To avoid crowds and enjoy the tranquility of the gardens, consider arriving early in the day.
- Dress comfortably: Wear comfortable clothing and shoes suitable for walking, as you'll want to explore the various gardens and trails.
- Bring a camera: Don't forget your camera or smartphone to capture the beautiful landscapes and vibrant flowers. The gardens provide countless photo opportunities.
- Check for events: Review the events calendar on the Gibbs Gardens website to see if any special programs or activities coincide with your visit.

Nearby Attractions

- Amicalola Falls State Park: Just a short drive away, Amicalola Falls is home to Georgia's tallest waterfall, cascading 729 feet. The park features hiking trails, picnic areas, and breathtaking views, making it an excellent spot for outdoor enthusiasts.

- Dahlonega: Known for its historic downtown and gold rush history, the charming town of Dahlonega is just a 30-minute drive from Gibbs Gardens. Visitors can explore local shops, dine at cozy restaurants, and visit the Dahlonega Gold Museum.

- Woody Gap Trailhead: For those looking to hike, the Woody Gap Trailhead offers access to the Appalachian Trail. This section of the trail provides stunning views of the surrounding mountains and is suitable for both novice and experienced hikers.

41 — HIGH MUSEUM OF ART

COUNTY: FULTON **CITY:** ATLANTA

DATE VISITED: **WHO I WENT WITH:**

RATING: ☆ ☆ ☆ ☆ ☆ **WILL I RETURN?** YES / NO

1280 Peachtree St NE
Atlanta, GA 30309
404-733-4400

High Museum of Art is an Atlanta's premier art museum and a vibrant hub of cultural engagement. Established in 1905, the High Museum houses an impressive collection of over 15,000 works of art, ranging from classic European paintings to contemporary American pieces. With its striking architecture, engaging exhibitions, and commitment to community outreach, the High Museum is a must-visit destination for art lovers and anyone looking to immerse themselves in Georgia's rich cultural scene.

The High Museum of Art aims to inspire and educate through art. Its mission is to foster an appreciation for the arts by providing access to diverse artistic expressions and engaging the community through educational programs and outreach initiatives.

American Art: The museum boasts a vast collection of American art from the 18th century to the present. Highlights include works by iconic artists such as Georgia O'Keeffe, Edward Hopper, and Jasper Johns. The American collection reflects the country's diverse cultural heritage and artistic innovation.

European Art: The High is home to an impressive selection of European paintings, including masterpieces by Rembrandt, Monet, and Van Gogh. These works provide insight into the evolution of European art and its impact on the global art scene.

African Art: The museum features a significant collection of African art, including masks, sculptures, and textiles from various regions. This collection highlights the rich artistic traditions and cultural expressions of the African continent.

The High Museum hosts a dynamic schedule of temporary exhibitions that explore various themes, artists, and movements. From contemporary art to historical retrospectives, these exhibitions provide fresh perspectives and engaging experiences for visitors. Be sure to check the museum's website for information on current and upcoming exhibitions, as well as special events and programs.

The museum itself is a work of art, designed by the renowned architect Richard Meier. Its stunning white façade, geometric forms, and natural light create an inviting atmosphere for visitors. The museum's expansion in 2005 added even more gallery space and features a beautiful outdoor plaza. Take time to appreciate the architecture and landscaping surrounding the museum, which enhances the overall visitor experience.

The High Museum offers a range of educational programs for all ages, including guided tours, workshops, and family activities. These programs aim to deepen visitors' understanding of art and foster creativity. Special events, such as "Art Walks" and "Family Fun Days," provide interactive experiences for families and art enthusiasts alike. Be sure to check the schedule for seasonal activities and community engagement opportunities.

The High Café offers a variety of dining options, including fresh salads, sandwiches, and seasonal dishes made with locally sourced ingredients. Enjoy your meal with views of the museum's outdoor gardens and plaza.

If you're looking to explore more dining options in the area, Midtown Atlanta boasts a diverse array of restaurants and cafés. From casual eateries to fine dining, you'll find something to suit every taste. Popular options include South City Kitchen for Southern cuisine and Ecco for Mediterranean-inspired dishes.

Tips

- Plan your visit: Take a moment to explore the museum's website before your visit to familiarize yourself with current exhibitions, events, and any special programming.
- Allow time to explore: With so much to see and experience, plan to spend at least a few hours at the museum to fully appreciate the collections and exhibitions.
- Join a guided tour: Enhance your experience by participating in a guided tour, where knowledgeable staff can provide insights and context about the art and artists featured in the museum.
- Visit the gift shop: Don't forget to stop by the museum's gift shop, where you can find unique art-inspired gifts, books, and souvenirs to remember your visit.

Nearby Attractions

- Atlanta Botanical Garden: Just a short walk away, the Atlanta Botanical Garden features stunning landscapes, themed gardens, and seasonal exhibits. Explore the beautiful plant collections and enjoy special events like the Garden Lights holiday display.

- Fox Theatre: A historic landmark in Atlanta, the Fox Theatre hosts Broadway shows, concerts, and special events throughout the year. Check the schedule for upcoming performances and consider catching a show during your visit.

- Piedmont Park: Located nearby, Piedmont Park is a sprawling urban park offering walking trails, picnic areas, and recreational facilities. Enjoy a leisurely stroll or relax in the park while taking in the views of the Atlanta skyline.

42 HISTORIC RIVER STREET

COUNTY: CHATHAM **CITY:** SAVANNAH

DATE VISITED: **WHO I WENT WITH:**

RATING: ☆ ☆ ☆ ☆ ☆ **WILL I RETURN?** YES / NO

River St.
Savannah, GA 31401

Historic River Street is one of Savannah's most iconic destinations, where history, culture, and Southern charm converge along the picturesque Savannah River. Once a bustling hub for cotton trading, River Street is now a vibrant waterfront promenade lined with cobblestone streets, shops, restaurants, and historic buildings. With its lively atmosphere and rich history, River Street offers a unique experience for visitors looking to explore the heart of Savannah.

Established in the early 18th century, River Street played a crucial role in Savannah's economic development. The riverfront was the site of cotton warehouses and shipping docks, making it a vital center for trade. Today, many of the historic buildings have been restored and repurposed, preserving the charm and character of this significant area.

River Street runs along the Savannah River, stretching from the Waving Girl Statue to the Factor's Walk. It is easily accessible from the downtown area and is a popular starting point for exploring Savannah.

As you stroll along River Street, you'll encounter beautifully preserved buildings that showcase Savannah's architectural heritage. Look for the distinctive 19th-century warehouses and brick buildings that have been converted into shops, restaurants, and galleries. The Rousakis Riverfront Plaza features lovely gardens, fountains, and art installations, providing a scenic backdrop for visitors to relax and take in the views of the river.

River Street is home to an array of unique shops offering everything from souvenirs and local crafts to art and antique finds. Don't miss the chance to explore the River Street Market Place, where you can find local artisans showcasing their work. The dining options along River Street are diverse, featuring both casual and fine dining establishments. Enjoy fresh seafood at The Crab Shack or indulge in Southern cuisine at A.J.'s Dockside. For a sweet treat, stop by River Street Sweets for their famous pralines and candies.

River Street is a lively area with plenty of entertainment options. From street performers and live music to seasonal festivals and events, there's always something happening along the riverfront. Take a leisurely riverboat cruise for a unique perspective of Savannah from the water. Various boat tours are available, ranging from dinner cruises to sightseeing excursions.

Explore several historic sites near River Street, including the Savannah History Museum, which offers insights into the city's past and its role in American history. Don't miss the Waving Girl Statue, a tribute to Florence Martus, who waved at passing ships for over 44 years. It's a popular spot for photos and a symbol of Savannah's maritime heritage.

River Street hosts a variety of events and festivals throughout the year, making it an exciting place to visit any time. Notable events include:

- Savannah Music Festival: Held in March and April, this festival showcases a wide range of musical genres and attracts artists from around the world.

- Savannah Riverfront Seafood Festival: Celebrated in September, this festival features local seafood, live music, and family-friendly activities.

- Holiday Celebrations: During the holiday season, River Street is adorned with festive decorations and lights, and the annual Savannah Holiday Market offers local crafts and seasonal goods.

Tips

- Wear comfortable shoes: With cobblestone streets and plenty of walking, be sure to wear comfortable footwear to enjoy your exploration fully.
- Stay hydrated: Bring water, especially during warmer months, as you'll likely spend hours walking and enjoying the sights.
- Plan for weather: Savannah can be humid, so check the weather forecast and dress accordingly. An umbrella may come in handy during the rainy season.
- Explore beyond river street: Take time to venture into nearby historic districts and neighborhoods to discover Savannah's charming streets and historic architecture.

Nearby Attractions

- Forsyth Park: Just a short distance away, Forsyth Park is a beautiful green space featuring walking paths, a stunning fountain, and picnic areas. It's a perfect spot to relax and enjoy the outdoors.

- Savannah College of Art and Design (SCAD): The SCAD campus is nearby and showcases impressive galleries and exhibitions featuring student and faculty work. Check the SCAD website for current exhibitions open to the public.

- Old Fort Jackson: Located along the river, this historic fort offers tours, exhibits, and live cannon demonstrations, providing a glimpse into Savannah's military history.

43 HISTORIC SAVANNAH THEATRE

COUNTY: CHATHAM	CITY: SAVANNAH
DATE VISITED:	WHO I WENT WITH:
RATING: ☆ ☆ ☆ ☆ ☆	WILL I RETURN? YES / NO

222 Bull Street
Savannah, GA 31401
912-233-7764

Historic Savannah Theatre is a cherished cultural institution and one of the oldest continually operating theaters in the United States. Located in the heart of Savannah, this iconic venue has been entertaining audiences since 1818 and is renowned for its vibrant performances, including musicals, plays, and special events. With its charming architecture and rich history, the Savannah Theatre offers a unique glimpse into the world of performing arts while celebrating Savannah's rich cultural heritage.

Originally built as a cotton warehouse, the Savannah Theatre was transformed into a performance venue in the early 19th century. Over the years, it has undergone several renovations and restorations, preserving its historic charm while adapting to modern performance standards. The theater has hosted a variety of notable performances, including vaudeville acts, Broadway shows, and concerts.

The Savannah Theatre features a stunning facade with intricate details and a welcoming marquee that beckons visitors to enter. The interior is equally captivating, with a beautifully restored auditorium that retains the elegance of its historical roots while providing modern amenities for guests.

The theater hosts a range of performances throughout the year, including musicals, comedies, and dramatic productions. Signature shows often celebrate Southern culture and heritage, featuring live music and talented local performers. Popular productions include holiday shows like "A Christmas Tradition" and classic performances such as "The Savannah Sipping Society." Be sure to check the theater's schedule for upcoming performances and ticket availability.

One of the unique aspects of the Savannah Theatre is its intimate setting, allowing audiences to experience performances up close and personal. With a seating capacity of just over 400, every seat in the house offers a great view of the stage, creating a warm and engaging atmosphere for both performers and guests.

The Savannah Theatre is not only a venue for entertainment but also a significant part of Savannah's cultural heritage. It is listed on the National Register of Historic Places and has been a focal point for the performing arts in the region for over two centuries. Guided tours may be available, providing insights into the theater's rich history and its role in Savannah's artistic community.

The Savannah Theatre offers concessions, including snacks and beverages, allowing you to enjoy refreshments during performances. Be sure to arrive early to grab a treat.

The area around the Savannah Theatre is home to a variety of dining options. Consider dining at The Collins Quarter for a blend of Australian and Southern cuisine or Cotton & Rye, which offers a modern twist on classic Southern dishes. Both restaurants are within walking distance of the theater.

Tips

- Book in advance: Popular performances can sell out quickly, so it's best to book your tickets in advance to secure your seats.
- Arrive early: Give yourself ample time to find parking and get settled before the show begins. Arriving early also allows you to explore the theater and take in its historic ambiance.
- Dress comfortably: While there's no strict dress code, many guests opt for smart casual attire. Wear comfortable shoes, especially if you plan to explore the surrounding area before or after the performance.
- Check the performance schedule: Visit the Savannah Theatre website for details on upcoming shows, including special events and seasonal performances.

Nearby Attractions

- Forsyth Park: Just a short walk away, Forsyth Park is a sprawling urban park featuring walking paths, gardens, and the iconic Forsyth Fountain. It's a great place to relax and enjoy the natural beauty of Savannah.

- Savannah History Museum: Located in the historic Central of Georgia Railway Passenger Station, the Savannah History Museum offers exhibits on the city's past, including its role in the Civil War and its development as a port city.

- The Juliette Gordon Low Birthplace: A short distance from the theater, this historic home is the birthplace of the founder of the Girl Scouts of the USA. The site offers guided tours that highlight the life and contributions of Juliette Gordon Low.

44 HOFWYL-BROADFIELD PLANTATION

COUNTY: GLYNN   **CITY:** BRUNSWICK

DATE VISITED: **WHO I WENT WITH:**

RATING: ☆ ☆ ☆ ☆ ☆   **WILL I RETURN?** YES / NO

5556 U.S. Highway 17 N
Brunswick, GA 31525
912-264-7333

Hofwyl-Broadfield Plantation is a beautifully preserved historical site located near the scenic marshes of the Altamaha River in Brunswick, Georgia. This plantation offers visitors a glimpse into the lives of those who lived and worked here from the early 19th century through the Civil War and beyond. With its rich history, stunning natural surroundings, and educational programs, Hofwyl-Broadfield Plantation is a must-visit destination for anyone interested in Georgia's agricultural heritage and antebellum history.

Established in 1806, Hofwyl-Broadfield Plantation was initially a rice plantation founded by the Hofwyl family. Over the years, it evolved into a cotton and sugar plantation, playing a significant role in Georgia's agricultural economy. The plantation is also known for its connection to the Lowe family, who managed it for several generations until the 1940s. In 1973, Hofwyl-Broadfield became a Georgia State Historic Site, preserving its historical significance and providing educational opportunities for visitors.

The centerpiece of the plantation is the historic main house, built in the early 19th century. Guided tours of the house provide insight into the lives of the families who resided there, showcasing original furnishings, artifacts, and architectural details that reflect the era. The house features a blend of Federal and Greek Revival architectural styles, with spacious rooms and a beautiful view of the surrounding marshlands.

Guided tours of Hofwyl-Broadfield Plantation offer a comprehensive overview of its history, agricultural practices, and the lives of enslaved people who worked on the plantation. Knowledgeable staff members share stories and details that bring the plantation's history to life.

Special programs and events are held throughout the year, including lectures, workshops, and seasonal celebrations that highlight various aspects of plantation life and Georgia's agricultural heritage.

The plantation is set against a backdrop of stunning natural beauty, with expansive views of the Altamaha River and lush marshlands. Visitors can enjoy walking trails that meander through the grounds, providing opportunities for birdwatching and appreciating the local flora and fauna. The property is also home to several ancient live oak trees draped in Spanish moss, creating a picturesque setting for photography and reflection.

Various exhibits throughout the plantation provide additional context about the history of Hofwyl-Broadfield and the agricultural practices that shaped the region. Interpretive displays offer information on rice and cotton cultivation, as well as the daily lives of those who lived and worked on the plantation.

Tips

- Plan ahead: check the plantation's website for information on guided tour times and special events to make the most of your visit.
- Wear comfortable shoes: The plantation grounds feature walking trails, so wear comfortable footwear for exploring the area.
- Bring a camera: With its stunning scenery and historic architecture, Hofwyl-Broadfield Plantation is a photographer's paradise. Capture the beauty of the landscape and the charm of the historic buildings.
- Stay hydrated: Bring water, especially during the warmer months, as you'll likely spend time outdoors exploring the grounds.

Nearby Attractions

- Fort King George Historic Site: Located just a short drive away, this historic fort offers insights into early colonial history in Georgia. Visitors can explore the reconstructed fort, visitor center, and beautiful views of the Satilla River.

- Glynn County Historical Society: Situated in Brunswick, the society showcases the local history of Glynn County, including exhibits on the region's development, culture, and notable figures.

- Jekyll Island: A short drive from the plantation, Jekyll Island offers beautiful beaches, historic sites, and outdoor activities, including biking, hiking, and exploring the Jekyll Island Museum.

----

45 JEKYLL ISLAND HISTORIC DISTRICT

COUNTY: GLYNN **CITY:** JEKYLL ISLAND

DATE VISITED: **WHO I WENT WITH:**

RATING: ☆ ☆ ☆ ☆ ☆ **WILL I RETURN?** YES / NO

Jekyll Island Historic District is a captivating area that showcases the rich history and architectural beauty of one of Georgia's barrier islands. Once a private retreat for America's wealthiest families in the late 19th and early 20th centuries, this historic district is now a National Historic Landmark District, offering visitors a unique glimpse into the past. With its stunning coastal views, preserved structures, and lush landscapes, the Jekyll Island Historic District is a must-visit destination for history enthusiasts and nature lovers alike.

Jekyll Island became a fashionable winter retreat for America's elite, including names like the Rockefellers, Morgans, and Vanderbilts. The island's historic district features the remains of the Jekyll Island Club, which was founded in 1886 and served as a social hub for these prominent families. After the club disbanded in the early 20th century, many of the buildings fell into disrepair, but restoration efforts have since revitalized the area, preserving its historical significance.

The historic district features a remarkable collection of buildings that reflect various architectural styles, including Romanesque, Gothic Revival, and tabby construction. Notable structures include the Jekyll Island Club Hotel, Crane Cottage, and the Faith Chapel, each telling a story of the island's opulent past. Visitors can explore the grounds and appreciate the craftsmanship and attention to detail that characterize these historic structures.

To fully appreciate the history of the district, consider joining a guided tour. Knowledgeable guides provide insights into the lives of the island's elite families, the club's influence on American history, and the architectural features of the buildings. Tours often include visits to several key sites within the district, allowing you to experience the rich history firsthand.

The Jekyll Island Museum, located in the historic district, offers a wealth of information about the island's history, ecology, and the stories of the families who once called it home. Exhibits feature artifacts, photographs, and multimedia displays that provide context to the island's development and its importance in

American society. The museum also offers educational programs and events throughout the year, including workshops, lectures, and family-friendly activities.

The historic district is surrounded by the natural beauty of Jekyll Island. Visitors can enjoy walking and biking trails that weave through the area, offering opportunities for wildlife viewing and enjoying the coastal scenery. The nearby beaches provide a perfect setting for relaxation, swimming, and beachcombing. Don't miss the chance to explore the island's tidal marshes and maritime forests, which are home to a variety of wildlife.

Tips

- Wear comfortable shoes: The historic district is best explored on foot, so wear comfortable walking shoes to enjoy the sights.
- Plan for weather: Jekyll Island has a warm coastal climate. Dress in layers and bring sunscreen and water, especially during the summer months.
- Take your time: Allow plenty of time to explore the historic district, as there's much to see and learn. Don't rush through; instead, take in the beauty and history at a leisurely pace.
- Explore beyond the District: Take time to explore other parts of Jekyll Island, including its beautiful beaches, nature trails, and additional attractions like the Jekyll Island Golf Club.

Nearby Attractions

- Driftwood Beach: A beautiful and unique beach known for its stunning driftwood sculptures and picturesque scenery. It's an excellent spot for photography and leisurely strolls along the shore.

- Georgia Sea Turtle Center: Located on Jekyll Island, this rehabilitation center and educational facility focuses on the conservation of sea turtles. Visitors can learn about sea turtle rescue efforts, watch rehabilitation in action, and explore interactive exhibits.

- Jekyll Island Club National Historic Landmark District: A short walk from the historic district, this area offers additional insights into the island's history with more preserved buildings, gardens, and scenic views.

----

46. JIMMY CARTER PRESIDENTIAL LIBRARY & MUSEUM

COUNTY: FULTON   **CITY:** ATLANTA

DATE VISITED: **WHO I WENT WITH:**

RATING: ☆ ☆ ☆ ☆ ☆   **WILL I RETURN?** YES / NO

441 John Lewis Freedom Parkway NE
Atlanta, Georgia, 30307
404-865-7100

Jimmy Carter Presidential Library & Museum is located in Atlanta, Georgia. This inspiring institution is dedicated to preserving and showcasing the life, work, and legacy of James Earl Carter Jr., the 39th President of the United States. Opened in 1986, the library is not only a repository of presidential documents but also a vibrant museum that highlights Carter's achievements in public service, peace efforts, and humanitarian work. Visitors will discover the remarkable journey of a man committed to making the world a better place.

Established in honor of President Carter, the library houses a vast collection of documents, photographs, and artifacts from his presidency (1977-1981) and personal life. The library is part of the Presidential Library System administered by the National Archives and Records Administration (NARA). Its mission is to preserve and provide access to the records of the Carter administration while promoting a deeper understanding of his impact on American history.

The museum features engaging exhibits that cover various aspects of President Carter's life, from his childhood in Plains, Georgia, to his time in the White House. Visitors can explore exhibits on his early life, military service, and political career, including key events like the Camp David Accords and the Iran Hostage Crisis. Interactive displays and multimedia presentations make the museum experience informative and engaging, appealing to visitors of all ages.

The library houses over 27 million pages of documents from Carter's presidency, including correspondence, speeches, and policy papers. While most of these materials are available for research, a dedicated reading room allows visitors to delve into primary source materials and gain insights into the decision-making processes of the Carter administration. Special collections also include materials related to the Carter Center, an organization founded by President Carter and his wife, Rosalynn, dedicated to promoting peace, democracy, and health initiatives worldwide.

The library is set on 35 acres of beautifully landscaped grounds, featuring native plants and walking trails. The architecture of the building itself is striking, designed to reflect the Southern landscape and culture. The outdoor spaces are ideal for relaxation and reflection, allowing visitors to connect with nature. Don't miss the lovely Rose Garden, which features a variety of blooms and provides a serene spot for photographs.

Throughout the year, the library hosts special events, lectures, and educational programs. These include discussions with historians, film screenings, and family-friendly activities that delve deeper into the themes of public service and civic engagement. Check the library's calendar for upcoming events and workshops to enhance your visit.

Tips

- Plan your visit: Consider spending at least two hours at the museum to fully explore the exhibits and enjoy the grounds. If possible, check the library's website for information on special events happening during your visit.
- Use guided tours: Take advantage of guided tours if available, as they provide valuable insights and context that enhance the experience.
- Bring a camera: The library and its gardens offer beautiful photo opportunities. Capture the moments and share your experience.
- Engage with staff: The staff at the library is knowledgeable and passionate about President Carter's legacy. Don't hesitate to ask questions and engage in discussions during your visit.

Nearby Attractions

- Martin Luther King Jr. National Historical Park: A short drive away, this park honors the legacy of Dr. King and includes his childhood home, church, and the Ebenezer Baptist Church, where he preached. It's a powerful reminder of the civil rights movement and its impact on American history.

- Fernbank Museum of Natural History: Located nearby, this museum features interactive exhibits, an IMAX theater, and beautiful walking trails. It's a great place for families and anyone interested in natural history and science.

- Atlanta Botanical Garden: Just a few miles from the library, this stunning garden showcases a diverse collection of plants, beautiful landscapes, and seasonal displays, including a tropical rainforest and a desert house.

🔴47 JULIETTE GORDON LOW BIRTHPLACE MUSEUM

COUNTY: CHATHAM　　　　　　　　　　　　　　　　**CITY:** SAVANNAH

DATE VISITED:　　　　　　　　**WHO I WENT WITH:**

　　　　RATING: ☆ ☆ ☆ ☆ ☆　　　　**WILL I RETURN?** YES / NO

10 East Oglethorpe Ave
Savannah, GA 31401
912-233-4501

Juliette Gordon Low Birthplace Museum is located in the historic district of Savannah, Georgia. This charming museum is dedicated to the life and legacy of Juliette Gordon Low, the founder of the Girl Scouts of the USA. Visitors to the birthplace can explore the rich history of this pioneering woman and her remarkable contributions to youth leadership and empowerment. The museum offers a unique opportunity to learn about Juliette's life, values, and the enduring impact of the Girl Scouts.

Juliette Gordon Low was born on October 31, 1860, in this beautifully restored home at 10 East Oglethorpe Avenue. She was a trailblazer in women's leadership and education, dedicating her life to inspiring girls to develop their leadership skills. In 1912, she founded the Girl Scouts in the United States, aiming to provide girls with opportunities for personal growth, community service, and outdoor adventure. The museum preserves her legacy, showcasing her life, achievements, and the founding principles of the Girl Scouts.

The museum offers guided tours led by knowledgeable staff who share the inspiring story of Juliette Gordon Low's life and her vision for the Girl Scouts. During the tour, visitors will learn about her childhood, her travels, and her commitment to empowering girls. The tours typically last about an hour and include access to several rooms in the historic home, showcasing original furnishings and personal artifacts belonging to Juliette and her family.

The birthplace is a beautifully restored Victorian townhouse, featuring period furnishings and décor that provide a glimpse into the life of Juliette and her family in the late 19th century. Key rooms to explore include the parlor, dining room, and Juliette's bedroom, each telling a part of her story. Exhibits throughout the museum showcase the history of the Girl Scouts, including memorabilia, photographs, and stories from girls and leaders who have been influenced by Juliette's vision.

The museum hosts a variety of educational programs and special events throughout the year, including workshops, camps, and community service projects for girls and families. These programs aim to instill the values of leadership, community engagement, and environmental stewardship that Juliette championed. Be sure to check the museum's calendar for upcoming events and activities that may coincide with your visit.

The museum features a small gift shop where visitors can purchase Girl Scout memorabilia, books, and educational materials. Proceeds from the shop help support the museum's programs and preservation efforts.

Tips

- Plan ahead: To make the most of your visit, consider scheduling your tour in advance, especially during peak tourist seasons.
- Explore the area: Savannah is a city rich in history and charm. Take time to explore the nearby squares, shops, and restaurants before or after your visit to the museum.
- Engage with staff: The museum staff is passionate about Juliette Gordon Low's legacy. Don't hesitate to ask questions and share your interest in the Girl Scouts.
- Capture the moment: Bring your camera to take photos of the beautiful architecture, gardens, and historic surroundings.

Nearby Attractions

- Savannah History Museum: Just a short walk away, this museum offers a comprehensive look at Savannah's rich history, featuring exhibits on the Revolutionary War, the Civil War, and the city's unique culture.

- Forsyth Park: A beautiful urban park located nearby, Forsyth Park is a great place to relax, enjoy a picnic, or take a leisurely stroll. Don't miss the iconic Forsyth Fountain, a popular spot for photos.

- Bonaventure Cemetery: A short drive from the museum, this historic cemetery is known for its stunning oak trees and beautiful monuments. It offers a peaceful place for reflection and is a popular site for history enthusiasts.

LENOX SQUARE

48

COUNTY: FULTON **CITY:** ATLANTA

DATE VISITED: **WHO I WENT WITH:**

RATING: ☆ ☆ ☆ ☆ ☆ **WILL I RETURN?** YES / NO

3393 Peachtree Rd NE
Atlanta, GA 30326
888-605-2801

Lenox Square is an Atlanta's premier shopping destination, located in the heart of Buckhead. With its stunning architecture, luxury retailers, and vibrant atmosphere, Lenox Square offers an unparalleled shopping experience for locals and visitors alike. Opened in 1959, this iconic mall has grown into a shopping and dining hub, attracting millions of shoppers each year. Whether you're looking for high-end fashion, unique gifts, or delicious cuisine, Lenox Square has something for everyone.

Lenox Square was one of the first indoor malls in the Southeastern United States. Over the years, it has undergone several renovations and expansions, solidifying its status as a landmark in Atlanta. Today, it features over 250 stores, ranging from luxury brands to popular retailers, making it a shopping paradise.

Lenox Square is home to an impressive array of retailers, including luxury brands such as Gucci, Louis Vuitton, and Chanel, as well as popular department stores like Macy's and Nordstrom. In addition, you'll find a mix of trendy boutiques, lifestyle shops, and specialty stores. The mall offers a variety of shopping experiences, whether you're looking for the latest fashion trends, electronics, home goods, or beauty products. Don't forget to explore the seasonal pop-up shops that often feature unique, locally made items.

After a day of shopping, take a break at one of Lenox Square's many dining options. The mall features a diverse selection of restaurants, cafes, and eateries. Enjoy a casual meal at The Cheesecake Factory, grab a quick bite at Panda Express, or indulge in fine dining at Sushi Hayakawa. For a quick snack or coffee, stop by Starbucks or Dulce Vegan Bakery & Cafe. With options to suit every palate, you're sure to find the perfect dining spot to recharge.

Throughout the year, Lenox Square hosts a variety of special events, including seasonal festivals, fashion shows, and holiday celebrations. Keep an eye on the mall's calendar for upcoming events that may coincide with your visit. The mall also features a spacious outdoor plaza, which is often used for community events, live music, and art displays, adding to the vibrant atmosphere of Lenox Square.

Lenox Square offers a range of amenities to enhance your shopping experience. Enjoy complimentary Wi-Fi throughout the mall, family-friendly facilities, and ample parking options, including valet services for convenience. The mall's concierge services can assist with directions, gift cards, and reservations for restaurants, ensuring that your visit is enjoyable and hassle-free.

Tips

- Arrive early: To avoid crowds, consider visiting during weekdays or early in the morning on weekends.
- Wear comfortable shoes: With so many stores to explore, wear comfortable shoes to make your shopping experience enjoyable.
- Stay hydrated: Bring a water bottle or take advantage of the dining options to stay refreshed during your visit.
- Check for deals: Before your visit, check the mall's website for any promotions, special sales, or coupons from your favorite retailers.

Nearby Attractions

- Phipps Plaza: Just a short walk away, this upscale shopping center features luxury retailers, fine dining, and an impressive AMC theater. Phipps Plaza is perfect for those looking to explore more shopping options or catch the latest movie.

- Atlanta History Center: Located a few miles from Lenox Square, this renowned history museum offers exhibits on Atlanta's past, beautiful gardens, and historic homes, including the Swan House. It's a great place to delve into the history of the region.

- Buckhead's Nightlife: After a day of shopping, explore Buckhead's vibrant nightlife. The area is home to an array of bars, lounges, and music venues where you can unwind and enjoy live entertainment.

----

49 LITTLE WHITE HOUSE

COUNTY: MERIWETHER   CITY: WARM SPRINGS

DATE VISITED: WHO I WENT WITH:

RATING: ☆ ☆ ☆ ☆ ☆   WILL I RETURN? YES / NO

401 Little White House Road
Warm Springs, GA 31830
706-655-5870

Little White House is a charming and historically significant site located in Warm Springs, Georgia. This former retreat of President Franklin D. Roosevelt offers a unique glimpse into the life and legacy of one of America's most revered leaders. Nestled in the picturesque countryside, the Little White House served as a refuge for Roosevelt during his battle with polio and is now a museum dedicated to his memory and the important role Warm Springs played in his life and presidency.

The Little White House was built in 1932 as a personal retreat for Franklin D. Roosevelt, who sought the therapeutic benefits of the warm springs in the area for his polio treatment. The house served as a place for relaxation and reflection during his presidency, where he conducted meetings and made critical decisions. Roosevelt died in the home on April 12, 1945, making it a site of historical significance.

The Little White House offers guided tours that take visitors through the rooms where Roosevelt lived and worked. Knowledgeable guides share fascinating stories about Roosevelt's time in Warm Springs, his policies, and the impact of his leadership on the nation. The tour typically lasts about an hour, allowing guests to see the living quarters, his bedroom, and the sunroom where he spent much of his time.

In addition to the house itself, visitors can explore a museum that features exhibits on Roosevelt's life, including his early years, political career, and contributions to the country during the Great Depression and World War II. The museum also showcases personal artifacts, photographs, and memorabilia that illustrate Roosevelt's time in Warm Springs and his dedication to improving the lives of others.

The Little White House is set on beautifully landscaped grounds, featuring gardens that reflect the natural beauty of the area. Visitors are encouraged to stroll through the gardens, which include native plants and flowering trees. The property also includes a historic swimming pool, where Roosevelt participated in therapy sessions, emphasizing the significance of the warm springs in his recovery.

Throughout the year, the Little White House hosts various special events, including educational programs, history lectures, and seasonal celebrations. These events provide an opportunity for visitors to engage more deeply with the history and legacy of Franklin D. Roosevelt. Check the official website for upcoming events that might coincide with your visit.

Tips

- Plan your tour: To make the most of your visit, consider joining a guided tour, as they provide valuable insights into Roosevelt's life and legacy.
- Bring a camera: The gardens and historic house offer beautiful photo opportunities. Capture the moments and share your experience with friends and family.
- Check for special events: Before your visit, check the museum's website for any special events, lectures, or programs that might enhance your experience.
- Explore the area: Allow time to explore the surrounding area, including the historic district and nearby parks, to fully appreciate the charm of Warm Springs.

Nearby Attractions

- Warm Springs Historic District: Take a leisurely stroll through the historic district, which features charming shops, galleries, and restaurants. The area is known for its quaint atmosphere and rich history.

- F.D. Roosevelt State Park: Just a short drive from the Little White House, this expansive state park offers hiking trails, picnic areas, and scenic views of the Appalachian foothills. It's a great spot for outdoor enthusiasts looking to explore Georgia's natural beauty.

- The Roosevelt Warm Springs Institute for Rehabilitation: This facility, founded by Roosevelt in 1927, continues to provide rehabilitation services today. While tours may not be available, the institute's history is closely tied to Roosevelt's legacy and the area's commitment to helping those with disabilities.

----

50 MARIETTA SQUARE

COUNTY: COBB   CITY: MARIETTA

DATE VISITED: WHO I WENT WITH:

RATING: ☆ ☆ ☆ ☆ ☆   WILL I RETURN?   YES / NO

4 Depot Street
Marietta, GA 30060

Marietta Square is the vibrant heart of Marietta, Georgia. This charming town square, rich in history and culture, is a perfect destination for families, history buffs, and anyone looking to experience Southern hospitality. Surrounded by beautiful historic buildings, unique shops, and delicious dining options, Marietta Square offers something for everyone. Whether you're exploring the local history, enjoying outdoor events, or indulging in tasty treats, Marietta Square is a must-visit destination.

Established in the early 1830s, Marietta Square has been the center of the community for nearly two centuries. The square was named after Mary Cobb, the wife of one of the town's founders, and it has been the site of important historical events, including the Civil War. Today, many of the buildings surrounding the square have been beautifully preserved, reflecting the town's rich heritage.

As you stroll through Marietta Square, you'll be captivated by the stunning architecture of the historic buildings that line the square. Notable structures include the Marietta City Hall, the Marietta Museum of History, and the Cobb County Courthouse, which features beautiful Neoclassical design elements. Take time to appreciate the detailed facades and unique styles that represent different eras of Marietta's history.

Marietta Square is home to a variety of charming shops and boutiques, offering everything from unique gifts and local art to clothing and home decor. Explore stores like The Nest, which specializes in home goods, and Marietta Wine Market, where you can find a selection of wines from around the world. Don't miss the Marietta Square Farmers Market, held every Saturday from 9 AM to noon, where local farmers and artisans offer fresh produce, handmade crafts, and delicious baked goods.

After shopping, treat yourself to a delicious meal at one of the many restaurants surrounding the square. Options range from casual eateries to fine dining, ensuring there's something for every palate. Popular spots include Copeland's of

New Orleans, known for its flavorful Cajun and Creole cuisine, and Big Pie In The Sky, famous for its giant pizza slices. For dessert, stop by Sweet Treats, a delightful bakery offering a variety of pastries and sweets.

Marietta Square is a hub for community events and festivals throughout the year. Don't miss seasonal events like the Marietta BBQ Festival, the Arts and Crafts Festival, and holiday celebrations that bring the community together for fun and festivities. The square also hosts live music performances, outdoor movie nights, and art exhibits, providing plenty of opportunities to enjoy local talent and entertainment.

The square features beautiful green spaces where visitors can relax and enjoy the outdoors. Glover Park, located at the center of the square, offers a lovely setting for picnics and leisurely strolls. It's an ideal spot to unwind and watch the world go by. In warmer months, you may find families enjoying the park's shade trees, kids playing, and couples strolling hand in hand.

Tips

- Dress comfortably: Wear comfortable shoes for walking, as you'll want to explore all the shops, dining options, and parks.
- Visit the Farmers Market: If you're in town on a Saturday, make sure to check out the Farmers Market for fresh produce and local crafts.
- Engage with locals: Don't hesitate to chat with shop owners and residents; they can offer great recommendations and insights into the area.
- Check the events calendar: Before your visit, look for events happening during your stay to make the most of your experience in Marietta Square.

Nearby Attractions

- Marietta Museum of History: Located just off the square, this museum offers exhibits that delve into the local history of Marietta and Cobb County. Learn about the city's past, including its role in the Civil War and the growth of the community.

- Kennesaw Mountain National Battlefield Park: A short drive from Marietta Square, this park preserves the site of one of the Civil War's significant battles. Visitors can explore hiking trails, visit the visitor center, and learn about the history of the area.

- Gone With the Wind Museum: Situated nearby, this museum is dedicated to the legacy of Margaret Mitchell's classic novel. Visitors can explore memorabilia, photographs, and exhibits related to the book and its film adaptation.

51 MARTIN LUTHER KING JR. NATIONAL HISTORIC SITE

COUNTY: FULTON **CITY:** ATLANTA

DATE VISITED: **WHO I WENT WITH:**

RATING: ☆ ☆ ☆ ☆ ☆   **WILL I RETURN?** YES / NO

450 Auburn Avenue NE
Atlanta, GA 30312
404-331-5190

Martin Luther King Jr. National Historic Site is a significant landmark in Atlanta, Georgia, dedicated to the life and legacy of civil rights leader Dr. Martin Luther King Jr. This historic site is a must-visit for anyone interested in learning about the American civil rights movement and the profound impact Dr. King had on the nation. The site encompasses several important locations that highlight Dr. King's life, activism, and the struggle for social justice.

Established as a national historic site in 1980, this area is a tribute to Dr. King's enduring legacy. It includes his childhood home, the church where he preached, and the King Center, which houses his tomb. The site serves as a reminder of the ongoing struggle for civil rights and equality in America.

Begin your visit at the Visitor Center, which provides an overview of Dr. King's life and the civil rights movement. The center features exhibits, photographs, and videos that highlight key events and figures in the struggle for equality. A short film, "King: A Filmed Record... Montgomery to Memphis," is shown regularly, offering insights into Dr. King's journey and the impact of his work.

Take a guided tour of the birth home of Dr. Martin Luther King Jr., located just a short walk from the Visitor Center. This home, where Dr. King was born in 1929, has been preserved to reflect the time period and offers a glimpse into his early life. Tours are free, but advance reservations are recommended, especially during peak seasons.

Visit Ebenezer Baptist Church, where Dr. King served as co-pastor with his father, Martin Luther King Sr. The church played a pivotal role in the civil rights movement and is known for its passionate sermons and community outreach. Services are held regularly, and visitors are welcome to attend. The church also offers guided tours that delve into its history and significance.

The King Center is dedicated to Dr. King's vision of peace and nonviolence. It houses the tombs of Dr. King and his wife, Coretta Scott King, and features an outdoor park with beautiful landscaping. Inside the center, you can explore exhibits related to Dr. King's philosophy, his writings, and the impact of his work on civil rights.

While visiting the national historic site, take time to explore the Sweet Auburn Historic District, recognized as one of the most significant African American neighborhoods in the country. This area was a hub of African American commerce and culture during the civil rights era. Key sites in the district include the Auburn Avenue Research Library, the Alonzo Herndon Home, and various murals and monuments that celebrate African American history.

Tips

- Plan ahead: Consider downloading the National Park Service app or visiting the official website to plan your visit and check for any events or programs happening during your stay.
- Take a guided tour: Guided tours of the birth home and Ebenezer Baptist Church provide valuable insights into Dr. King's life and the history of the civil rights movement.
- Dress comfortably: Wear comfortable shoes, as you'll be walking between several locations and exploring the historic district.
- Engage with park rangers: The park rangers are knowledgeable and passionate about Dr. King's legacy. Don't hesitate to ask questions during your visit.

Nearby Attractions

- Atlanta Botanical Garden: Just a short drive away, this beautiful garden features a stunning collection of plants, flowers, and themed gardens, offering a peaceful escape in the city.

- The National Center for Civil and Human Rights: Located downtown, this museum showcases the history of the civil rights movement in America and highlights contemporary human rights issues worldwide.

- Fox Theatre: An iconic Atlanta landmark, the Fox Theatre is renowned for its stunning architecture and hosts a variety of performances, including Broadway shows, concerts, and special events.

----

52 MERCER WILLIAMS HOUSE MUSEUM

COUNTY: CHATHAM　　　　　　　　　　　　　　　　**CITY:** SAVANNAH

DATE VISITED:　　　　　　　　**WHO I WENT WITH:**

RATING: ☆ ☆ ☆ ☆ ☆　　　　**WILL I RETURN?** YES / NO

429 Bull Street
Savannah, GA 31401
912-238-0208

Mercer-Williams House Museum is a stunning historic home located in the heart of Savannah, Georgia. Known for its striking architecture and rich history, this beautifully preserved house offers visitors a glimpse into the life of one of Savannah's most prominent families. The Mercer-Williams House is also famous for its connection to the acclaimed novel "Midnight in the Garden of Good and Evil" by John Berendt, which has further increased its allure. Whether you're an architecture enthusiast, a history buff, or a literary fan, the Mercer-Williams House Museum is a must-visit destination in Savannah.

The Mercer-Williams House was designed by noted architect Hugh B. B. McAlpin and built in 1860 for General Hugh Mercer, a prominent figure in Savannah's history. The house later became home to Jim Williams, an influential Savannah antique dealer and preservationist, who meticulously restored the home. The Mercer-Williams House gained national attention after being featured in Berendt's book, which details a murder that took place within its walls.

The Mercer-Williams House Museum offers guided tours that last approximately 45 minutes. These tours provide an in-depth look at the history of the house, its architectural features, and the stories of the Mercer and Williams families. Knowledgeable guides share fascinating anecdotes about Jim Williams, his collection of antiques, and the events surrounding the murder that brought national attention to the house.

The house is a prime example of Italianate architecture, characterized by its tall windows, decorative cornices, and intricate ironwork. Visitors can admire the beautifully restored interiors, including the grand foyer, parlor, and dining room, all filled with period furnishings and art. The house features a stunning spiral staircase and intricate plaster moldings, showcasing the craftsmanship of the era.

The Mercer-Williams House is home to an impressive collection of art and antiques that reflect the taste and refinement of its former residents. Highlights include fine paintings, decorative arts, and unique historical artifacts. The museum provides insight into the art and history of Savannah through its curated collections, making it a rewarding experience for art lovers.

The museum features a lovely courtyard garden that complements the beauty of the house. Visitors can enjoy a stroll through the landscaped gardens, which offer a peaceful retreat in the bustling city. The garden is also home to various native plants and flowers, providing a glimpse of Savannah's natural beauty.

The Mercer-Williams House gained international fame due to its prominent role in John Berendt's "Midnight in the Garden of Good and Evil." Fans of the book will appreciate the opportunity to learn more about the characters and events depicted in the story. The museum often features displays related to the book, offering visitors a chance to connect with Savannah's literary history.

Tips

- Plan your tour: Guided tours are highly recommended to fully appreciate the history and significance of the Mercer-Williams House. Arriving early can help you secure your spot.
- Explore the surrounding area: After your tour, take time to explore the beautiful historic district of Savannah, which is filled with charming squares, shops, and restaurants.
- Bring a camera: The architecture and gardens provide great photo opportunities, so don't forget your camera.
- Read the book: If you haven't already, consider reading "Midnight in the Garden of Good and Evil" before your visit to enhance your experience and understanding of the site.

Nearby Attractions

- Forsyth Park: A short walk from the museum, Forsyth Park is one of Savannah's most beloved green spaces. The park features walking paths, beautiful fountains, and plenty of space for picnics and relaxation.

- Savannah History Museum: Located in the old passenger depot, this museum provides a comprehensive look at Savannah's history, from its founding to the present day. Exhibits include artifacts from the Civil War and local culture.

- Savannah College of Art and Design (SCAD): SCAD has several buildings and galleries in the area, showcasing the work of talented artists and designers. The SCAD Museum of Art, in particular, is worth a visit for contemporary art lovers.

MERCIER ORCHARDS

53

COUNTY: FANNIN   **CITY:** BLUE RIDGE

DATE VISITED: **WHO I WENT WITH:**

RATING: ☆ ☆ ☆ ☆ ☆   **WILL I RETURN?** YES / NO

8660 Blue Ridge Dr
Blue Ridge, GA 30513
706-632-3411

Mercier Orchards is a family-owned farm and apple orchard located in the scenic town of Blue Ridge, Georgia. Known for its breathtaking mountain views and abundant harvests, Mercier Orchards is the perfect destination for families, nature lovers, and anyone looking to enjoy fresh, delicious produce and outdoor activities. Open year-round, this charming orchard offers a variety of seasonal fruits, homemade goods, and fun events that make it a must-visit spot in North Georgia.

Established in 1943, Mercier Orchards has grown from a small family farm into one of the largest apple orchards in Georgia. With over 300 acres of land, the orchard produces a wide variety of fruits, including apples, peaches, blueberries, and strawberries, alongside a selection of homemade products.

Visit during the fall harvest season for the ultimate apple-picking experience. With over 20 varieties of apples, guests can pick their own apples directly from the trees. Enjoy the crisp mountain air as you explore the orchard and select your favorite fruits. Check the orchard's website for the picking schedule, as it varies by season and weather conditions.

The on-site Farm Market offers a wide range of fresh produce, homemade jams, jellies, and baked goods. Don't miss out on their famous apple cider donuts, pies, and apple butter, all made from the freshest ingredients. Browse through local products, including honey, syrups, and artisanal cheeses, perfect for taking home as souvenirs or gifts.

Mercier Orchards features a Cider House where visitors can sample a variety of hard ciders made from their own apples. Enjoy tastings in a welcoming atmosphere while learning about the cider-making process. The orchard also produces wines from their own grapes. Pair your cider and wine tastings with local cheeses for a delightful culinary experience.

Throughout the year, Mercier Orchards hosts a variety of events, including seasonal festivals, farm tours, and workshops. From the Apple Festival in the fall to berry-picking days in the summer, there's always something happening at the orchard. Check their calendar for family-friendly activities, live music, and themed events that offer a fun day out for all ages.

The orchard is located in the picturesque Blue Ridge Mountains, providing ample opportunities for outdoor exploration. Enjoy scenic hiking trails nearby, or relax in the orchard's picnic areas, where you can enjoy the beauty of nature while savoring your fresh-picked fruits and baked goods. The area is also known for fishing and boating on Lake Blue Ridge, just a short drive away.

Tips

- Dress comfortably: Wear comfortable clothing and sturdy shoes, especially if you plan on picking apples or exploring the outdoor areas.
- Check the picking schedule: Before your visit, confirm which fruits are in season to maximize your experience and enjoyment.
- Bring a picnic: If you prefer, pack a picnic to enjoy in one of the orchard's designated areas amidst the beautiful scenery.
- Arrive early: To avoid crowds, consider arriving early, especially on weekends during the busy harvest season.

Nearby Attractions

- Blue Ridge Scenic Railway: Experience a delightful train ride along the Toccoa River, offering stunning views of the mountains and valleys. The journey includes stops in charming towns where you can shop and explore.

- Lake Blue Ridge: This beautiful lake is perfect for outdoor activities such as fishing, kayaking, and hiking. Enjoy a day by the water and take in the breathtaking views of the surrounding mountains.

- Aska Adventure Area: A short drive from the orchard, this area offers hiking, mountain biking, and picnic spots in the lush Chattahoochee National Forest. Explore the trails and discover stunning vistas.

----

54 MOUNTAIN VALLEY FARM

COUNTY: GILMER **CITY:** ELLIJAY

DATE VISITED: **WHO I WENT WITH:**

RATING: ☆ ☆ ☆ ☆ ☆ **WILL I RETURN?** YES / NO

2021 Homer Wright Road
Ellijay, GA 30536
706-889-1426

Mountain Valley Farm is a picturesque family-owned farm located in the stunning landscapes of North Georgia. Nestled in the heart of the Appalachian Mountains, this charming farm offers a unique blend of agriculture, outdoor activities, and Southern hospitality. Known for its breathtaking views and diverse offerings, Mountain Valley Farm is an ideal destination for families, couples, and anyone looking to escape into nature and enjoy a taste of rural life.

Mountain Valley Farm has deep roots in North Georgia agriculture. Established by the Smith family, the farm has been in operation for over three generations. With a commitment to sustainable farming practices, the Smiths cultivate a variety of fruits and vegetables, while also providing a welcoming environment for visitors to experience farm life.

Visitors can enjoy guided tours of Mountain Valley Farm, where you'll learn about sustainable farming practices, the history of the land, and the various crops grown on the farm. Tours are interactive and family-friendly, allowing guests to participate in activities like feeding animals, picking fruits and vegetables, and learning about farm equipment.

Depending on the season, guests can participate in the U-Pick experience, where you can harvest your own fruits and vegetables directly from the fields. Common crops include strawberries, blueberries, peaches, and pumpkins. This hands-on experience allows families to enjoy the thrill of picking fresh produce while connecting with nature.

The on-site Farm Store offers a wide selection of fresh produce, homemade jams, jellies, and local honey. Visitors can also find farm-fresh eggs and artisanal products from local vendors. Don't miss the chance to try the farm's famous apple cider and other seasonal treats, perfect for taking home as souvenirs.
Seasonal Events and Festivals

Mountain Valley Farm hosts various seasonal events throughout the year, including Harvest Festivals, Apple Picking Days, and Christmas Tree Sales. These events are great for families and often feature live music, food vendors, and activities for children. Check the farm's website for the calendar of events to plan your visit around these exciting gatherings.

The farm is surrounded by beautiful hiking trails and scenic picnic areas, making it an excellent spot for outdoor enthusiasts. Enjoy a leisurely hike through the woods, or set up a picnic with the fresh produce you've picked. The area is also perfect for birdwatching and wildlife observation, offering a peaceful retreat into nature.

Tips

- Dress appropriately: Wear comfortable clothing and sturdy shoes, especially if you plan to pick fruits or hike on the trails.
- Bring cash: While most places accept cards, it's a good idea to have cash on hand for small purchases and local vendors at events.
- Check the harvest calendar: Before your visit, review the farm's harvest calendar to see what fruits and vegetables will be available for picking during your trip.
- Plan for weather: Check the weather forecast and plan accordingly. Bring sunscreen or rain gear as needed to ensure a comfortable visit.

Nearby Attractions

- Helen, Georgia: Just a short drive away, this charming Bavarian-style village offers unique shops, restaurants, and outdoor activities, including tubing on the Chattahoochee River.

- Unicoi State Park: This beautiful state park features hiking trails, fishing, and stunning views of the surrounding mountains. Enjoy a day of outdoor fun, or simply relax by the lake.

- North Georgia Wine Country: Explore the nearby wineries and vineyards, where you can sample local wines and enjoy scenic views of the vineyards. Many wineries offer tastings, tours, and events throughout the year.

MUSEUM OF AVIATION

55

COUNTY: HOUSTON **CITY:** WARNER ROBINS

DATE VISITED: **WHO I WENT WITH:**

RATING: ☆ ☆ ☆ ☆ ☆ **WILL I RETURN?** YES / NO

1942 Heritage Blvd
Warner Robins, GA 31098
478-926-6870

Museum of Aviation is located in Warner Robins, Georgia. As one of the largest aviation museums in the United States, this impressive facility is dedicated to preserving and showcasing the rich history of aviation and the role of the United States Air Force. With an extensive collection of aircraft, interactive exhibits, and educational programs, the Museum of Aviation is an exciting destination for aviation enthusiasts, families, and history buffs alike.

Established in 1984, the Museum of Aviation is situated on the grounds of the Robins Air Force Base. The museum was created to honor the contributions of the U.S. Air Force and to educate the public about aviation history, military aircraft, and aerospace technology.

The Museum of Aviation boasts an impressive collection of over 90 aircraft, ranging from historic military planes to modern jets. Highlights include the Boeing B-17 Flying Fortress, McDonnell Douglas F-4 Phantom II, and the Lockheed C-130 Hercules. Many aircraft are displayed outdoors in the museum's expansive aircraft park, allowing visitors to get up close and personal with these remarkable machines.

The museum features several indoor galleries that explore various aspects of aviation history. Exhibits cover topics such as World War II aviation, the Cold War, and the history of the Air Force. Interactive displays and multimedia presentations make the exhibits engaging for visitors of all ages. Don't miss the Space Exhibit, which showcases the U.S. space program and its impact on aviation technology.

The Museum of Aviation offers a range of educational programs and workshops for students, scouts, and groups. These programs are designed to inspire interest in science, technology, engineering, and mathematics (STEM) through hands-on activities and learning experiences. Special events, such as guest speaker series and workshops, are held throughout the year, providing additional opportunities for learning and engagement.

This dedicated space within the museum highlights the history of Robins Air Force Base and its significance to the U.S. Air Force. The Heritage Center includes exhibits on the base's role in aircraft maintenance and logistics, as well as the men and women who served there. Visitors can learn about the technological advancements and historical milestones achieved at the base over the years.

The museum features a gift shop where visitors can purchase aviation-themed souvenirs, books, and educational materials. It's a great place to find unique gifts and memorabilia to take home. The on-site café offers a selection of snacks and beverages, making it a convenient stop during your visit.

Tips

- Plan your tour: Consider taking a guided tour to learn more about the exhibits and aircraft from knowledgeable staff members. Guided tours may be available for groups and special events.
- Check the events calendar: Review the museum's events calendar before your visit to see if any special programs or activities are happening during your stay.
- Bring your camera: The museum's impressive aircraft displays and historical exhibits provide fantastic photo opportunities. Capture your memories of this unique experience.
- Allow plenty of time: With so much to see and explore, plan to spend several hours at the museum to fully enjoy all the exhibits and activities.

Nearby Attractions

- Houston Lake: Just a short drive away, this picturesque lake is perfect for outdoor activities such as fishing, boating, and picnicking. The park surrounding the lake offers walking trails and scenic views.

- Peach County Courthouse: Located in nearby Fort Valley, this historic courthouse is a beautiful example of neoclassical architecture and offers a glimpse into the local history of the area.

- Georgia National Fairgrounds & Agricenter: Located in Perry, this venue hosts various events throughout the year, including the Georgia National Fair, rodeos, and exhibitions. It's a great place to experience local culture and entertainment.

----

56 NATIONAL CENTER FOR CIVIL AND HUMAN RIGHTS

COUNTY: FULTON	CITY: ATLANTA

DATE VISITED:	WHO I WENT WITH:

RATING: ☆ ☆ ☆ ☆ ☆	WILL I RETURN? YES / NO

100 Ivan Allen Jr. Boulevard
Atlanta, GA 30313
678-999-8990

National Center for Civil and Human Rights is located in the heart of Atlanta, Georgia. This powerful and moving museum is dedicated to the history of the American civil rights movement and the ongoing struggle for human rights globally. Through interactive exhibits, powerful artifacts, and educational programs, the Center invites visitors to reflect on the past and consider their role in advocating for justice and equality today.

Opened in 2014, the National Center for Civil and Human Rights was established to honor the legacy of civil rights leaders and movements in the United States while highlighting contemporary human rights issues. The Center serves as a beacon of hope and a catalyst for action, encouraging visitors to engage with the principles of equality and justice.

The National Center features several compelling exhibits that immerse visitors in the civil rights movement and its impact. The "Rolls of Courage" exhibit showcases the stories of courageous individuals who fought for civil rights, using multimedia displays to bring their stories to life. The "Human Rights" exhibit connects the civil rights movement in the U.S. with contemporary global human rights issues, encouraging visitors to think critically about justice, equity, and activism.

One of the most powerful features of the Center is the "Lunch Counter" exhibit, which allows visitors to experience the tension and bravery of the civil rights sit-ins. This interactive simulation immerses guests in the historical context of the protests, fostering a deeper understanding of the struggles faced by those fighting for equality.

The National Center for Civil and Human Rights offers a variety of educational programs and workshops tailored for students, educators, and community groups. These programs aim to promote dialogue and understanding around civil and human rights issues, using history as a foundation for discussion and action. Special events, such as guest lectures, panel discussions, and film screenings, are held regularly, featuring activists, scholars, and thought leaders in the field of civil rights.

The museum houses an extensive collection of artifacts from the civil rights movement, including photographs, letters, and personal items from influential figures such as Dr. Martin Luther King Jr., Rosa Parks, and more. These artifacts provide a personal connection to the historical events that shaped the movement, allowing visitors to witness the sacrifices made for equality.

The on-site gift shop features a variety of books, educational materials, and unique souvenirs related to civil rights and human rights. It's a great place to find gifts that promote awareness and understanding of these important issues. The café offers a selection of refreshments and snacks, providing a comfortable space to relax and reflect on your visit.

Tips

- Allow time for reflection: Plan to spend at least two to three hours at the Center to fully engage with the exhibits and reflect on their impact.
- Participate in programs: If available, consider attending a workshop or lecture to deepen your understanding of civil rights issues and learn how to get involved in advocacy efforts.
- Be prepared for emotion: The exhibits may evoke strong emotions as they address difficult topics. Take your time to process what you see and learn, and feel free to discuss your thoughts with companions or staff.
- Visit the website: Before your visit, check the Center's website for information on special events, temporary exhibits, and any changes to hours or admission fees.

Nearby Attractions

- Martin Luther King Jr. National Historical Park: Just a short drive away, this park includes the historic Ebenezer Baptist Church, the Martin Luther King Jr. Birth Home, and exhibits about his life and legacy.

- Atlanta History Center: This expansive history museum offers exhibits on the Civil War, Southern history, and the development of Atlanta, along with beautiful gardens and historic homes.

- Centennial Olympic Park: A beautiful urban park built for the 1996 Summer Olympics, it features fountains, walking paths, and hosts various events and concerts throughout the year.

57. NATIONAL CIVIL WAR NAVAL MUSEUM

COUNTY: MUSCOGEE	CITY: COLUMBUS
DATE VISITED:	WHO I WENT WITH:
RATING: ☆ ☆ ☆ ☆ ☆	WILL I RETURN? YES / NO

1002 Victory Drive
Columbus, GA 31901
706-327-9798

National Civil War Naval Museum is located in Columbus, Georgia. This unique museum is dedicated to preserving and interpreting the naval history of the Civil War, focusing on the contributions and experiences of the Confederate and Union navies. With its extensive collection of artifacts, exhibits, and educational programs, the museum provides a captivating insight into the naval warfare that played a critical role during this tumultuous period in American history.

Established in 2004, the National Civil War Naval Museum is built on the legacy of the original Columbus Iron Works, which played a significant role in shipbuilding for the Confederacy. The museum seeks to educate visitors about the naval aspects of the Civil War and highlight the stories of those who served at sea.

The National Civil War Naval Museum features an impressive collection of over 100 artifacts, including ship models, uniforms, weaponry, and personal items from naval officers. The exhibits showcase the technology, strategies, and challenges faced by both the Union and Confederate navies. Highlights include the CSS Jackson, a full-scale replica of a Confederate ironclad warship, and various models that illustrate the evolution of naval warfare during the Civil War.

Engaging and interactive displays throughout the museum allow visitors to experience naval history hands-on. Exhibits include simulations of naval battles and the opportunity to explore shipbuilding techniques of the era. A dedicated children's area provides educational activities that make learning about history fun for younger visitors, fostering curiosity and engagement.

The museum offers a variety of educational programs, workshops, and lectures that cater to students, educators, and history enthusiasts. These programs focus on naval history, engineering, and the social aspects of the Civil War. Special events, including reenactments and guest speakers, are scheduled throughout the year, providing opportunities for deeper exploration of specific topics related to naval history.

The museum offers guided tours led by knowledgeable staff who provide in-depth insights into the exhibits and the historical context of naval operations during the Civil War. These tours can enhance your understanding and appreciation of the artifacts and their significance.

Before you leave, stop by the museum gift shop, which features a variety of books, memorabilia, and educational materials related to the Civil War and naval history. It's an excellent place to find unique gifts and souvenirs to commemorate your visit.

Tips

- Plan for a few hours: Allocate at least two to three hours for your visit to fully explore the exhibits and participate in any available programs.
- Join a guided tour: If possible, join a guided tour to gain deeper insights into the exhibits and the naval history of the Civil War.
- Check for special events: Before your visit, look at the museum's calendar for any special events, lectures, or activities that may coincide with your trip.
- Capture the moment: Bring your camera to capture the impressive displays and exhibits throughout the museum.

Nearby Attractions

- The Chattahoochee RiverWalk: This scenic walking and biking path runs along the Chattahoochee River, offering beautiful views, picnic areas, and access to recreational activities like kayaking and fishing.

- Columbus Museum: Located nearby, the Columbus Museum features a diverse collection of American art and regional history, making it a great complement to your visit to the naval museum.

- Oxbow Meadows Environmental Learning Center: This nearby center offers exhibits on local ecology, walking trails, and opportunities to learn about the native wildlife of the region, perfect for nature lovers.

NATIONAL INFANTRY MUSEUM AND SOLDIER CENTER

(58)

COUNTY: MUSCOGEE **CITY:** COLUMBUS

DATE VISITED: **WHO I WENT WITH:**

RATING: ☆ ☆ ☆ ☆ ☆ **WILL I RETURN?** YES / NO

1775 Legacy Way
Columbus, GA 31903
706-685-5800

National Infantry Museum and Soldier Center is located in Columbus, Georgia. This state-of-the-art museum is dedicated to honoring the service and sacrifices of the United States Army Infantry and all soldiers. With interactive exhibits, personal stories, and historical artifacts, the museum offers a comprehensive look at the history of the Infantry and its vital role in American military operations.

Opened in 2009, the National Infantry Museum and Soldier Center was established to recognize the contributions of the Infantry in safeguarding freedom throughout American history. The museum is situated on a site that has been pivotal for military training, close to Fort Benning, the home of the U.S. Army Infantry School.

The museum features over 40,000 square feet of exhibits, showcasing the history of the Infantry from the Revolutionary War to the present day. Artifacts include weapons, uniforms, and equipment used by soldiers throughout various conflicts. Key exhibits highlight pivotal moments in military history, such as the Civil War, World War I, World War II, and modern-day conflicts. Each exhibit is designed to educate visitors about the sacrifices made by soldiers and the evolution of Infantry tactics and technology.

Engage with history through interactive displays that allow visitors to experience military training simulations and view video testimonies from veterans. These immersive experiences provide insight into the life of a soldier, enhancing understanding of their challenges and triumphs. The "Walk of Honor" features engraved bricks and plaques dedicated to soldiers, offering a personal connection to the sacrifices made by service members and their families.

The Soldier Center houses a theater that shows films about Infantry history and the experiences of soldiers. The theater frequently hosts special presentations and guest speakers, providing additional context to the exhibits. The center also includes a gift shop where visitors can purchase military-themed souvenirs, books, and educational materials related to the Infantry and its history.

The National Infantry Museum offers a variety of educational programs designed for school groups, military families, and community organizations. Programs cover topics ranging from military history to leadership and teamwork. Special events, including commemorations, reenactments, and lectures by historians and military experts, are held throughout the year. Check the museum's calendar for upcoming events.

The museum's grounds feature several memorials honoring fallen soldiers and their sacrifices. Visitors can explore these outdoor spaces and reflect on the bravery and dedication of those who served. The Infantry Soldier Monument, a prominent feature outside the museum, pays tribute to the Infantry soldiers and their service to the nation.

Tips

- Plan for a few hours: Allocate at least two to three hours for your visit to fully explore the exhibits and participate in any available programs or events.
- Join a guided tour: If available, consider joining a guided tour to gain deeper insights into the exhibits and the history of the Infantry.
- Check the events calendar: Before your visit, review the museum's events calendar for any special programs or guest speakers scheduled during your stay.
- Be respectful: As the museum honors the sacrifices of soldiers, maintain a respectful demeanor while exploring the exhibits and grounds.

Nearby Attractions

- Fort Benning: Just a short drive away, Fort Benning is home to various military training programs and offers opportunities for visitors to learn more about the U.S. Army's role in the region.

- Columbus Museum: Located downtown, this museum features a collection of American art and regional history, including exhibits on the history of Columbus and its contributions to the arts.

- Chattahoochee RiverWalk: A beautiful scenic path along the Chattahoochee River, perfect for walking, biking, and enjoying outdoor activities. The RiverWalk connects various parks and recreational areas.

----

59 NATIONAL MUSEUM OF THE MIGHTY EIGHTH AIR FORCE

COUNTY: CHATHAM　　　　　　　　　　　　　　　　　　　　CITY: POOLER

DATE VISITED:　　　　　　　　　　WHO I WENT WITH:

RATING: ☆ ☆ ☆ ☆ ☆　　　　WILL I RETURN?　YES / NO

175 Bourne Avenue
Pooler, GA 31322
912-748-8888

National Museum of the Mighty Eighth Air Force is located in Pooler, Georgia, just a short drive from Savannah. This remarkable museum is dedicated to preserving the history and legacy of the Eighth Air Force, which played a pivotal role in the air war against Nazi Germany during World War II. Through a variety of exhibits, artifacts, and educational programs, the museum honors the brave men and women who served in the Eighth Air Force and their significant contributions to the war effort.

The museum opened its doors in 2000 and has since become a vital institution for preserving the history of the Eighth Air Force, which was formed in 1942. It focuses on the airmen who flew in combat, as well as the support personnel who made those missions possible.

The National Museum features over 100,000 square feet of exhibit space, showcasing a wide array of artifacts, photographs, and memorabilia related to the Eighth Air Force. Exhibits detail the history of the Eighth from its formation to its pivotal role in various missions during WWII. Highlights include original uniforms, aircraft models, and a variety of weapons used during the air campaigns. Notable exhibits focus on significant missions such as the bombing of Germany and the liberation of concentration camps.

One of the museum's most impressive features is its collection of historic aircraft, including a B-17 Flying Fortress and a B-24 Liberator. These planes are displayed both indoors and outdoors, allowing visitors to appreciate their size and engineering marvel. The B-17G "Thunderbird" and the B-24J "Wabash Cannonball" are not only historically significant but also provide a glimpse into the life of an airman during WWII.

Engage with history through interactive exhibits that allow visitors to learn about the daily lives of airmen and the technical aspects of flying these bombers. Interactive stations provide hands-on learning experiences that are especially enjoyable for younger visitors. The museum also offers flight simulators that let guests experience what it was like to be in the cockpit of a WWII bomber.

The National Museum of the Mighty Eighth Air Force offers a variety of educational programs for students, families, and history enthusiasts. Programs include guided tours, lectures, and workshops that explore various aspects of military aviation and WWII history. The museum frequently hosts special events, such as veteran reunions, lectures from historians, and film screenings, which provide opportunities for deeper engagement with the subject matter.

Before you leave, be sure to visit the museum gift shop, which features a wide range of books, memorabilia, and educational materials related to the Eighth Air Force and WWII. It's a great place to find unique gifts and souvenirs. The on-site café offers a selection of snacks and beverages, providing a convenient spot to relax and reflect on your visit.

Tips

- Plan for a few hours: Allocate at least two to three hours for your visit to fully engage with the exhibits and aircraft displays.
- Participate in programs: Check the museum's schedule for any special events or programs during your visit and consider joining a guided tour for a more in-depth experience.
- Take your time: The exhibits are rich in detail and history, so take your time to read and reflect on the stories and artifacts presented.
- Capture the moment: Don't forget your camera to document your visit, especially when exploring the outdoor aircraft displays.

Nearby Attractions

- Savannah Historic District: Just a short drive away, Savannah's historic district is known for its stunning architecture, charming squares, and rich history. Enjoy walking tours, shops, and restaurants in this picturesque area.

- Fort Pulaski National Monument: Located nearby, this historic fort played a key role in the Civil War and features beautiful grounds, walking trails, and educational exhibits.

- Oatland Island Wildlife Center: This wildlife center is home to native animals and offers walking trails through marshland and forest. It's an excellent spot for families and nature lovers.

NORTH GEORGIA WILDLIFE PARK

60

COUNTY: WHITE **CITY:** CLEVELAND

DATE VISITED: **WHO I WENT WITH:**

RATING: ☆ ☆ ☆ ☆ ☆ **WILL I RETURN?** YES / NO

2912 Paradise Valley Rd
Cleveland, GA 30528
706-348-7279

North Georgia Wildlife Park is located in Cleveland, Georgia! This enchanting wildlife park is dedicated to the conservation and education of various animal species while providing an interactive experience for visitors of all ages. With a focus on rehabilitation, rescue, and education, North Georgia Wildlife Park offers a unique opportunity to learn about wildlife and the importance of protecting their habitats.

Established to provide a safe haven for animals in need, North Georgia Wildlife Park promotes wildlife education and rehabilitation. The park serves as a sanctuary for both native and exotic species, allowing visitors to understand the importance of wildlife conservation.

The park features a wide variety of animals, including exotic species like lemurs, kangaroos, and capybaras, as well as native wildlife such as deer, foxes, and birds of prey. Visitors have the chance to get up close and personal with some of these animals during guided encounters and educational sessions. Interactive experiences, such as feeding sessions and photo opportunities, allow guests to create unforgettable memories while learning about the animals' behaviors and habitats.

North Georgia Wildlife Park offers numerous educational programs aimed at promoting awareness about wildlife conservation. Programs are designed for all age groups, making them perfect for families, schools, and youth groups. Topics include animal behavior, habitat preservation, and the importance of conservation efforts. The knowledgeable staff provide engaging presentations that inspire visitors to respect and protect wildlife.

The park hosts daily wildlife shows that showcase the talents and behaviors of various animals. These entertaining presentations provide insights into the animals' natural habits and highlight the challenges they face in the wild. Visitors can enjoy learning about the park's rescue and rehabilitation efforts, as well as the role of each species in the ecosystem.

Explore the beautiful grounds of the park through well-maintained nature trails that wind through the natural landscape. The trails offer opportunities for birdwatching and appreciating the local flora and fauna. Picnic areas are available for families and groups to enjoy a meal surrounded by nature, making it a great spot for relaxation after exploring the park.

Before you leave, be sure to check out the park's gift shop, which features a variety of animal-themed merchandise, educational books, and souvenirs. It's a great place to find unique gifts while supporting the park's conservation efforts. Light snacks and refreshments are available at the park, allowing you to refuel during your visit.

Tips

- Plan for a half-day: Allocate at least 2 to 4 hours for your visit to fully enjoy the animal encounters, shows, and trails.
- Check the schedule: Before your visit, check the park's website for show times and any special events happening during your stay.
- Dress comfortably: Wear comfortable shoes and clothing suitable for outdoor activities, as you'll be walking around the park.
- Bring a camera: Capture your memories and experiences at the park, especially during animal encounters.

Nearby Attractions

- Cleveland: This charming small town offers quaint shops, local restaurants, and scenic views. Stroll through downtown and enjoy the hospitality of the North Georgia mountains.

- Helen, Georgia: Just a short drive away, the picturesque Bavarian-style town of Helen is known for its unique architecture, shops, and outdoor activities like tubing on the Chattahoochee River.

- Unicoi State Park: Located near Helen, this beautiful state park offers hiking trails, fishing, and stunning views of the mountains and nearby Smithgall Woods State Park.

OAKLAND CEMETERY

COUNTY: FULTON **CITY:** ATLANTA

DATE VISITED: **WHO I WENT WITH:**

RATING: ☆ ☆ ☆ ☆ ☆ **WILL I RETURN?** YES / NO

248 Oakland Ave SE
Atlanta, GA 30312
404-549-8932

Oakland Cemetery is a historic and beautifully landscaped cemetery located in the heart of Atlanta, Georgia. Established in 1850, Oakland Cemetery is not only a resting place for the city's early citizens but also a serene park filled with rich history, stunning architecture, and lush gardens. This unique site serves as both a cemetery and an outdoor museum, making it an ideal destination for history buffs, nature lovers, and those seeking a peaceful retreat.

Founded in 1850, Oakland Cemetery is the oldest cemetery in Atlanta. It reflects the city's history and evolution, with many notable figures buried here, including Civil War veterans, local leaders, and influential citizens. The cemetery was initially established as a public burial ground, and over the years, it has expanded to include elaborate mausoleums, family plots, and beautifully carved headstones.

Oakland Cemetery is home to a wide array of historic monuments, sculptures, and intricate headstones. The cemetery's design features a mix of architectural styles, including Victorian, Gothic, and Neoclassical, showcasing the artistry of the time. Notable gravesites include those of Margaret Mitchell, author of Gone with the Wind, and Maynard Jackson, Atlanta's first African American mayor.

The cemetery offers guided walking tours that delve into the rich history of the site and the stories of those buried here. Tours cover various themes, including Civil War history, Victorian funerary customs, and notable residents. Special tours are available during significant anniversaries and holidays, providing insights into the cemetery's history and cultural significance.

Oakland Cemetery features beautifully landscaped gardens, walking paths, and serene green spaces. The combination of blooming flowers, towering trees, and historic architecture creates a peaceful environment perfect for contemplation and reflection. The Bell Tower, surrounded by vibrant gardens, offers a picturesque spot to relax and enjoy the natural beauty of the cemetery.

Throughout the year, Oakland Cemetery hosts various events, including art exhibits, music performances, and historical reenactments. These events aim to engage the community and celebrate the cemetery's rich history. The Sunday in the Park event is a popular annual gathering featuring local artists, musicians, and food vendors, transforming the cemetery into a vibrant community space.

The cemetery's visitor center provides information about the cemetery's history, notable figures, and upcoming events. Staff members are available to answer questions and offer recommendations for exploring the site. The gift shop features a selection of books, souvenirs, and unique gifts related to the cemetery's history and Atlanta's cultural heritage.

Tips

- Take your time: Allocate at least 1-2 hours to explore the grounds and soak in the history. Don't rush; the beauty of the cemetery lies in its details.
- Wear comfortable shoes: Bring comfortable walking shoes, as you'll be exploring the cemetery's varied terrain.
- Respect the space: As a cemetery, Oakland is a place of remembrance. Be respectful of those who are interred here and maintain a quiet demeanor.
- Capture the beauty: Bring a camera to capture the stunning architecture, beautiful gardens, and unique monuments that the cemetery has to offer.

Nearby Attractions

- Historic Fourth Ward Park: A beautiful park that offers walking trails, picnic areas, and a playground. It's a great place to enjoy the outdoors and take in the scenery.

- Martin Luther King Jr. National Historical Park: Located a short distance away, this park includes the childhood home of Dr. King and the Ebenezer Baptist Church where he preached. It's an important site for understanding the Civil Rights Movement.

- Krog Street Market: A trendy market featuring local vendors, shops, and restaurants. It's an excellent place to grab a bite to eat or shop for unique gifts.

----

62 OATLAND ISLAND WILDLIFE CENTER

COUNTY: CHATHAM   **CITY:** SAVANNAH

DATE VISITED: **WHO I WENT WITH:**

RATING: ☆ ☆ ☆ ☆ ☆   **WILL I RETURN?** YES / NO

711 Sandtown Road
Savannah, GA 31410
912-395-1212

Oatland Island Wildlife Center is a beautiful 175-acre wildlife sanctuary located just a short drive from downtown Savannah, Georgia. Nestled along the marshes and maritime forests, this center is dedicated to the conservation and rehabilitation of native wildlife. It offers visitors a unique opportunity to connect with nature and learn about the animals that inhabit the Southeastern United States.

Established in the late 1990s, Oatland Island Wildlife Center began as a mission to rescue and rehabilitate injured and orphaned native wildlife. Over the years, it has evolved into an educational facility that promotes wildlife conservation and environmental stewardship.

Oatland Island Wildlife Center features various native animal exhibits showcasing species such as red foxes, bobcats, owls, and alligators. Each exhibit is designed to mimic the animals' natural habitats, providing a realistic and enriching experience for both the animals and visitors. The center emphasizes the importance of local wildlife and their roles in the ecosystem, making it an educational experience for all ages.

Visitors have the chance to participate in up-close animal encounters, where they can learn more about specific species and their behaviors. These interactions are led by knowledgeable staff members who share insights about the animals and their conservation needs. The encounters provide a memorable way to connect with wildlife and promote awareness about the importance of protecting their habitats.

Explore the scenic nature trails that wind through Oatland Island's diverse ecosystems, including wetlands, forests, and salt marshes. The trails are well-maintained and provide opportunities for birdwatching and enjoying the area's natural beauty. Don't miss the chance to stroll along the Boardwalk Trail, which offers stunning views of the marsh and a peaceful setting for reflection and relaxation.

Oatland Island Wildlife Center offers a variety of educational programs designed for visitors of all ages. Programs include guided tours, workshops, and seasonal events that focus on wildlife conservation and environmental education. Special events, such as Wildlife Day, allow families to engage in hands-on activities, meet local wildlife experts, and participate in fun educational games.

The visitor center provides information about the center's mission, exhibits, and events. Staff members are available to answer questions and offer recommendations for exploring the area. The gift shop features a variety of wildlife-themed merchandise, educational books, and souvenirs, allowing you to take a piece of Oatland Island home with you.

Tips

- Plan for a half-day: Allocate at least 2 to 4 hours for your visit to fully enjoy the animal exhibits, trails, and educational programs.
- Dress comfortably: Wear comfortable clothing and shoes suitable for outdoor activities, as you'll be exploring the trails and exhibits.
- Bring water and snacks: While the center has a small gift shop, it's a good idea to bring water and snacks, especially if you plan to spend several hours exploring the grounds.
- Respect the wildlife: Remember to maintain a respectful distance from the animals and follow the center's guidelines for interacting with wildlife.

Nearby Attractions

- Savannah Historic District: Just a short drive away, Savannah's historic district offers beautiful architecture, charming squares, and a rich history. Enjoy walking tours, shops, and restaurants in this picturesque area.

- Fort Pulaski National Monument: Located nearby, this historic fort features beautiful grounds and educational exhibits about the Civil War and coastal defense.

- Tybee Island: A quick drive from the center, Tybee Island is known for its beautiful beaches, historic lighthouse, and relaxed atmosphere. It's perfect for a day of sun and sand after your wildlife adventure.

⓺⓷ OCMULGEE MOUNDS NATIONAL HISTORICAL PARK

COUNTY: BIBB	CITY: MACON

DATE VISITED:	WHO I WENT WITH:

RATING: ☆ ☆ ☆ ☆ ☆	WILL I RETURN? YES / NO

1207 Emery Hwy
Macon, GA 31217
478-752-8257

Ocmulgee Mounds National Historical Park is a captivating site rich in Native American history and culture, located in Macon, Georgia. This national park preserves ancient earth mounds and archaeological features created by the ancestors of the Creek Nation, providing a unique opportunity to explore the area's deep-rooted heritage. The park is not only a place of historical significance but also a serene natural setting for outdoor enthusiasts.

The site dates back to 1000 BCE, with evidence of continuous habitation for over 10,000 years. The mounds, built by indigenous peoples, served various purposes, including ceremonial sites, burial grounds, and community gatherings. In the 19th century, the park became a site of interest for archaeologists, leading to its designation as a national monument in 1936 and later a national historical park in 2019.

The park features several impressive mounds, including the Great Temple Mound, which rises 55 feet and offers breathtaking views of the surrounding area. These mounds were used for various ceremonial purposes and reflect the engineering skills of the Native American cultures that inhabited the region. The mounds are linked by a network of trails, allowing visitors to explore the site and learn about its historical significance.

The park's visitor center provides a wealth of information about the history of the mounds and the people who built them. Exhibits include artifacts, photographs, and interactive displays that bring the site's history to life. Park rangers are available to answer questions and provide insights into the park's features and the cultural heritage of the Native American tribes in the area.

Ocmulgee Mounds offers a variety of guided tours and educational programs throughout the year. These tours provide an in-depth understanding of the mounds, the archaeological significance of the site, and the cultural practices of the indigenous peoples. Special events, such as Cultural Heritage Days and Archaeology Month, feature demonstrations, workshops, and presentations that engage visitors in the park's history and significance.

The park is home to several miles of scenic walking and biking trails that wind through the lush landscape, including wetlands, forests, and fields. Trails vary in difficulty, offering something for everyone, from casual walkers to more experienced hikers. Keep an eye out for local wildlife, including birds, deer, and various species of plants native to the region.

Ocmulgee Mounds offers designated picnic areas where visitors can enjoy a meal amidst the natural beauty of the park. These spots provide a great opportunity to relax and take in the views after exploring the mounds. The park's peaceful setting makes it an excellent place for families to spend the day together, enjoying both nature and history.

Tips

- Plan for a half-day: Allocate at least 2 to 4 hours for your visit to fully explore the mounds, visitor center, and trails.
- Wear comfortable shoes: Comfortable walking shoes are recommended, as you will be exploring various terrains throughout the park.
- Bring water and snacks: While there are picnic areas available, it's a good idea to bring your own refreshments to enjoy during your visit.
- Respect the site: As a historical site, please be respectful of the mounds and surrounding nature. Stay on designated paths and avoid climbing on the mounds.

Nearby Attractions

- Museum of Arts and Sciences: Located in Macon, this museum features art exhibits, a planetarium, and natural history displays, offering a fun and educational experience for visitors of all ages.

- Hay House: A stunning example of Italian Renaissance Revival architecture, Hay House is a historic home that offers guided tours, showcasing its beautiful furnishings and rich history.

- Macon's Historic District: Stroll through the charming streets of Macon's historic district, where you can find antebellum homes, local shops, and delicious restaurants.

---

64   OKEFENOKEE SWAMP PARK

COUNTY: WARE **CITY:** WAYCROSS

DATE VISITED: **WHO I WENT WITH:**

RATING: ☆ ☆ ☆ ☆ ☆ **WILL I RETURN?** YES / NO

5700 Okefenokee Swamp Park Rd
Waycross, Georgia 31503
912-283-0583

Okefenokee Swamp Park is an extraordinary destination located in Waycross, Georgia. This vast and fascinating swamp, spanning over 400,000 acres, is one of the largest blackwater swamps in North America. The park offers a unique opportunity to explore diverse ecosystems, rich wildlife, and the cultural heritage of the region. Whether you're an adventure seeker or a nature lover, Okefenokee Swamp Park is a must-visit.

The Okefenokee Swamp has a rich history that dates back thousands of years. It has been home to Native American tribes, including the Creek and Seminole peoples. The swamp was designated a national wildlife refuge in 1937 and later became a state park. Today, the park aims to educate visitors about the swamp's ecology and history while promoting conservation efforts.

The park offers a variety of guided swamp tours, including boat tours and canoe/kayak rentals. These tours provide an intimate look at the swamp's unique ecosystem, with opportunities to see alligators, herons, turtles, and a variety of other wildlife. The Swamp Boat Tour takes visitors through the heart of the swamp, where experienced guides share fascinating stories about the flora and fauna, as well as the cultural history of the area.

Explore several miles of nature trails that wind through the stunning landscapes of the park. These trails allow visitors to experience the beauty of the swamp up close, including its lush vegetation and diverse wildlife. The Chesser Island Boardwalk is a popular trail that provides scenic views and a chance to spot wildlife, including birds and reptiles, while enjoying the tranquility of the environment.

Okefenokee Swamp Park is a haven for wildlife enthusiasts. Keep your eyes peeled for alligators lounging in the sun, colorful birds, and a variety of other animals that call the swamp home. The park offers wildlife observation platforms, making it easy to catch glimpses of animals in their natural habitats without disturbing them.

The park features educational exhibits that highlight the ecology and cultural history of the Okefenokee Swamp. Interactive displays provide insight into the importance of wetlands and the species that inhabit them. Seasonal programs and events are offered throughout the year, including workshops, guided nature walks, and children's programs designed to engage and educate visitors about the swamp's ecosystem.

The visitor center is the perfect starting point for your adventure at Okefenokee Swamp Park. It provides maps, information about tours and activities, and insights into the park's history and ecology. Don't forget to stop by the gift shop, where you can find unique souvenirs, educational materials, and locally made crafts to remember your visit.

Tips

- Dress appropriately: Wear comfortable clothing and sturdy shoes, as you'll be walking on various terrains. Consider lightweight, breathable fabrics, and don't forget sunscreen and a hat for sun protection.
- Stay hydrated: Bring water, especially during the warmer months, as you'll be spending time outdoors in the sun.
- Bring binoculars: If you enjoy birdwatching or wildlife observation, binoculars will enhance your experience and help you see animals up close.
- Respect nature: Follow park rules and guidelines, including staying on designated paths and not disturbing wildlife.

Nearby Attractions

- Stephen C. Foster State Park: Located at the western edge of the swamp, this park offers additional opportunities for hiking, fishing, and canoeing, as well as camping facilities.

- The Okefenokee Heritage Center: Situated in Waycross, this center features exhibits that showcase the history and culture of the region, including the heritage of the Native American tribes and early settlers.

- Screven County Historic Site: A short drive from the park, this historic site includes several landmarks that highlight the rich history of the area, including antebellum homes and local museums.

OLD FORT JACKSON

COUNTY: CHATHAM **CITY:** SAVANNAH

DATE VISITED: **WHO I WENT WITH:**

RATING: ☆ ☆ ☆ ☆ ☆ **WILL I RETURN?** YES / NO

1 Fort Jackson Rd
Savannah, GA 31404
912-232-3945

Old Fort Jackson is a historic fortification located on the banks of the Savannah River in Savannah, Georgia. As one of the oldest standing brick forts in Georgia, Old Fort Jackson offers a fascinating glimpse into the military history of the region, particularly during the War of 1812 and the Civil War. With its well-preserved architecture and engaging exhibits, it's a must-visit for history buffs and families alike.

Constructed in 1808, Old Fort Jackson was named after James Jackson, a prominent Georgia politician and general. The fort played a critical role in defending the city of Savannah from naval attacks and served as a military outpost during various conflicts. Today, it stands as a testament to the rich history of coastal defense in Georgia.

Visitors can explore the fort's historic structures, including its impressive brick walls, gun emplacements, and powder magazines. Guided tours are available, providing in-depth insights into the fort's history and its significance in American military heritage. The exhibits within the fort showcase artifacts, historical photographs, and information about military life, the construction of the fort, and the various conflicts it was involved in.

One of the highlights of a visit to Old Fort Jackson is the daily cannon demonstrations, where knowledgeable staff members showcase the firing of historic cannons. This exciting experience gives visitors a sense of what military life was like during the 19th century and the fort's role in coastal defense. The demonstrations often include explanations of the cannons' mechanics and the tactics used during battles, making it an educational experience for all ages.

The fort is situated along the scenic Savannah River, offering stunning views of the water and the surrounding landscape. The historic architecture of the fort provides a picturesque backdrop for photography enthusiasts. The park grounds around the fort also feature beautiful walking paths, making it a lovely place to enjoy a leisurely stroll while taking in the sights.

Old Fort Jackson hosts various educational programs and special events throughout the year, including reenactments, workshops, and lectures focused on military history. These programs engage visitors of all ages and offer hands-on learning opportunities. Check the fort's schedule for upcoming events during your visit, as they often include family-friendly activities and interactive exhibits.

The visitor center provides essential information about the fort, its history, and the various programs offered. Friendly staff members are available to answer questions and assist with planning your visit. The gift shop features a variety of souvenirs, books, and historical memorabilia, allowing you to take home a piece of your experience.

Tips

- Plan for 1-2 hours: Allocate enough time to explore the fort, watch the cannon demonstrations, and take in the exhibits. A visit typically lasts between one and two hours.
- Dress comfortably: Wear comfortable shoes and clothing suitable for walking and outdoor activities. Consider bringing a hat and sunscreen, especially during the warmer months.
- Stay hydrated: Bring water, especially during the summer heat, to ensure a comfortable experience while exploring the grounds.
- Respect the historic site: Follow all park guidelines, and be mindful of the historical significance of the fort and its surroundings.

Nearby Attractions

- River Street: Just a short drive away, River Street is a vibrant waterfront area filled with shops, restaurants, and historic buildings. Stroll along the cobblestone streets and enjoy the lively atmosphere.

- Savannah History Museum: Located in the historic district, this museum offers exhibits on Savannah's rich history, including its role in the Revolutionary War and the Civil War.

- Forsyth Park: This large public park in the heart of Savannah features beautiful walking paths, a fountain, and plenty of green space for picnics or leisurely strolls.

----

66 OWENS-THOMAS HOUSE & SLAVE QUARTERS

COUNTY: CHATHAM	CITY: SAVANNAH
DATE VISITED:	WHO I WENT WITH:
RATING: ☆ ☆ ☆ ☆ ☆	WILL I RETURN? YES / NO

124 Abercorn St
Savannah, GA 31401
912-790-8800

Owens-Thomas House & Slave Quarters is an architectural masterpiece and historical site located in the heart of Savannah, Georgia. Built in 1816, this stunning example of Regency architecture offers a profound insight into both the grandeur of the antebellum South and the complex history of slavery in America. As a designated National Historic Landmark, the Owens-Thomas House serves as a testament to Savannah's rich cultural heritage.

The Owens-Thomas House was designed by the prominent architect William Jay for Richard Richardson Owens, a successful Savannah businessman. The house features a blend of architectural styles and advanced features for its time, including indoor plumbing and a unique ventilation system. The Slave Quarters, located behind the main house, provide a stark contrast to the elegance of the home, offering visitors a glimpse into the lives of the enslaved individuals who lived and worked there.

Visitors can take guided tours of the Owens-Thomas House, which typically last about 45 minutes. Knowledgeable guides share engaging stories about the house's history, its architectural significance, and the lives of the people who inhabited it. The tours include both the main house and the Slave Quarters, providing a comprehensive understanding of the social and economic dynamics of the time.

The Owens-Thomas House features beautiful period furnishings, exquisite plasterwork, and intricate wood details that reflect the style of early 19th-century Southern architecture. The double parlor, spiral staircase, and garden are particularly noteworthy, showcasing the elegance of the home and the lifestyle of its original occupants.

The Slave Quarters, a significant part of the tour, offers a sobering perspective on the lives of enslaved individuals. The quarters are restored to reflect the living conditions and challenges faced by those who worked in the household. Exhibits in the Slave Quarters provide context on the historical realities of slavery in

Savannah, exploring the roles, relationships, and struggles of enslaved people.

The Owens-Thomas House hosts various educational programs and special events throughout the year, including lectures, workshops, and themed tours that delve deeper into specific aspects of the site's history. Seasonal events often celebrate the culture and heritage of the African American community in Savannah, providing additional layers of understanding about the city's past.

The visitor center offers resources for planning your visit, including maps, brochures, and information about other historic sites in Savannah. Staff members are available to answer questions and provide insights into the house and its history. The gift shop features a selection of books, local crafts, and unique souvenirs that reflect the rich history and culture of Savannah.

Tips

- Plan for 1-2 hours: Allocate enough time to take a guided tour and explore the surrounding gardens and exhibits. A visit typically lasts between one and two hours.
- Dress comfortably: Wear comfortable shoes and clothing suitable for walking, as you will be exploring both the house and its grounds.
- Stay engaged: Don't hesitate to ask questions during your tour. The guides are knowledgeable and eager to share fascinating stories about the site.
- Respect the historic site: Follow all guidelines while touring the house and grounds, and be mindful of the site's significance in American history.

Nearby Attractions

- Savannah History Museum: Located just a short walk away, this museum offers extensive exhibits on Savannah's history, including its role in the Revolutionary War and the Civil War.

- Forsyth Park: A beautiful urban park featuring walking paths, a large fountain, and plenty of green space. It's a perfect spot for a leisurely stroll or a picnic.

- Juliette Gordon Low Birthplace: The childhood home of the founder of the Girl Scouts of the USA, this historic site offers guided tours that explore the life and legacy of Juliette Gordon Low.

PIEDMONT PARK

COUNTY: FULTON **CITY:** ATLANTA

DATE VISITED: **WHO I WENT WITH:**

RATING: ☆ ☆ ☆ ☆ ☆ **WILL I RETURN?** YES / NO

1320 Monroe Dr NE
Atlanta, GA 30306
404-875-7275

Piedmont Park is Atlanta's most important green space and a beloved urban oasis located in the heart of the city. Covering 189 acres, this vibrant park offers a perfect escape for locals and visitors alike. Whether you're looking to enjoy outdoor activities, attend events, or simply relax in a beautiful setting, Piedmont Park has something for everyone.

Established in the late 1800s, Piedmont Park was originally designed by Frederick Law Olmsted, the landscape architect behind New York's Central Park. The park has undergone various renovations and expansions, becoming a central hub for recreation, cultural events, and community gatherings in Atlanta.

The park features multiple sports facilities, including tennis courts, basketball courts, and baseball fields. Whether you want to join a pickup game or play a friendly match, there are plenty of options for sports enthusiasts. Enjoy the park's scenic trails, perfect for walking, jogging, or biking. The paths wind through beautiful landscapes, offering picturesque views of the city skyline and surrounding greenery.

Piedmont Park has several well-maintained playgrounds, making it a great destination for families. Children can enjoy the slides, swings, and climbing structures while parents relax nearby. The park offers numerous picnic areas equipped with tables and grills. Pack a lunch and enjoy a leisurely meal surrounded by nature.

Piedmont Park is home to numerous annual events and festivals, including the Atlanta Dogwood Festival, Music Midtown, and the Atlanta Pride Festival. These events bring the community together and showcase local artists, musicians, and vendors. The park also hosts weekly farmers' markets and outdoor movie nights, providing fun and entertainment for visitors throughout the year.

One of the highlights of Piedmont Park is its breathtaking views of the Atlanta skyline. The Legacy Fountain and the Piedmont Park Conservancy offer beautiful spots for photography and relaxation. The park features diverse flora and fauna, including a variety of trees, flowers, and wildlife. The Piedmont Park Conservancy maintains the park's gardens, including the Sylvan Grove and the Jacqueline D. Smith Pavilion, which showcase native plants and seasonal blooms.

The Piedmont Park Conservancy operates a visitor center where you can find maps, information about park events, and tips for enjoying your visit. The friendly staff can assist with any questions and provide insights into the park's history and activities. Restrooms and water fountains are conveniently located throughout the park, ensuring a comfortable experience for visitors.

Tips

- Plan your activities: Consider what activities you want to enjoy during your visit, such as sports, picnicking, or attending an event. This will help you make the most of your time in the park.
- Check the event calendar: Before your visit, check the park's event calendar to see if any festivals, markets, or performances are scheduled during your stay.
- Bring essentials: Pack water, snacks, sunscreen, and any sports equipment you might need for a day of fun and relaxation.
- Respect the park: Follow park rules and guidelines, and be mindful of the environment. Keep the park clean by disposing of trash properly.

Nearby Attractions

- Atlanta Botanical Garden: Located adjacent to the park, the Atlanta Botanical Garden features stunning floral displays, themed gardens, and a tropical rainforest. It's a must-visit for garden enthusiasts.

- Fox Theatre: Just a short drive away, the historic Fox Theatre hosts Broadway shows, concerts, and cultural events in a beautifully restored venue. Check the schedule for upcoming performances during your visit.

- High Museum of Art: A short distance from the park, the High Museum of Art boasts an impressive collection of American and European art, as well as contemporary works. The museum frequently hosts special exhibitions and events.

---

68 PIN POINT HERITAGE MUSEUM

COUNTY: CHATHAM **CITY:** SAVANNAH

DATE VISITED: **WHO I WENT WITH:**

RATING: ☆ ☆ ☆ ☆ ☆   **WILL I RETURN?** YES / NO

9924 Pin Point Avenue
Savannah, GA 31406
912-355-0064

Pin Point Heritage Museum is a hidden gem located in the historic community of Pin Point, Georgia, just a short drive from Savannah. This museum is dedicated to preserving and showcasing the rich cultural heritage and history of the Gullah-Geechee people, who are descendants of enslaved Africans living along the coastal regions of South Carolina and Georgia. Through its exhibits and programs, the museum tells the story of this unique community and their contributions to the region's history.

The Pin Point Heritage Museum is housed in a former school building that served the local African American community for over 50 years. The museum was established to honor the legacy of the Gullah-Geechee culture and to educate visitors about the history of Pin Point and its residents. The museum also highlights the importance of the local seafood industry, which has been a vital part of the community's economy and culture.

The museum features a variety of exhibits that showcase the history, culture, and traditions of the Gullah-Geechee people. Artifacts, photographs, and documents help to illustrate the daily life and struggles of the community over the years. Visitors can learn about traditional crafts, music, and culinary practices that have been passed down through generations, enriching the cultural tapestry of the region.

Guided tours are available, providing visitors with in-depth insights into the exhibits and the history of Pin Point. Knowledgeable staff and volunteers share stories about the community's past and its significance within the broader context of American history. The tours often highlight the impact of the seafood industry, focusing on how local residents have sustainably harvested and celebrated the rich natural resources of the area.

The museum regularly hosts cultural programs, workshops, and events that celebrate Gullah-Geechee heritage. These may include storytelling sessions, craft demonstrations, and cooking classes, allowing visitors to engage directly with the culture. Special events often coincide with local festivals and heritage celebrations, providing opportunities to experience Gullah music, dance, and cuisine firsthand.

The museum is set against the backdrop of beautiful marshlands and waterways, offering picturesque views and a tranquil setting for visitors. Take time to explore the outdoor areas, which provide insight into the natural environment that has shaped the Gullah-Geechee way of life. Walking paths around the museum allow for leisurely strolls, where you can enjoy the sights and sounds of the coastal ecosystem.

The visitor center offers maps, brochures, and additional resources to enhance your experience. Staff members are available to answer questions and provide recommendations for further exploration in the area. The gift shop features a selection of locally crafted items, books on Gullah-Geechee culture, and unique souvenirs to commemorate your visit.

Tips

- Plan for 1-2 hours: Allow enough time to explore the exhibits, participate in a guided tour, and enjoy the outdoor spaces. A visit typically lasts between one and two hours.
- Engage with staff: Take the opportunity to ask questions and engage with staff members. They are passionate about the history and culture of the Gullah-Geechee people and can provide valuable insights.
- Check for events: Before your visit, check the museum's schedule for any special events or programs that may be happening during your stay.
- Respect the space: Follow all museum guidelines and be mindful of the importance of preserving this cultural heritage for future generations.

Nearby Attractions

- Fort Pulaski National Monument: Just a short drive away, this well-preserved Civil War fort offers tours, walking trails, and beautiful views of the marsh. Learn about the fort's history and its role in the defense of Savannah.

- Skidaway Island State Park: A nearby natural haven, this state park features hiking trails, picnic areas, and opportunities for wildlife viewing. It's a great place to immerse yourself in the region's natural beauty.

- Savannah National Wildlife Refuge: Located a bit further, this refuge is perfect for birdwatching and exploring the wetlands. The scenic driving tour allows visitors to see diverse wildlife in their natural habitat.

PONCE CITY MARKET

69

COUNTY: FULTON   CITY: ATLANTA

DATE VISITED: WHO I WENT WITH:

RATING: ☆ ☆ ☆ ☆ ☆   WILL I RETURN?   YES / NO

675 Ponce De Leon Ave NE
Atlanta, GA 30308
404-900-7900

Ponce City Market, is one of Atlanta's most vibrant destinations that seamlessly combines history, shopping, dining, and entertainment! Housed in the former Ponce de Leon Amusement Park and the historic Sears, Roebuck & Co. building, Ponce City Market has transformed into a bustling hub of activity that captures the spirit of Atlanta's rich history while embracing modern urban culture.

Built in 1926, the Ponce City Market was originally a Sears department store and later served as a vital retail center for decades. In 2014, the building was revitalized and reopened as a mixed-use community space, featuring shops, restaurants, offices, and residential units. The restoration maintains much of the building's original architecture, adding character and charm to this unique destination.

Ponce City Market offers a diverse mix of shops, from local boutiques to well-known brands. Explore unique retailers selling everything from clothing and accessories to home goods and artisanal products. Don't miss the opportunity to browse through the Central Food Hall, where you'll find a variety of local vendors showcasing gourmet snacks, handmade crafts, and specialty goods.

With an impressive selection of dining options, Ponce City Market caters to all tastes. From casual eateries to upscale restaurants, you can indulge in a variety of cuisines, including Southern comfort food, international dishes, and vegan options.

- Kevin Rathbun's Krog Street Market: Known for its innovative dishes and vibrant atmosphere.
- H&F Burger: Famous for its mouthwatering burgers and milkshakes.
- El Tesoro: A must-visit for fans of Mexican cuisine, offering delicious tacos and margaritas.

Ponce City Market is directly connected to the Atlanta BeltLine, a network of walking and biking trails that encircle the city. Take a stroll along the BeltLine for scenic views and access to additional parks and attractions.

Enjoy breathtaking views of the Atlanta skyline at the Ponce City Market Rooftop. With mini-golf, games, and a bar, it's a perfect spot to unwind after a day of shopping and dining.

Throughout the year, Ponce City Market hosts a variety of events, including seasonal festivals, food tastings, art exhibitions, and live music. Check the event calendar for upcoming activities during your visit.

The market is home to several art installations and public spaces that showcase local artists. Explore the murals and sculptures that celebrate Atlanta's vibrant culture. Don't miss the opportunity to visit the Historic Ponce City Market Tour, which offers insights into the building's rich history and its significance to the community.

Ponce City Market provides various amenities for visitors, including restrooms, free Wi-Fi, and comfortable seating areas for relaxation. The market is family-friendly, with spaces for children to play and engage in creative activities.

Tips

- Plan your day: Allocate sufficient time to explore the shops, enjoy a meal, and visit the rooftop. A visit can easily take a few hours, especially if you participate in events or activities.
- Stay updated on events: Check the Ponce City Market website for a schedule of events happening during your visit to enhance your experience.
- Bring your camera: Capture the beautiful architecture, art installations, and stunning skyline views, especially from the rooftop.
- Engage with local vendors: Support local businesses by purchasing unique items and enjoying delicious food from vendors throughout the market.

Nearby Attractions

- Atlanta Botanical Garden: A stunning 30-acre garden featuring beautiful landscapes, exotic plants, and seasonal displays. Just a short distance away, it's perfect for nature lovers.

- Martin Luther King Jr. National Historic Park: A significant site honoring the life and legacy of Dr. Martin Luther King Jr. Explore the historic Ebenezer Baptist Church and the King Center.

- Fernbank Museum of Natural History: A family-friendly destination showcasing exhibits on natural history, science, and culture, including a giant dinosaur skeleton and an IMAX theater.

70 PROVIDENCE CANYON STATE PARK

COUNTY: STEWART **CITY:** LUMPKIN

DATE VISITED: **WHO I WENT WITH:**

RATING: ☆ ☆ ☆ ☆ ☆ **WILL I RETURN?** YES / NO

8930 Canyon Road
Lumpkin, GA 31815
229-838-6202

Providence Canyon State Park is often referred to as "Georgia's Little Grand Canyon." Located in the southwestern part of the state, this stunning park is renowned for its breathtaking canyons, unique geological formations, and diverse wildlife. Whether you're a nature enthusiast, a hiking aficionado, or just looking for a serene getaway, Providence Canyon offers a memorable outdoor experience.

Providence Canyon was formed in the 19th century due to poor agricultural practices, including over-farming and deforestation, which led to severe erosion. The canyons were designated a state park in 1971 and have since become a site for conservation and education, showcasing the importance of sustainable land management.

The park features several canyons, some reaching depths of up to 150 feet and exhibiting a variety of colorful soils. The contrasting hues of red, orange, yellow, and white create a striking landscape that attracts photographers and nature lovers alike. There are multiple overlooks providing breathtaking views of the canyons, making them perfect spots for photos or quiet reflection.

Canyon Loop Trail: This 3-mile loop trail takes you down into the canyon and back up, offering stunning views of the canyon walls and unique geological features. Expect moderate terrain with some steep sections.

The park features several shorter nature trails that allow you to explore the area's rich biodiversity. Look for native plants, wildflowers, and local wildlife along the way.

Providence Canyon State Park offers both primitive camping and picnic areas for visitors. Campsites are equipped with picnic tables and fire rings, providing a perfect setting for a night under the stars. Several picnic spots are available throughout the park, making it an ideal place for families to enjoy a meal in a beautiful natural setting.

The park hosts various educational programs, workshops, and guided tours throughout the year. These events focus on local ecology, geology, and the importance of conservation. Check the park's calendar for special events such as guided hikes, ranger talks, and seasonal festivities.

The park features a visitor center where you can find maps, brochures, and educational materials about the park's geology and ecology. Knowledgeable staff can provide recommendations and answer any questions you may have. Restrooms and water fountains are available for visitor convenience.

Tips

- Dress appropriately: Wear sturdy hiking shoes and dress in layers, as temperatures can vary throughout the day. Don't forget sunscreen and a hat for sun protection.
- Stay hydrated: Bring plenty of water, especially if you plan to hike the longer trails. Staying hydrated is essential for enjoying your outdoor adventures.
- Follow Leave No Trace principles: Help preserve the park's beauty by packing out all trash and respecting wildlife and plant life.
- Check weather conditions: Be aware of weather forecasts before your visit, as conditions can change rapidly in outdoor environments.

Nearby Attractions

- Florence Marina State Park: Located just a short drive away, this park offers beautiful views of Lake Walter F. George, fishing opportunities, and additional hiking trails. It's a great spot for water activities and picnicking.

- Kolomoki Mounds Historic Park: About 30 minutes from Providence Canyon, this archaeological site features ancient Native American mounds, a museum, and hiking trails. It's a fascinating glimpse into Georgia's prehistoric past.

- Historic Downtown Lumpkin: Take some time to explore the charming downtown area of Lumpkin, where you can find local shops, restaurants, and historical sites that reflect the region's heritage.

RIVERWALK

(71)

COUNTY: RICHMOND **CITY:** AUGUSTA

DATE VISITED: **WHO I WENT WITH:**

RATING: ☆ ☆ ☆ ☆ ☆   **WILL I RETURN?** YES / NO

10th Street
Augusta, GA 30901

Riverwalk in Augusta, Georgia. Stretching along the picturesque Savannah River, the Riverwalk is a vibrant waterfront area that offers a delightful blend of scenic views, recreational activities, and cultural attractions. This beautifully landscaped promenade is the perfect place for a leisurely stroll, a family outing, or an afternoon of exploration in one of Georgia's most historic cities.

The Riverwalk was developed as part of Augusta's downtown revitalization efforts in the 1980s, transforming an underutilized area along the river into a thriving public space. It is now a centerpiece for recreation, arts, and community events, drawing locals and visitors alike.

The Riverwalk features stunning views of the Savannah River, with beautiful landscapes and historic architecture lining the promenade. Benches and shaded areas provide perfect spots to relax and take in the scenery. Enjoy watching boats navigate the river, or catch sight of local wildlife, including birds and turtles, in their natural habitat.

Walking and Biking: The paved pathways along the Riverwalk are ideal for walking, jogging, or biking. The trails are well-maintained and accessible for people of all ages and abilities.

Fishing and Boating: Anglers can enjoy fishing along the riverbank, while boaters can launch their vessels from nearby docks. Kayaking and paddleboarding are also popular activities in the area.

Play Areas: Families can take advantage of playgrounds and green spaces along the Riverwalk, making it a great destination for children to play and explore.

Augusta Museum of History: Located at the start of the Riverwalk, this museum showcases the rich history of Augusta through engaging exhibits, including the history of the Masters Tournament and local contributions to music and art.

The Imperial Theatre: A historic venue that hosts a variety of performances, including concerts, plays, and community events. Check the schedule for upcoming shows during your visit.

Art Installations: Throughout the Riverwalk, you'll find public art displays, sculptures, and murals that reflect the cultural heritage and artistic spirit of Augusta.

The Riverwalk is home to several restaurants and cafes offering diverse dining options. Enjoy everything from Southern cuisine to casual bites with river views. Explore nearby shops and boutiques in the downtown area, featuring local crafts, gifts, and souvenirs that reflect Augusta's charm.

The Riverwalk hosts various events throughout the year, including concerts, farmers' markets, and holiday celebrations. Keep an eye on the local calendar for special happenings during your visit.

Tips

- Plan your route: Consider starting at the Augusta Museum of History to get a sense of the area's heritage before exploring the Riverwalk.
- Bring your camera: The scenic views along the Riverwalk provide excellent opportunities for photography, especially during sunrise and sunset.
- Check the weather: Dress appropriately for the weather and bring sunscreen if you plan to spend time outdoors.
- Stay hydrated: Bring water, especially if you plan to walk or bike along the Riverwalk for an extended period.

Nearby Attractions

- The Masters Tournament: If you're visiting in early April, experience the excitement of the famous golf tournament held at Augusta National Golf Club. While the tournament itself is not at the Riverwalk, it's a significant event in the city.

- Phinizy Swamp Nature Park: Just a short drive from the Riverwalk, this park offers walking trails, boardwalks, and opportunities for birdwatching in a serene natural setting.

- Meadow Garden: The historic home of George Walton, a signer of the Declaration of Independence, offers guided tours and beautiful gardens to explore.

72 ROCK CITY GARDENS

COUNTY: WALKER   **CITY:** LOOKOUT MOUNTAIN

DATE VISITED: **WHO I WENT WITH:**

RATING: ☆ ☆ ☆ ☆ ☆   **WILL I RETURN?** YES / NO

1400 Patten Rd
Lookout Mountain, GA 30750

Rock City Gardens is a breathtaking natural attraction located atop Lookout Mountain in Georgia. Renowned for its stunning vistas, unique rock formations, and enchanting gardens, Rock City Gardens offers a magical experience for visitors of all ages. Whether you're a nature enthusiast, a family looking for adventure, or a romantic couple seeking beautiful scenery, Rock City Gardens has something for everyone.

Established in the 1930s by Garnet and Frieda Carter, Rock City was initially developed as a private garden. It quickly transformed into a popular tourist destination, showcasing the area's natural beauty and geological wonders. Today, Rock City Gardens continues to enchant visitors with its whimsical landscapes and rich history.

One of the highlights of Rock City is the See Seven States viewpoint, where visitors can gaze across the stunning landscape and see seven states at once: Georgia, Alabama, Tennessee, South Carolina, North Carolina, Kentucky, and Virginia. Lover's Leap is another spectacular overlook that provides breathtaking views of the surrounding mountains and valleys, perfect for photography and enjoying the natural beauty.

The Enchanted Trail spans 4,100 feet and leads visitors through a magical landscape filled with unique rock formations, lush gardens, and fascinating features. The trail is suitable for all ages and offers several resting spots along the way. Explore captivating formations like the Balanced Rock, which seems to defy gravity, and the Needle's Eye, a narrow passage through which visitors can walk.

Rock City Gardens is home to a variety of beautifully landscaped gardens featuring thousands of flowering plants. The vibrant seasonal displays include azaleas, rhododendrons, and wildflowers, providing a colorful backdrop year-round. The Fairyland Caverns and Gnome Valley add a whimsical touch, featuring charming sculptures and hidden surprises throughout the garden.

Children will love exploring the trails and discovering hidden gems along the way. Interactive exhibits and educational signage make the experience engaging for young visitors. Seasonal events, such as the Enchanted Garden of Lights during the winter holidays and spring flower festivals, offer additional fun activities for families.

Enjoy delicious Southern cuisine at Café 7, located at the top of Lookout Mountain. The café offers a diverse menu with fantastic views, making it an ideal spot for a relaxing meal. Visit the gift shop for unique souvenirs, local crafts, and garden-related items to commemorate your visit.

Tips

- Wear comfortable shoes: The walking trails involve some uphill and uneven terrain, so be sure to wear sturdy footwear for your adventure.
- Bring a camera: The stunning views and unique rock formations provide countless opportunities for photography, so don't forget your camera or smartphone.
- Check the weather: Be aware of the weather forecast, as conditions can change quickly in the mountains. Dress in layers and bring water for your hike.
- Plan your day: Allocate several hours to fully enjoy the park, especially if you want to experience all the trails and viewpoints.

Nearby Attractions

- Ruby Falls: Just a short drive away, Ruby Falls is a stunning underground waterfall located in a cave 1,120 feet beneath Lookout Mountain. Guided tours take you through the cave to see this natural wonder.

- Lookout Mountain Incline Railway: Known as one of the steepest railways in the world, this historic incline railway offers a scenic ride up Lookout Mountain with stunning views along the way.

- Chickamauga and Chattanooga National Military Park: Explore the rich Civil War history of the region through this extensive park, featuring trails, monuments, and historical sites.

----

73 SAVANNAH HISTORIC DISTRICT

COUNTY: CHATHAM **CITY:** SAVANNAH

DATE VISITED: _____ **WHO I WENT WITH:** _____

RATING: ☆ ☆ ☆ ☆ ☆   **WILL I RETURN?** YES / NO

301 Martin Luther King Jr Blvd
Savannah, GA 31401

Savannah Historic District is a beautifully preserved area that captures the charm and history of one of America's oldest cities. Known for its stunning architecture, lush public squares, and vibrant culture, Savannah's Historic District offers a unique glimpse into the past. Whether you're a history buff, an architecture enthusiast, or simply looking to enjoy the Southern hospitality, the Historic District has something for everyone.

Founded in 1733, Savannah was the first city in Georgia and served as its colonial capital. The Historic District was designed by James Oglethorpe, who laid out the city's grid system and public squares. Today, it is one of the largest National Historic Landmark Districts in the United States, showcasing over 20 city squares, historic buildings, and monuments.

The district is home to 22 picturesque squares, each with its own unique character and historical significance. Notable squares include Chippewa Square, famous for its role in the movie Forrest Gump, and Forsyth Park, which features a stunning fountain and walking paths. Each square is surrounded by beautiful oak trees draped in Spanish moss, making them perfect spots for a leisurely stroll or a picnic.

Explore the stunning architecture of the district, featuring styles ranging from Georgian and Federal to Victorian and Gothic Revival. Don't miss the Cathedral of St. John the Baptist, a magnificent example of Gothic architecture with stunning stained glass windows. Other must-see buildings include the Savannah History Museum, located in the old Central of Georgia Railway depot, and the historic Juliette Gordon Low Birthplace, the founder of the Girl Scouts.

Savannah History Museum: Discover the rich history of Savannah through engaging exhibits and artifacts, including a section dedicated to the city's role in the Civil War.

Telfair Museums: Comprising three museums (Telfair Academy, Owens-Thomas

House & Slave Quarters, and Jepson Center), these institutions showcase American and European art, decorative arts, and the history of the area.

Broughton Street: Known for its vibrant shopping scene, this street is lined with boutiques, galleries, and local shops offering everything from art to clothing.

Experience Savannah's culinary scene with a variety of restaurants offering Southern cuisine. Don't miss iconic spots like The Olde Pink House and Mrs. Wilkes' Dining Room, known for their delicious Southern comfort food.

Savannah is known for its rich history and ghostly tales. Join a guided ghost tour to explore the district's haunted history and visit reputedly haunted sites, such as the Pirate's House and the Colonial Park Cemetery. Historical walking tours are also available, providing insights into the city's storied past, architecture, and cultural heritage.

Tips

- Wear comfortable shoes: The Historic District is best explored on foot, so wear comfortable walking shoes to enjoy the cobblestone streets and pathways.
- Stay hydrated: Especially during warmer months, bring water and take breaks in the shaded squares to stay cool.
- Plan your itinerary: With so much to see, consider planning your visit to include both the major attractions and hidden gems within the district.
- Check for events: Savannah hosts various festivals and events throughout the year. Check local listings for happenings during your visit.

Nearby Attractions

- Forsyth Park: A sprawling 30-acre park featuring walking paths, gardens, and the iconic Forsyth Fountain. It's a great place to relax or enjoy outdoor activities.

- River Street: Just a short walk away, River Street offers a lively waterfront area with shops, restaurants, and beautiful views of the Savannah River. It's a popular spot for dining and entertainment.

- Bonaventure Cemetery: A short drive from the Historic District, this hauntingly beautiful cemetery is known for its historic graves, stunning statuary, and picturesque pathways lined with moss-draped trees.

74 SCADSTORY

COUNTY: CHATHAM **CITY:** SAVANNAH
DATE VISITED: **WHO I WENT WITH:**
RATING: ☆ ☆ ☆ ☆ ☆   **WILL I RETURN?** YES / NO

342 Bull St
Savannah, GA 31401
912-525-5505

SCADstory is a captivating experience that showcases the legacy and creativity of the Savannah College of Art and Design (SCAD). Located in the heart of Savannah, SCADstory is an immersive space designed to celebrate the university's contributions to the arts and culture while inspiring visitors of all ages. Whether you are an art enthusiast, prospective student, or simply curious about the vibrant world of creativity, SCADstory offers a unique glimpse into the dynamic SCAD community.

SCAD was founded in 1978 by Paula Wallace, and since then, it has grown into one of the largest art and design universities in the United States. SCADstory was created to tell the story of the university's journey, its impact on the local community, and the extraordinary achievements of its students and alumni.

SCADstory features interactive exhibits that highlight the university's innovative programs, notable alumni, and contributions to the art world. Visitors can explore various mediums, from graphic design and fashion to film and fine arts. The exhibits include video installations, digital displays, and hands-on activities that engage visitors in the creative process.

SCADstory offers a range of educational programs and workshops designed for all ages. These programs cover various artistic disciplines and are led by experienced faculty and industry professionals. Workshops may include topics such as painting, animation, fashion design, and photography, providing participants with the chance to develop their skills and creativity.

The center regularly hosts exhibitions featuring student and faculty work, showcasing the latest trends and innovations in the art and design fields. Check the schedule for upcoming exhibitions and events during your visit. SCADstory also hosts lectures, panels, and film screenings featuring prominent artists, designers, and alumni who share their experiences and insights with the community.

As you explore SCADstory, you'll be surrounded by the vibrant energy of student creativity. The space itself is designed to inspire, featuring artistic decor, colorful installations, and engaging visual displays. Take a moment to relax in the lounge area, where you can enjoy student work and artwork from various disciplines.

The SCADshop located within SCADstory offers a selection of unique merchandise, including prints, art supplies, and SCAD-branded apparel. It's a perfect place to find a memorable souvenir or gift that reflects the artistic spirit of SCAD.

Tips

- Explore at your own pace: Take your time to enjoy the exhibits and activities at SCADstory. Engage with interactive displays and ask questions to staff members for a deeper understanding.
- Plan ahead: If you're interested in attending a workshop or event, check the SCAD website in advance to reserve your spot and learn about any fees.
- Bring a notebook: If you're inspired by what you see, consider bringing a notebook or sketchpad to jot down ideas or sketch your impressions.
- Stay informed: Follow SCADstory on social media or sign up for their newsletter to stay updated on upcoming events, workshops, and exhibitions.

Nearby Attractions

- Savannah Historic District: Just a short walk away, the Historic District features stunning architecture, beautiful public squares, and a wealth of history. Explore the charming streets, shops, and restaurants.

- Forsyth Park: A beautiful 30-acre park featuring walking paths, gardens, and the iconic Forsyth Fountain. It's a great place to relax and enjoy the outdoors.

- Telfair Museums: Comprising several museums (Telfair Academy, Owens-Thomas House & Slave Quarters, and Jepson Center), Telfair Museums showcases a diverse collection of art and historical exhibits, making it a great complement to your visit to SCADstory.

----

75 SHIPS OF THE SEA MARITIME MUSEUM

COUNTY: CHATHAM	CITY: SAVANNAH

DATE VISITED:	WHO I WENT WITH:

RATING: ☆ ☆ ☆ ☆ ☆	WILL I RETURN? YES / NO

41 Martin Luther King Jr. Blvd
Savannah, GA 31401
912-232-1511

Ships of the Sea Maritime Museum is a unique gem nestled in the heart of Savannah, Georgia. This museum is dedicated to preserving and showcasing the rich maritime history of the region, highlighting the significance of ships and the sea in shaping Savannah's cultural heritage. Whether you're a history enthusiast, a maritime lover, or simply looking for a fascinating place to explore, the Ships of the Sea Maritime Museum offers an engaging and educational experience.

Established in 1966, the museum is housed in the historic William Scarbrough House, built in 1819. The house itself is an architectural treasure, showcasing the Federal style typical of Savannah's historic homes. The museum was founded by a group of maritime enthusiasts to preserve the city's maritime artifacts and educate the public about the importance of seafaring in the region.

The Ships of the Sea Maritime Museum features an impressive collection of ship models, maritime paintings, and artifacts that tell the story of Savannah's maritime history. The exhibits cover various topics, including shipbuilding, navigation, and the impact of the maritime industry on the city's development. One of the museum's highlights is the stunning collection of handcrafted ship models, meticulously created by skilled artisans. These models range from historical ships to modern vessels, showcasing the art of shipbuilding.

The museum boasts beautifully landscaped gardens that provide a tranquil escape from the bustling city. The gardens are designed in the style of traditional Southern gardens, featuring lush plants, blooming flowers, and serene pathways. Visitors can relax in the gardens, enjoying the sights and sounds of nature while learning about the relationship between the sea and the environment.

The Ships of the Sea Maritime Museum offers a variety of educational programs, including guided tours, lectures, and workshops. These programs are designed to engage visitors of all ages and provide a deeper understanding of maritime history. Special events, such as maritime-themed festivals and family days, are held throughout the year, offering interactive experiences and activities for children and adults alike.

Don't forget to visit the museum's gift shop, where you can find a selection of maritime-themed merchandise, books, and souvenirs. From nautical decor to educational materials, the gift shop offers unique items that celebrate the maritime heritage of Savannah.

The museum is wheelchair accessible, ensuring that all visitors can enjoy the exhibits and gardens. Restrooms are available on-site for visitor convenience.

Tips

- Plan your time: Allocate at least 1-2 hours to explore the museum and gardens fully. Take your time to enjoy the exhibits and soak in the atmosphere.
- Engage with staff: The museum staff is knowledgeable and passionate about maritime history. Don't hesitate to ask questions or seek recommendations for your visit.
- Check for events: Visit the museum's website to stay informed about upcoming events, workshops, and special exhibitions during your visit.
- Explore nearby attractions: Take advantage of the museum's central location by exploring other nearby attractions, making for a full day of cultural experiences.

Nearby Attractions

- Savannah History Museum: Just a short walk away, this museum offers a comprehensive overview of Savannah's history, featuring exhibits on the Revolutionary War, the Civil War, and the city's cultural heritage.

- Forsyth Park: A beautiful 30-acre park featuring walking paths, gardens, and the iconic Forsyth Fountain. It's an ideal spot for a leisurely stroll or a picnic.

- River Street: A vibrant waterfront area filled with shops, restaurants, and entertainment. Enjoy stunning views of the Savannah River while sampling local cuisine or browsing unique boutiques.

----

76 SKIDAWAY ISLAND STATE PARK

COUNTY: CHATHAM **CITY:** SAVANNAH

DATE VISITED: **WHO I WENT WITH:**

RATING: ☆ ☆ ☆ ☆ ☆ **WILL I RETURN?** YES / NO

52 Diamond Causeway
Savannah, GA 31411
912-598-2300

Skidaway Island State Park is a hidden gem located just a few miles from Savannah, Georgia. This serene and picturesque park offers a unique blend of natural beauty, recreational opportunities, and rich history. With its lush landscapes, diverse wildlife, and extensive trails, Skidaway Island State Park is the perfect destination for outdoor enthusiasts, families, and anyone looking to escape the hustle and bustle of city life.

Established in 1980, Skidaway Island State Park was created to preserve the natural environment of the area while providing a space for public enjoyment. The park is situated on the site of a former maritime forest and is home to several archaeological sites that date back thousands of years, highlighting the area's rich history.

The park features a network of well-maintained trails that meander through lush forests, salt marshes, and along scenic waterways. The Skidaway Island Trail offers a leisurely 1.5-mile loop that is perfect for hiking, jogging, or leisurely strolls. Wildlife enthusiasts will delight in spotting various bird species, including herons, egrets, and even the occasional osprey. Keep an eye out for deer, raccoons, and other native wildlife as you explore the park.

Skidaway Island State Park offers interpretive programs and guided nature walks that provide insights into the park's ecology, history, and wildlife. These programs are designed for all ages and can enhance your understanding of the unique environment. The park's visitor center features educational displays that highlight the flora and fauna of the area, along with information about the park's history and conservation efforts.

For those looking to extend their visit, Skidaway Island State Park offers a family-friendly campground with sites suitable for tents and RVs. Each campsite is equipped with picnic tables and fire pits, making it an ideal spot for a weekend getaway in nature. Numerous picnic areas throughout the park are perfect for family outings, providing scenic spots to relax and enjoy a meal surrounded by the beauty of the outdoors.

The park provides access to the waterways, making it a great spot for fishing and crabbing. Anglers can cast a line from the shore or launch a kayak for a more adventurous experience. Make sure to check local regulations and obtain any necessary licenses before fishing.

Enjoy biking along the park's trails, which are suitable for both novice and experienced cyclists. The peaceful surroundings and scenic views make for a delightful ride. Birdwatching is a popular activity in the park, with several designated birding areas. Bring your binoculars and enjoy the sights and sounds of nature as you observe the diverse birdlife.

Tips

- Dress appropriately: Wear comfortable clothing and sturdy shoes suitable for hiking and outdoor activities. Don't forget sunscreen and insect repellent.
- Bring water and snacks: Staying hydrated is essential while exploring the park. Pack water and snacks, especially if you plan to spend the day hiking or picnicking.
- Check the weather: Be sure to check the weather forecast before your visit, as conditions can change rapidly, especially in coastal areas.
- Respect nature: Practice Leave No Trace principles by disposing of waste properly and staying on marked trails to protect the park's natural resources.

Nearby Attractions

- Fort McAllister State Park: Located just a short drive away, this historic site features preserved Civil War earthworks, a museum, and scenic views of the Ogeechee River. Take a tour to learn about its history and significance.

- Savannah National Wildlife Refuge: A short drive from the park, this wildlife refuge offers excellent opportunities for birdwatching, hiking, and photography. The refuge is home to alligators, deer, and a variety of bird species.

- Downtown Savannah: Just a short drive from Skidaway Island, the historic district of Savannah is filled with charming squares, historic homes, and vibrant shops and restaurants. Spend some time exploring this iconic Southern city.

ST. SIMONS ISLAND

77

COUNTY: GLYNN   CITY: ST. SIMONS ISLAND

DATE VISITED: WHO I WENT WITH:

RATING: ☆ ☆ ☆ ☆ ☆   WILL I RETURN?   YES / NO

St. Simons Island is a charming coastal paradise located along Georgia's picturesque Golden Isles. Renowned for its stunning beaches, rich history, and vibrant community, St. Simons Island is an idyllic destination for families, couples, and solo travelers alike. Whether you're looking for relaxation, adventure, or a glimpse into the island's storied past, St. Simons Island has something for everyone.

St. Simons Island has a rich history dating back to the 16th century when Spanish explorers first arrived. The island played significant roles during the Revolutionary War and the Civil War. Today, it retains its historical charm through well-preserved landmarks and historic sites, making it a great place to explore Georgia's heritage.

St. Simons Island boasts several miles of beautiful sandy beaches, perfect for sunbathing, swimming, and beachcombing. East Beach is popular for families, while Massengale Park offers picnic areas and easy beach access. Take a leisurely stroll along the shoreline at sunset to witness breathtaking views of the Atlantic Ocean.

St. Simons Lighthouse Museum: Climb to the top of the lighthouse for panoramic views of the island and the sea. The museum features exhibits on the island's maritime history and the lighthouse's significance. Fort Frederica National Monument: Explore the ruins of this 18th-century fort built to protect the colony from Spanish invasion. Walk the trails, visit the visitor center, and learn about the fort's role in American history.

Christ Church: Visit this historic church founded in 1736, known for its beautiful architecture and serene grounds. The church is still active and offers a glimpse into the island's colonial past.

St. Simons Island features several miles of scenic bike paths and walking trails. Rent a bike and explore the island at your own pace, enjoying the lush landscapes and coastal views.

Rent a kayak or paddleboard to explore the island's waterways. Glide through salt marshes, spot wildlife, and enjoy the tranquility of nature. Guided tours are available for those looking to learn more about the local ecology.

Anglers can try their luck at catching fish from the shore or on a chartered fishing trip. Golf enthusiasts will appreciate the island's golf courses, including the scenic Sea Island Golf Club.

Village Pier: The charming Village area offers boutique shops, art galleries, and restaurants. Stroll along the pier, enjoy local art, and savor fresh seafood at one of the waterfront restaurants.

Seafood and Southern Cuisine: Don't miss the chance to try local dishes at restaurants such as The Crab Trap, Gnat's Landing, and ECHO. Fresh seafood, Southern comfort food, and local favorites await your taste buds.

St. Simons Island hosts various festivals and events throughout the year, including the St. Simons Island Shrimp & Grits Festival, the Island Arts Festival, and seasonal celebrations. Check the island's events calendar to see what's happening during your visit.

Tips

- Plan your itinerary: Prioritize the sites and activities you want to experience to make the most of your visit. Be sure to leave time for relaxation on the beach.
- Pack essentials: Bring sunscreen, a hat, and plenty of water, especially during the warmer months. Comfortable shoes are a must for walking and exploring.
- Check the weather: Coastal weather can be unpredictable. Check the forecast and be prepared for sudden changes, especially if you're planning outdoor activities.
- Respect nature and wildlife: Enjoy the natural beauty of St. Simons Island while being respectful of wildlife and the environment. Follow local guidelines to preserve the area's delicate ecosystems.

Nearby Attractions

- Jekyll Island: A short drive away, Jekyll Island is home to beautiful beaches, the historic Jekyll Island Club, and the Georgia Sea Turtle Center. It's perfect for a day trip filled with exploration and outdoor fun.

- Little St. Simons Island: This private island is accessible only by boat and offers a unique opportunity for nature lovers to explore pristine beaches, maritime forests, and wildlife habitats. Guided eco-tours are available.

- Brunswick: The nearby city of Brunswick offers additional dining, shopping, and cultural experiences. Explore the historic downtown area and try local cuisine.

78 ST. SIMONS LIGHTHOUSE MUSEUM

COUNTY: GLYNN	CITY: ST. SIMONS ISLAND
DATE VISITED:	WHO I WENT WITH:
RATING: ☆ ☆ ☆ ☆ ☆	WILL I RETURN? YES / NO

610 Beachview Drive
St. Simons Island, GA 31522
912-638-4666

St. Simons Lighthouse Museum is a historic gem located on St. Simons Island, Georgia. This iconic lighthouse and its accompanying museum offer visitors a fascinating glimpse into the island's maritime history and the important role lighthouses played in coastal navigation. With its stunning views, educational exhibits, and rich heritage, the St. Simons Lighthouse Museum is a must-visit destination for history buffs, families, and anyone looking to explore the beauty of Georgia's coast.

The St. Simons Lighthouse was first built in 1810, making it one of the oldest lighthouses in Georgia. The current structure, completed in 1872, stands 104 feet tall and has been guiding ships safely since its completion. The lighthouse is still an active aid to navigation, making it a vital part of the coastal community's heritage.

Visitors can climb the 129 steps to the top of the lighthouse for breathtaking panoramic views of the surrounding area, including the Atlantic Ocean and the lush landscapes of St. Simons Island. The climb is rewarding, and the view from the top is not to be missed. The lighthouse itself is a striking white brick structure with a black lantern, providing a beautiful photo opportunity. Surrounding the lighthouse are picturesque grounds perfect for a leisurely stroll or picnic.

The museum houses a variety of exhibits that explore the history of the lighthouse, the role of lighthouses in maritime navigation, and the life of the lighthouse keepers. You'll find artifacts, photographs, and informative displays that tell the story of the lighthouse and its significance to the island's history. Special exhibits often highlight the local maritime culture, shipwrecks, and the ecological importance of the coastal region.

The museum features a gift shop where visitors can purchase unique souvenirs, including nautical-themed items, books on local history, and handmade crafts by local artisans. It's a great place to find a keepsake to remember your visit.

The St. Simons Lighthouse Museum hosts various events and educational programs throughout the year, including guided tours, lectures, and seasonal festivals. Check the museum's calendar for upcoming events that may coincide with your visit.

Tips

- Plan your climb: If you wish to climb the lighthouse, arrive early in the day to avoid crowds. The climb can be strenuous, so wear comfortable shoes and take your time.
- Check the weather: Coastal weather can change quickly. Be sure to check the forecast and dress appropriately for your visit, especially if you plan to be outdoors.
- Take your time: Allow plenty of time to explore the museum exhibits and enjoy the views from the lighthouse. Take a moment to relax in the beautiful grounds surrounding the lighthouse.
- Bring a camera: The views from the top of the lighthouse are stunning, and the entire area is picturesque. Capture your memories with plenty of photos.

Nearby Attractions

- Fort Frederica National Monument: Just a short drive away, this historic site features the ruins of an 18th-century fort and offers trails and a visitor center. Learn about the fort's role in protecting the colony and explore its beautiful grounds.

- Christ Church: A short distance from the lighthouse, this historic church is known for its stunning architecture and peaceful grounds. It was founded in 1736 and continues to serve the local community.

- East Beach: This popular beach is perfect for sunbathing, swimming, and enjoying the ocean. The nearby Massengale Park offers picnic areas and convenient access to the beach.

----

(79) STATE BOTANICAL GARDEN OF GEORGIA

COUNTY: CLARKE CITY: ATHENS

DATE VISITED: WHO I WENT WITH:

RATING: ☆ ☆ ☆ ☆ ☆   WILL I RETURN?   YES / NO

2450 S. Milledge Avenue
Athens, GA 30605
706-542-1244

State Botanical Garden of Georgia is a stunning 313-acre oasis located in Athens, Georgia. This beautiful garden is a part of the University of Georgia and serves as a hub for education, research, and conservation. Visitors can immerse themselves in the beauty of nature, explore diverse plant collections, and enjoy a variety of recreational activities. Whether you're a nature enthusiast, a family looking for a fun day out, or someone seeking tranquility, the State Botanical Garden has something to offer everyone.

Established in 1968, the State Botanical Garden of Georgia was created to promote the study and conservation of Georgia's diverse plant life. It has since grown to include numerous themed gardens, walking trails, and educational facilities. The State Botanical Garden features a variety of themed gardens, including:

- Flower Garden: A vibrant display of seasonal blooms showcasing the beauty of native and ornamental plants.
- Herb Garden: Discover culinary and medicinal herbs while learning about their uses and history.
- Tropical Garden: Step into a lush tropical paradise filled with exotic plants and vibrant flowers.
- Shade Garden: A serene area that highlights shade-loving plants, perfect for quiet contemplation.

The garden boasts several miles of walking trails that meander through beautiful landscapes, offering visitors a chance to connect with nature. The trails are well-maintained and provide a peaceful setting for walking, jogging, or simply enjoying the sights and sounds of nature.

The Visitor Center serves as the main hub for information and education. Here, you can learn about the garden's programs, events, and ongoing conservation efforts. The Gift Shop offers a selection of botanical-themed merchandise, books, and unique gifts that make perfect souvenirs from your visit.

The State Botanical Garden hosts a variety of educational programs throughout the year, including workshops, guided tours, and family-friendly events. Check the garden's calendar for upcoming programs that may coincide with your visit.

The garden is a haven for wildlife, including birds, butterflies, and other native species. Bring your binoculars and camera to capture the beauty of the diverse ecosystem.

Tips

- Plan your visit: Review the garden map and plan which areas you'd like to explore. Consider downloading the garden's app for interactive maps and information on plant collections.
- Dress comfortably: Wear comfortable shoes for walking and dress in layers to accommodate changing weather conditions. Don't forget sunscreen and a hat for sunny days.
- Bring a picnic: Enjoy a leisurely lunch in the garden by bringing a picnic. There are several designated picnic areas where you can relax and enjoy the natural beauty around you.
- Check the events calendar: Look for special events or workshops that may be happening during your visit. Participating in these activities can enhance your experience and provide unique learning opportunities.

Nearby Attractions

- University of Georgia: Located just a short drive away, the University of Georgia campus offers beautiful historic buildings, museums, and a vibrant college atmosphere. The Georgia Museum of Art and Founders Garden are notable spots to visit.

- Downtown Athens: Known for its eclectic mix of shops, restaurants, and music venues, downtown Athens is a great place to grab a bite to eat or explore local culture. Don't miss iconic spots like the Georgia Theatre and The Foundry.

- Sandy Creek Park: Just a few minutes away, this park offers additional outdoor recreational opportunities, including hiking trails, fishing, and picnic areas.

STATE FARM ARENA

80

COUNTY: FULTON   CITY: ATLANTA

DATE VISITED: WHO I WENT WITH:

RATING: ☆ ☆ ☆ ☆ ☆   WILL I RETURN?   YES / NO

1 State Farm Drive
Atlanta, GA 30303
404-878-3000

State Farm Arena is a premier sports and entertainment venue located in the heart of downtown Atlanta, Georgia. Known for its vibrant atmosphere and state-of-the-art facilities, the arena is home to the NBA's Atlanta Hawks and hosts a wide array of concerts, events, and shows year-round. Whether you're a sports fan, music lover, or looking for a fun outing with family and friends, State Farm Arena has something for everyone.

Originally opened as the Omni Coliseum in 1972, the arena has undergone several renovations and name changes. It was rebranded as State Farm Arena in 2018, following a significant $200 million renovation that enhanced its amenities and fan experience.

State Farm Arena hosts a wide variety of events, including:
- NBA Games: Catch the Atlanta Hawks in action as they compete against top teams in the league.
- Concerts: The arena welcomes major artists and bands for live performances across genres, from pop and rock to hip-hop and country.
- Family Shows: Enjoy family-friendly events such as Disney on Ice, Cirque du Soleil, and other touring productions.

The arena features modern amenities designed to enhance the fan experience:
- Concessions: A diverse selection of food and beverage options is available, including local favorites, healthy choices, and traditional stadium snacks.
- Merchandise Shops: Purchase official team merchandise, concert memorabilia, and unique souvenirs to commemorate your visit.
- Luxury Suites and Club Seating: For a premium experience, consider renting a luxury suite or club seat for a more upscale viewing experience with additional amenities.

State Farm Arena is committed to providing a welcoming environment for all guests. The venue is equipped with accessible seating, restrooms, and entrances. Wheelchairs are available for rent at Guest

Enjoy pre-game and post-game festivities at the arena, including interactive fan zones, live entertainment, and special events. Arrive early to soak up the atmosphere and participate in the excitement.

Tips

- Plan ahead: Check the event schedule in advance to secure tickets and plan your visit around your chosen event.
- Arrive early: Give yourself plenty of time to navigate traffic, find parking, and explore the arena before the event begins. Arriving early allows you to enjoy the pre-game atmosphere or grab a bite to eat.
- Stay hydrated: If you're attending a concert or sporting event, consider bringing a refillable water bottle. Water stations are available throughout the arena to help you stay refreshed.
- Follow arena policies: Familiarize yourself with the arena's policies on prohibited items, including outside food and drink, to ensure a smooth entry.

Nearby Attractions

- Mercedes-Benz Stadium: Just a short walk away, this state-of-the-art stadium is home to the NFL's Atlanta Falcons and hosts major events such as concerts and college football championships. Don't miss a chance to tour the stadium if time allows!

- World of Coca-Cola: Experience the history of the world-famous beverage at this interactive museum located about a mile from the arena. Sample Coca-Cola products from around the globe and explore exhibits that celebrate the brand's heritage.

- Georgia Aquarium: One of the largest aquariums in the world, the Georgia Aquarium is a must-visit attraction featuring a diverse range of marine life, including whale sharks and beluga whales. It's a fun and educational experience for visitors of all ages.

----

81 STONE MOUNTAIN CARVING

COUNTY: DEKALB **CITY:** STONE MOUNTAIN

DATE VISITED: **WHO I WENT WITH:**

RATING: ☆ ☆ ☆ ☆ ☆ **WILL I RETURN?** YES / NO

1000 Robert E. Lee Blvd
Stone Mountain, GA 30083

Stone Mountain Carving is a monumental tribute to American history and a stunning feat of artistry located in Stone Mountain Park, Georgia. The carving, which features the likenesses of three Confederate leaders—Jefferson Davis, Robert E. Lee, and Thomas "Stonewall" Jackson—has become an iconic symbol of the South. Nestled amidst beautiful natural scenery, this site offers visitors a unique blend of history, culture, and recreation.

The carving was initiated in 1923 by sculptor Gutzon Borglum, who later went on to create Mount Rushmore. The project faced numerous delays and challenges and was ultimately completed in 1972 by the Stone Mountain Memorial Association. The carving spans 90 feet high and 190 feet wide, making it the largest bas-relief sculpture in the world.

The best views of the carving can be enjoyed from several vantage points within the park. The Confederate Hall Historical & Environmental Education Center offers informative displays and the option to view the carving up close.

Enjoy scenic trails that lead to various lookout points, providing excellent opportunities for photography and appreciating the grandeur of the carving from different angles. The park features over 15 miles of trails, including the challenging hike up Stone Mountain itself, which provides breathtaking views of the surrounding area. Take a scenic skyride to the summit of Stone Mountain for panoramic views of the Atlanta skyline and the Appalachian Mountains.

In the warmer months, the park hosts a spectacular laser light show projected onto the carving, accompanied by music and pyrotechnics, creating a memorable evening experience.

The Stone Mountain Museum within the park provides a deep dive into the history of the carving and the cultural significance of the site. Exhibits include artifacts, photographs, and interactive displays that offer insights into the challenges faced during the carving's creation and the legacy of the Confederacy.

Tips

- Plan ahead: Check the weather before your visit and dress appropriately. Comfortable footwear is recommended for hiking and exploring the park.
- Bring water and snacks: While there are dining options available, packing a picnic can enhance your experience as you enjoy the natural surroundings.
- Respect the site: Given the complex history associated with the carving, visitors are encouraged to approach the site with respect and consideration for its historical context.
- Engage with park rangers: Take advantage of the knowledge of park rangers who often lead tours and offer insights into the site's history and ecology.

Nearby Attractions

- Stone Mountain Park: Beyond the carving itself, the park offers numerous activities, including picnic areas, playgrounds, and a historic train ride that provides a scenic tour of the park's natural beauty.

- Sweetwater Creek State Park: Located a short drive away, this state park features hiking trails, fishing spots, and remnants of the New Manchester Manufacturing Company, providing visitors with a blend of natural beauty and historical exploration.

- Atlanta Botanical Garden: A bit further afield, this beautiful garden showcases a variety of themed plant collections, seasonal displays, and stunning outdoor art installations. It's a perfect spot for nature lovers and families.

SUMMIT SKYRIDE

82

COUNTY: DEKALB　　　　　　　　　　　　　　　　　　　　**CITY:** STONE MOUNTAIN

DATE VISITED:　　　　　　　　　　**WHO I WENT WITH:**

　　　　RATING: ☆ ☆ ☆ ☆ ☆　　　　**WILL I RETURN?** YES / NO

1000 Robert E. Lee Blvd Stone Mountain Park
Stone Mountain, GA 30083
478-478-6686

Summit Skyride is one of the most exhilarating experiences at Stone Mountain Park in Georgia. This scenic aerial tramway takes you on an unforgettable journey to the summit of Stone Mountain, providing breathtaking views of the surrounding landscape, including the Atlanta skyline and the Blue Ridge Mountains. Whether you're an adventure seeker or a family looking for a fun outing, the Summit Skyride offers a unique perspective of this iconic landmark.

What is the Summit Skyride? The Summit Skyride is a state-of-the-art aerial tramway that transports visitors to the top of Stone Mountain, where they can enjoy panoramic views and access various activities. The ride covers a distance of about 1,200 feet and ascends approximately 825 feet in elevation.

As you ascend, you'll be treated to stunning views of the natural beauty surrounding Stone Mountain. Look out for the lush forests, serene lakes, and the distant skyline of Atlanta as you ride. The Skyride features comfortable, enclosed gondolas that accommodate up to six passengers, making it perfect for families and groups. The ride is smooth, ensuring an enjoyable experience for everyone.

Once you reach the top, you'll find a spacious observation area where you can take in the breathtaking vistas. There are plenty of photo opportunities to capture the moment. Explore the various hiking trails that lead from the summit. The Walk-up Trail is a popular choice for those seeking a challenge, offering stunning views and a closer look at the mountain's unique granite formations.

Skyride Connector: The Skyride connects visitors to several other attractions within Stone Mountain Park, including the Historic Square, Summit Snack Shack, and The Great Barn—an interactive play area for children.

Laser Show: In the summer months, don't miss the famous Stone Mountain Laser Show, which is projected onto the mountain face. The Skyride provides a great view of the show, so consider timing your visit accordingly.

Tips

- Check the weather: Since the Summit Skyride is an outdoor experience, check the weather forecast before your visit. Clear days provide the best views, while foggy or rainy conditions may limit visibility.
- Dress comfortably: Wear comfortable clothing and sturdy shoes, especially if you plan to hike or explore the summit trails after your ride.
- Capture the moment: Don't forget your camera! The views from the Skyride and the summit are spectacular, making for great photo opportunities.
- Stay hydrated: Bring a water bottle, especially during warmer months. There are refill stations at the park to keep you refreshed.

Nearby Attractions

- Stone Mountain Park: Beyond the Skyride, the park is home to a wide range of activities, including hiking, biking, and picnicking. Check out the Stone Mountain Carving, the largest bas-relief sculpture in the world.

- Historic Stone Mountain Village: Just a short drive away, this charming village features shops, restaurants, and historical sites, providing a glimpse into the area's rich history and culture.

- Sweetwater Creek State Park: Located nearby, this state park is ideal for hiking, fishing, and enjoying nature. The park's trails wind through beautiful landscapes and along the banks of Sweetwater Creek.

----

83 SWAN HOUSE

COUNTY: FULTON **CITY:** ATLANTA
DATE VISITED: **WHO I WENT WITH:**
RATING: ☆ ☆ ☆ ☆ ☆ **WILL I RETURN?** YES / NO

130 West Paces Ferry Road NW
Atlanta, GA 30305
404-814-4000

Swan House is a stunning example of classical architecture and a cherished historic site located in Atlanta, Georgia. Nestled within the beautiful Atlanta History Center, this grand estate provides visitors with a glimpse into the elegant lifestyle of the early 20th century. From its meticulously preserved interiors to its picturesque gardens, the Swan House is a must-visit for anyone interested in history, architecture, or Southern culture.

Built in 1928 for Edgar and Josephine H. Thornton, the Swan House reflects the opulence of the time. Designed by renowned architect H.entz, Reid & Adler, it features a mix of Classical Revival and Mediterranean styles. The estate was donated to the Atlanta History Center in 1966, preserving its legacy for future generations.

Guided tours are available to take you through the beautifully restored rooms of the Swan House. You'll learn about the Thornton family, the architectural details, and the history of the house itself. Tours typically last around 45 minutes and provide insights into the lifestyle and social norms of the 1920s and 1930s.

The Swan House is characterized by its grand entrance, stately columns, and elegant terraces. The iconic swan motifs throughout the estate, which inspired its name, add a whimsical touch to the sophisticated design. Inside, you'll find luxurious furnishings, original art, and intricate details that showcase the opulence of the era. Key rooms include the great hall, dining room, and library, each reflecting the Thornton family's lifestyle and the architectural trends of the time.
Gardens and Grounds

The grounds surrounding the Swan House feature meticulously manicured gardens, fountains, and pathways. The gardens are a perfect spot for leisurely strolls, photography, and enjoying nature. The gardens not only enhance the beauty of the estate but also reflect the design philosophies of the early 20th century, emphasizing the connection between architecture and nature.

Tips

- Plan your tour: Guided tours can fill up quickly, especially on weekends. It's advisable to book your tour in advance, especially if you're visiting with a large group.
- Take your time: Allow yourself time to explore the gardens and grounds after your tour. The serene environment is perfect for relaxation and reflection.
- Photography: Photography is encouraged, but be mindful of any restrictions in certain indoor areas. The gardens offer plenty of picturesque backdrops for photos.
- Dress comfortably: Wear comfortable clothing and shoes, especially if you plan to explore the grounds and gardens.

Nearby Attractions

- Atlanta History Center: The Swan House is part of the Atlanta History Center, which also includes the Kenan Research Center, Smith Family Farm, and Woodruff-Belcher Gardens. The center hosts a variety of exhibitions and programs focused on Georgia's history and culture.

- The Atlanta Botanical Garden: Just a short drive away, this stunning garden features a diverse collection of plants, themed displays, and seasonal exhibitions. Don't miss the Canopy Walk, which takes you through the treetops for a unique perspective on the garden.

- Piedmont Park: This expansive urban park offers a variety of recreational opportunities, including walking trails, sports facilities, and beautiful green spaces. It's a great place to relax or enjoy a picnic after your visit to the Swan House.

----

84 TALLULAH GORGE STATE PARK

COUNTY: RABUN **CITY:** TALLULAH FALLS

DATE VISITED: **WHO I WENT WITH:**

RATING: ☆ ☆ ☆ ☆ ☆ **WILL I RETURN?** YES / NO

338 Jane Hurt Yarn Drive
Tallulah Falls, GA 30573
706-754-7981

Tallulah Gorge State Park is a breathtaking natural wonder located in the heart of the North Georgia mountains. This stunning gorge, carved by the Tallulah River, features dramatic cliffs, cascading waterfalls, and lush forests, making it a popular destination for outdoor enthusiasts, nature lovers, and anyone seeking adventure. With a variety of recreational activities and spectacular views, Tallulah Gorge is a must-visit destination for your next trip to Georgia.

Tallulah Gorge has been a significant site for thousands of years, with evidence of Native American presence in the area. The gorge was formed over millennia through erosion, resulting in its steep cliffs and beautiful waterfalls. The park was established in 1992 to preserve its natural beauty and provide recreational opportunities.

The gorge is approximately 1,000 feet deep and 2 miles long, offering breathtaking views from various overlooks. The panoramic vistas are particularly stunning in the fall when the foliage turns vibrant shades of red and gold. The park is home to several beautiful waterfalls, including Lula Falls, Hurricane Falls, and Tugaloo Falls, each offering unique views and photo opportunities.

Tallulah Gorge features a network of trails ranging from easy strolls to challenging hikes. The Hurricane Falls Trail leads to the base of the gorge, while the North and South Rim Trails offer stunning views from above. For those seeking a challenge, the Tallulah Gorge Trail includes steep steps and rugged terrain, rewarding hikers with breathtaking views of the waterfalls and the gorge itself.

Stop by the park's visitor center to learn more about the geology, ecology, and history of Tallulah Gorge. Interactive exhibits and knowledgeable staff provide valuable information about the area. The visitor center also offers restrooms, picnic areas, and a small gift shop featuring local crafts and park souvenirs.

Tallulah Gorge is a popular destination for rock climbing, with various routes available for climbers of all skill levels. Climbers must register at the visitor center before attempting climbs.

During specific times of the year, the park allows whitewater kayaking and rafting on the Tallulah River, providing an exhilarating experience for adventure seekers. Check the park's website for water release schedules and safety guidelines.

The park's diverse ecosystems provide ample opportunities for photography and birdwatching. Bring your camera and binoculars to capture the beauty of the gorge and its wildlife, including deer, foxes, and various bird species.

Tips

- Check weather conditions: Before your visit, check the weather forecast, as conditions can change rapidly in the mountains. Dress in layers to accommodate varying temperatures throughout the day.
- Plan your hike: Choose a trail that matches your skill level and experience. Make sure to allow enough time for your hike, especially if you plan to take photographs or enjoy the scenery along the way.
- Stay hydrated: Bring enough water for your hike, especially during warmer months. There are limited water sources available on the trails.

Nearby Attractions

- Tallulah Falls: The charming town of Tallulah Falls offers scenic views and local shops. Visit the Tallulah Falls Bridge for picturesque photo opportunities of the gorge.

- Black Rock Mountain State Park: Just a short drive away, this state park features hiking trails, camping, and stunning mountain views. The Black Rock Mountain Overlook is a must-see.

- Raven Cliff Falls: Located about 30 minutes from Tallulah Gorge, this park features a scenic hike to the spectacular Raven Cliff Falls, providing a lovely day trip option for nature lovers.

----

85 TELLUS SCIENCE MUSEUM

COUNTY: BARTOW **CITY:** CARTERSVILLE

DATE VISITED: **WHO I WENT WITH:**

RATING: ☆ ☆ ☆ ☆ ☆ **WILL I RETURN?** YES / NO

100 Tellus Drive
Cartersville, GA 30120
770-606-5700

Tellus Science Museum is a fascinating destination that celebrates the wonders of science, technology, and natural history in Cartersville, Georgia. This interactive museum offers visitors of all ages the chance to explore the universe, Earth's geological wonders, and the marvels of technology through engaging exhibits, hands-on activities, and educational programs. Whether you're a science enthusiast, a curious child, or a family looking for a fun outing, Tellus Science Museum is an exciting place to discover and learn.

Founded in 2009, Tellus Science Museum is part of the Tellus Foundation, which aims to promote science education in Georgia. The museum was designed to inspire curiosity and a love of learning about the natural world and the universe.

Explore the museum's impressive collection of dinosaur fossils and learn about prehistoric life. Don't miss the life-sized dinosaur skeletons that will take you back to the Mesozoic era. Journey through the universe in the museum's SkyTrek exhibit, which features interactive displays about planets, stars, and galaxies. The planetarium offers regular shows that bring the night sky to life, showcasing constellations and celestial events.

Marvel at the dazzling display of gems, minerals, and fossils. Learn about the geological processes that shape our planet and the valuable resources found beneath our feet. Discover the forces that shape our environment, including earthquakes, volcanoes, and weather phenomena. Engaging hands-on exhibits allow you to see these processes in action.

Energy and Robotics: Delve into the world of technology with exhibits on renewable energy sources, robotics, and the science behind everyday gadgets. Kids can participate in hands-on activities that teach the principles of engineering and design.

Automobile Gallery: Explore the history of automobiles with a unique collection of vintage cars and learn about the evolution of automotive technology.

Hands-On Learning: The museum offers various hands-on activities and demonstrations throughout the day, allowing visitors to engage with science in a fun and interactive way. Check the schedule upon arrival for any special programs.

Planetarium Shows: The Tellus Planetarium features daily shows that explore different themes related to space and astronomy. These immersive experiences are perfect for visitors of all ages, offering a chance to learn more about our universe.

Special Events: The museum hosts special events throughout the year, including science fairs, family nights, and seasonal celebrations. Check the museum's website for a calendar of upcoming events to make the most of your visit.

Tips

- Plan ahead: Arrive early to take full advantage of the exhibits and activities. Check the museum's website for any special events or planetarium showtimes to schedule your day.
- Interactive experience: Encourage kids to participate in hands-on activities and demonstrations, making the learning experience more enjoyable and memorable.
- Comfortable attire: Wear comfortable shoes, as you'll be walking and exploring various exhibits throughout the day. Dress in layers to accommodate the temperature inside the museum and outside.

Nearby Attractions

- Etowah Indian Mounds: Located just a short drive away, this archaeological site offers a glimpse into the lives of the Native American tribes that once inhabited the region. Visitors can explore the mounds, museum, and walking trails along the Etowah River.

- Red Top Mountain State Park: This beautiful state park is located on Lake Allatoona and offers hiking trails, fishing, and picnicking opportunities. It's a perfect spot for outdoor enthusiasts looking to unwind after a visit to the museum.

- Barnsley Resort: For a touch of luxury, visit Barnsley Resort, which features beautiful gardens, hiking trails, and fine dining. The resort is a great place to relax and enjoy nature after a day of learning.

86. THE OLD SORREL WEED HOUSE MUSEUM & TOURS

COUNTY: CHATHAM   **CITY:** SAVANNAH

DATE VISITED: **WHO I WENT WITH:**

RATING: ☆ ☆ ☆ ☆ ☆   **WILL I RETURN?** YES / NO

6 West Harris St
Savannah, GA 31401
912-257-2223

Old Sorrel Weed House Museum & Tours is a historical gem located in the heart of Savannah, Georgia. This beautifully preserved house is one of the finest examples of antebellum architecture in the city and offers a unique glimpse into the past. With its intriguing history, stunning architecture, and stories of the people who lived here, the Old Sorrel Weed House is a must-visit for history buffs and anyone looking to immerse themselves in Savannah's rich cultural heritage.

Built in the 1840s by successful businessman Francis Sorrel, the Old Sorrel Weed House has a fascinating history, including tales of tragedy, love, and the paranormal. It is reputed to be one of Savannah's most haunted locations, adding to its allure as a historical site. The house is named after its original owner and has been meticulously restored to reflect its original grandeur.

Explore the house through guided tours that provide insight into its history, architecture, and the lives of its former residents. Knowledgeable guides share captivating stories about the Sorrel family, the house's design, and its role in Savannah's history. For those interested in the supernatural, the Old Sorrel Weed House offers special paranormal tours that delve into its ghostly legends and reported hauntings. Learn about the eerie experiences reported by visitors and staff, making for a spine-tingling adventure.

The house features stunning Greek Revival architecture, characterized by its grand columns, spacious verandas, and elaborate decorative details. Take your time to admire the craftsmanship and learn about the architectural elements that define this historical treasure. The museum's restoration efforts have preserved many original features, including antique furnishings, intricate plasterwork, and period-appropriate decor, providing an authentic glimpse into 19th-century life.

Throughout the house, visitors can view a collection of artifacts and memorabilia that showcase the Sorrel family's history and the social context of their time. These items contribute to a deeper understanding of life in Savannah during the antebellum period.

Engage with the past through storytelling sessions that bring to life the experiences of the Sorrel family and other historical figures connected to the house. These sessions often include personal anecdotes and dramatic reenactments.

The picturesque architecture and charming gardens provide ample opportunities for photography. Capture the beauty of the Old Sorrel Weed House and its surroundings, making for great memories of your visit.

The museum hosts various special events throughout the year, including holiday celebrations, educational workshops, and themed tours. Check the museum's website for a calendar of upcoming events and activities.

Tips

- Plan your tour: Arrive early to ensure you have enough time to explore the house and grounds. Consider booking your tour in advance, especially for popular paranormal tours, as they can fill up quickly.
- Engage with guides: Don't hesitate to ask questions during your tour. The guides are knowledgeable and eager to share fascinating stories and details about the house and its history.
- Wear comfortable shoes: You may be walking through the house and its gardens, so wear comfortable shoes to make the most of your visit.

Nearby Attractions

- Savannah History Museum: Located just a short distance away, this museum offers a comprehensive look at Savannah's history, featuring exhibits on everything from the American Revolution to the Civil War.

- Forsyth Park: A short walk from the museum, Forsyth Park is a beautiful green space perfect for a leisurely stroll, picnic, or simply enjoying the iconic fountain and surrounding oak trees draped with Spanish moss.

- Bonaventure Cemetery: Just a short drive away, this famous cemetery is known for its stunning monuments, historical significance, and hauntingly beautiful landscapes. It's a serene place to explore and reflect.

THE OLDE PINK HOUSE

87

COUNTY: CHATHAM **CITY:** SAVANNAH

DATE VISITED: **WHO I WENT WITH:**

RATING: ☆ ☆ ☆ ☆ ☆ **WILL I RETURN?** YES / NO

23 Abercorn St
Savannah, GA 31401
912-232-4286

The Olde Pink House is one of Savannah's most iconic and charming restaurants. Located in a beautifully restored 18th-century mansion, this historic venue combines fine dining with rich Southern hospitality and a touch of local history. Whether you're a food enthusiast or a history buff, The Olde Pink House promises a unique culinary experience in an enchanting atmosphere.

Built in 1771, The Olde Pink House is one of Savannah's oldest structures. Originally serving as a residence for the Habersham family, it has witnessed significant events in the city's history. The house was transformed into a restaurant in 1979 and has since become a beloved culinary destination.

The Olde Pink House features classic Southern architecture with its iconic pink exterior, beautiful ironwork, and inviting front porch. Inside, you'll find elegant dining rooms adorned with antique furnishings and period decor that reflect the home's storied past. Dine in one of several rooms, each with its own character. From the cozy parlor to the elegant dining room, each space offers a warm and inviting atmosphere perfect for a romantic dinner or special occasion.

The menu at The Olde Pink House showcases the best of Southern cuisine, featuring local ingredients and traditional recipes. Signature dishes include fried green tomatoes, shrimp and grits, and pecan-crusted fish. For those looking to experience a range of flavors, consider trying the chef's tasting menu, which offers a curated selection of the restaurant's finest dishes paired with wine.

The bar offers an extensive selection of craft cocktails, featuring local spirits and innovative mixes. Try the restaurant's signature drinks, which often incorporate seasonal ingredients for a unique twist. The Olde Pink House boasts an impressive wine list, carefully curated to complement the menu and enhance your dining experience.

Due to the popularity of The Olde Pink House, it is highly recommended to make reservations in advance, especially during peak dining hours or special occasions.

Online booking is available through their website.

While primarily a restaurant, The Olde Pink House also offers occasional historical tours that delve into the rich history of the building and its significance in Savannah. Check their website for any scheduled tours during your visit.

The restaurant hosts special events throughout the year, including themed dinners, holiday celebrations, and wine tastings. Keep an eye on their event calendar for opportunities to enjoy unique dining experiences.

Tips

- Make reservations: Plan ahead and secure your reservation early, especially during weekends or busy tourist seasons. This ensures you won't miss out on the chance to dine in this iconic establishment.
- Arrive early: Arriving a bit early allows you to explore the exterior of the building and take photos, as well as enjoy a pre-dinner drink at the bar.
- Try the specials: Be sure to ask about daily specials, as the chef often creates unique dishes using seasonal ingredients that are not on the regular menu.

Nearby Attractions

- Savannah Historic District: Stroll through the picturesque streets of Savannah's historic district, where you can admire beautifully preserved architecture, charming squares, and lush parks.

- Chippewa Square: Just a short walk away, this iconic square is famous for its role in the movie Forrest Gump. It's a perfect spot to relax and enjoy the sights of Savannah.

- Forsyth Park: A bit further down, Forsyth Park offers beautiful walking paths, fountains, and plenty of green space to unwind after your meal. Don't forget to take a photo with the iconic Forsyth Fountain.

----

88 TOCCOA FALLS

COUNTY: STEPHENS　　　　　　　　　　　　　　　　　　　　　**CITY:** TOCCOA

DATE VISITED:　　　　　　　　　　　**WHO I WENT WITH:**

RATING: ☆ ☆ ☆ ☆ ☆　　　　**WILL I RETURN?**　YES / NO

107 Kincaid Dr campus of Toccoa Falls College
Toccoa, GA 30598
706-914-8679

Toccoa Falls is one of Georgia's most stunning natural attractions! Nestled in the picturesque Toccoa Falls College campus, this breathtaking waterfall is the highest in the state, cascading 186 feet into a serene pool below. With its breathtaking beauty and tranquil surroundings, Toccoa Falls is a must-visit destination for nature lovers, hikers, and anyone seeking a peaceful escape.

The area around Toccoa Falls has a rich history, with Native American roots and early European settlers. The waterfall is named after the Toccoa River, and its beauty has attracted visitors for generations. The falls are also known for the legend of the "Toccoa Falls," which speaks of a tragic love story intertwined with the landscape.

Toccoa Falls is renowned for its majestic drop and picturesque surroundings. Visitors can enjoy various vantage points for photography, allowing you to capture the natural beauty of the falls. The area is surrounded by beautiful gardens, walking paths, and wooded areas, making it a serene setting for relaxation and contemplation.

The Toccoa Falls Visitor Center offers information about the falls, the history of the area, and details about the local flora and fauna. You can also find helpful staff members who can answer questions and provide guidance for your visit.

A short, well-maintained walking path leads from the Visitor Center to the base of the falls. The trail is easy to navigate, making it suitable for visitors of all ages. Take a leisurely stroll through the surrounding woods, where you can enjoy the sights and sounds of nature. Keep an eye out for local wildlife and various plant species along the way.

There are designated picnic areas where you can enjoy a meal surrounded by the beauty of nature. Bring your lunch and unwind while soaking in the peaceful atmosphere.

The falls and surrounding landscape provide numerous opportunities for stunning photographs. Early morning or late afternoon offers the best lighting for capturing the falls' beauty.

Toccoa Falls College occasionally hosts events and festivals throughout the year, including concerts, educational programs, and seasonal celebrations. Check their website or contact the Visitor Center for information on upcoming events.

Tips

- Wear comfortable shoes: The short walk to the falls is relatively easy, but comfortable footwear is recommended for the best experience.
- Bring water and snacks: Staying hydrated and having a few snacks on hand will enhance your visit, especially if you plan to explore the surrounding area.
- Plan for weather: Check the weather forecast before your visit, as rain can affect trail conditions. Dress in layers, as temperatures can fluctuate throughout the day.

Nearby Attractions

- Currahee Mountain: Located just a short drive away, Currahee Mountain offers hiking trails with stunning panoramic views of the surrounding area. The mountain has historical significance as it was a training site for paratroopers during World War II.

- Toccoa River: Enjoy outdoor activities such as fishing, kayaking, and tubing along the scenic Toccoa River. Several outfitters in the area offer equipment rentals and guided tours.

- Toccoa Train Depot: Visit the historic Toccoa Train Depot, which dates back to the 1800s and is now a museum. Learn about the area's railway history and its significance to Toccoa's development.

----

89 TOCCOA RIVER SWINGING BRIDGE

COUNTY: FANNIN　　　　　　　　　　　　　　　　**CITY:** BLUE RIDGE

DATE VISITED:　　　　　　**WHO I WENT WITH:**

RATING: ☆ ☆ ☆ ☆ ☆　　　**WILL I RETURN?** YES / NO

Hwy 60 Benton MacKaye Trail
Blue Ridge, GA 30513

Toccoa River Swinging Bridge is a captivating destination that offers a unique blend of adventure and stunning natural beauty. Spanning the Toccoa River in Blue Ridge, Georgia, this swinging bridge is an exhilarating way to experience the breathtaking views of the surrounding mountains and lush landscapes. Whether you're an outdoor enthusiast or just looking for a memorable outing, this attraction is sure to impress.

Originally built in 1970 as part of a local hiking trail, the bridge has become a beloved spot for visitors seeking adventure and scenic views. The bridge spans approximately 270 feet and offers a thrilling experience as you walk across it.

As you traverse the bridge, enjoy breathtaking views of the Toccoa River and the surrounding mountains. The sights change with the seasons, from vibrant fall foliage to the lush greens of summer, making it a great destination year-round. Capture the beauty of the river, the bridge, and the landscape from various angles. The unique perspective from the bridge offers fantastic photo opportunities.

The bridge sways gently as you walk, adding an element of excitement to your crossing. It's a fun experience for both children and adults, making it an ideal spot for families. After crossing the bridge, explore the surrounding hiking trails that wind along the river. There are several trails ranging in difficulty, perfect for both novice and experienced hikers.

Enjoy a picnic by the river. There are designated areas with picnic tables and benches where you can relax, have lunch, and soak in the tranquil atmosphere.

The Toccoa River is known for its excellent fishing opportunities. Bring your fishing gear and try your luck at catching trout and other species in the river. Ensure you have the appropriate fishing license if you plan to fish.

For the more adventurous, consider renting a kayak or inner tube to explore the

Toccoa River. Paddling or floating down the river provides a unique perspective and allows you to enjoy the scenery from the water.

Keep an eye out for local wildlife along the river and in the surrounding woods. You might spot deer, various bird species, and other animals that call this area home.

Tips

- Dress for the weather: Wear appropriate clothing and sturdy shoes, especially if you plan to hike or spend time outdoors. Be prepared for changes in weather, as conditions can vary throughout the day.
- Bring water and snacks: Staying hydrated and having snacks on hand will enhance your visit, especially if you plan to hike or spend time exploring the area.
- Plan your timing: Visiting during weekdays or early mornings can help you avoid crowds, allowing for a more peaceful experience on the bridge and surrounding areas.

Nearby Attractions

- Blue Ridge Lake: Just a short drive away, Blue Ridge Lake offers opportunities for boating, fishing, and hiking. The scenic views around the lake are perfect for a relaxing afternoon.

- Blue Ridge Scenic Railway: Experience the beauty of the North Georgia mountains by taking a scenic train ride on the Blue Ridge Scenic Railway. Enjoy stunning views of the countryside as you travel along the Toccoa River.

- Aska Adventure Area: This outdoor recreation area features hiking, biking, and more. With various trails and breathtaking scenery, it's perfect for those looking to immerse themselves in nature.

----

90 TYBEE ISLAND LIGHT STATION AND MUSEUM

COUNTY: CHATHAM	CITY: TYBEE ISLAND
DATE VISITED:	WHO I WENT WITH:
RATING: ☆ ☆ ☆ ☆ ☆	WILL I RETURN? YES / NO

30 Meddin Dr
Tybee Island, GA 31328
912-786-5801

Tybee Island Light Station and Museum is one of Georgia's most iconic landmarks. Located on the scenic Tybee Island, this historic lighthouse has guided mariners for over 270 years, making it a must-visit destination for history enthusiasts, beachgoers, and families alike. Explore the fascinating history, breathtaking views, and unique experiences that await you at this coastal gem.

Constructed in 1736, the lighthouse has undergone several renovations and restorations throughout its history. The current structure was built in 1916 and stands 154 feet tall, offering a glimpse into the maritime heritage of the region.

Visitors can climb the 178 steps to the top of the lighthouse for a panoramic view of Tybee Island and the Atlantic Ocean. The experience is exhilarating, and the view is well worth the effort. The lighthouse features its original Fresnel lens, which is on display for visitors to admire. Learn about the technology used in lighthouses and the significance of lightkeeping in maritime history.

The museum houses a collection of maritime artifacts, photographs, and displays that tell the story of Tybee Island's history and its role as a vital navigational aid. Explore the exhibits that highlight the life of lighthouse keepers and the maritime culture of the area. Don't forget to stop by the gift shop for unique souvenirs, local crafts, and maritime-themed items to remember your visit.

The lighthouse grounds include several historic buildings, such as the Lighthouse Keeper's Cottage and the Oil House, which are part of the museum complex. Enjoy the beautifully landscaped gardens surrounding the lighthouse, which provide a perfect spot for photos and relaxation.

Guided tours are available and provide in-depth information about the lighthouse's history, the surrounding area, and the importance of maritime navigation. Tours are offered during peak season and on weekends.

The picturesque lighthouse and its stunning surroundings make for excellent photography opportunities. Early morning or late afternoon is the best time for capturing the perfect shot.

The Tybee Island Light Station hosts various events throughout the year, including educational programs, lighthouse tours, and community gatherings. Check their website for upcoming events and activities.

Tips

- Wear comfortable shoes: The climb to the top of the lighthouse requires sturdy footwear. Make sure to wear comfortable shoes for the best experience.
- Check the weather: Since many activities are outdoors, check the weather forecast before your visit. Be prepared for sunny conditions and bring sunscreen, especially during the summer months.
- Bring water and snacks: Staying hydrated and having snacks on hand will enhance your visit, especially if you plan to spend time exploring the area.

Nearby Attractions

- Tybee Island Beach: Enjoy the sun, sand, and surf at Tybee Island's beautiful beaches. Spend a day swimming, sunbathing, or beachcombing along the coast.

- Fort Pulaski National Monument: Just a short drive away, Fort Pulaski is a well-preserved Civil War fort that offers historical exhibits, walking trails, and stunning views of the Savannah River. It's a great spot for history buffs and outdoor enthusiasts alike.

- Dolphin Tours: Explore the waters around Tybee Island by taking a dolphin-watching tour. These tours provide a unique opportunity to see dolphins in their natural habitat and learn about the local ecosystem.

----

91 UHUBURG

COUNTY: WHITE   **CITY:** HELEN

DATE VISITED: **WHO I WENT WITH:**

RATING: ☆ ☆ ☆ ☆ ☆   **WILL I RETURN?** YES / NO

571 Ridge Road
Helen, GA 30545
312-339-5878

Nestled in the picturesque landscape of Georgia, Uhuburg is a stunning Renaissance castle that serves as a remarkable testament to the country's rich history and architectural heritage. This hidden gem, often overlooked by travelers, offers a unique glimpse into the past and is an essential stop for history enthusiasts and adventurers alike.

Uhuburg Castle, constructed during the Renaissance period, dates back to the 16th century. It was built as a strategic fortress to protect the region from invaders and has witnessed countless historical events. The castle is named after the nearby village of Uhuburg, which adds to its charm and allure. Over the centuries, the castle has undergone various renovations, preserving its original architecture while adapting to modern needs.

The castle showcases classic Renaissance architecture characterized by its symmetrical design, elegant arches, and intricate stone carvings. Visitors will be captivated by the stunning facades, the grand entrance, and the well-preserved interiors that reflect the opulence of the era. The castle's towers offer panoramic views of the surrounding valleys and mountains, making it a perfect spot for photography enthusiasts.

Uhuburg Castle was strategically built on a hilltop, providing a commanding view of the surrounding valleys and mountain passes. This location not only made it a formidable fortress against invaders but also allowed for effective communication and signal relay between nearby settlements.

The castle features a blend of local architectural styles and influences from the Italian Renaissance, which is evident in its ornate stonework, large windows, and grand entrance. The use of natural materials, such as local stone, enhances its harmony with the surrounding landscape.

Throughout its history, Uhuburg has served various roles, from a military stronghold to a royal residence. It has been associated with several prominent historical figures in Georgian history, including noble families and military leaders who played crucial roles in the region's defense.

In recent years, significant restoration efforts have been undertaken to preserve the castle's structure and historical features. These initiatives aim to maintain the castle's integrity while making it accessible to the public, allowing visitors to appreciate its history and beauty.

Uhuburg Castle is steeped in local legends and folklore. Stories of secret passages, hidden treasures, and ghostly apparitions add an air of mystery to the site. Local guides often share these tales, enhancing the visitor experience with a sense of adventure.

The castle is not just a historical site; it also serves as a cultural hub for the region. It hosts various art exhibitions, music festivals, and traditional performances that celebrate Georgian culture. These events provide an opportunity for visitors to engage with local artists and experience the vibrant traditions of the area.

The natural beauty surrounding Uhuburg Castle is breathtaking. Visitors can enjoy hiking trails that lead through lush forests and offer stunning views of the nearby mountains. The area is also rich in biodiversity, making it a great spot for nature enthusiasts and photographers.

After exploring the castle, visitors can indulge in local Georgian cuisine at nearby restaurants. Traditional dishes, such as khachapuri (cheese-filled bread) and khinkali (dumplings), are a must-try. Pairing these dishes with local wines offers a delightful culinary experience.

Uhuburg Castle is equipped with visitor facilities, including information centers, rest areas, and gift shops. Visitors can find souvenirs, local crafts, and historical books about the castle and the region.

Tips

- Dress comfortably: Wear comfortable shoes for exploring the castle grounds and surrounding areas.
- Photography: Bring a camera to capture the stunning architecture and beautiful landscapes.

Nearby Attractions

- Unicoi State Park: Just a short drive from Uhuburg, Unicoi State Park is a beautiful natural area offering a variety of outdoor activities. Visitors can enjoy hiking trails, fishing, and kayaking in the park's serene lake. The park features stunning mountain views, picnic areas, and access to the Anna Ruby Falls, where two waterfalls cascade into a picturesque setting, making it a perfect spot for nature lovers.

- Helen Tubing & Waterpark: Located in the heart of Helen, this popular attraction offers a fun-filled day for families and thrill-seekers alike. Guests can float down the Chattahoochee River in inflatable tubes or enjoy the water slides and pools at the waterpark. It's a great way to relax during the summer months and experience the charming Bavarian-style village of Helen.

- Nacoochee Village Antique Mall: Just a few minutes from Uhuburg, this antique mall is a treasure trove for those interested in vintage finds and unique collectibles. The mall features a wide variety of antiques, from furniture to jewelry, making it an ideal spot for browsing and discovering hidden gems. Additionally, visitors can enjoy local art and handmade crafts, offering a glimpse into the creative spirit of the region.

92 UNICOI STATE PARK

COUNTY: WHITE **CITY:** HELEN

DATE VISITED: **WHO I WENT WITH:**

RATING: ☆ ☆ ☆ ☆ ☆ **WILL I RETURN?** YES / NO

1788 Highway 356
Helen, GA 30545
706-878-2201

Unicoi State Park is a top destination for outdoor enthusiasts, families, and anyone looking to immerse themselves in nature. Covering over 1,000 acres of pristine forestland, the park offers a variety of activities, breathtaking scenery, and a perfect escape from the hustle and bustle of everyday life. Whether you're seeking adventure or simply a peaceful retreat, Unicoi State Park has something for everyone.

Unicoi State Park is located just outside the charming town of Helen, Georgia, about 90 miles northeast of Atlanta. The park's proximity to Helen makes it an ideal spot for those wanting to combine natural exploration with the town's unique Bavarian-inspired atmosphere.

Unicoi State Park is renowned for its diverse activities and natural beauty. Whether you're looking to hike, fish, or simply relax, there's something here for everyone.

The park boasts over 12 miles of hiking trails, catering to all skill levels. Some of the most popular trails include:

- Unicoi Lake Loop Trail: This moderate 2.5-mile loop encircles the beautiful Unicoi Lake, offering stunning views of the water and surrounding mountains. It's perfect for a relaxing walk or morning jog.
- Anna Ruby Falls Trail: A short drive from the park, this easy 0.8-mile trail leads to the breathtaking Anna Ruby Falls, a twin waterfall that's one of the region's most iconic natural features.
- Smith Creek Trail: For a more challenging adventure, this 8-mile trail connects Unicoi State Park to Anna Ruby Falls and takes hikers through lush forests, creeks, and mountain ridges.

At the heart of the park lies Unicoi Lake, a sparkling 53-acre lake that provides a serene setting for various water-based activities. Rentals are available for kayaks, canoes, and paddleboards. Glide across the peaceful waters while soaking in the scenic beauty that surrounds you. Unicoi Lake is stocked with trout, bass, and other fish, making it a haven for anglers. Whether you're a seasoned fisherman or a beginner, the lake offers excellent opportunities to cast a line. During warmer months, visitors can cool off in the designated swimming area, complete with a sandy beach.

For thrill-seekers, Unicoi offers a Zipline Adventure that takes you soaring through the treetops. With multiple ziplines ranging from beginner to advanced, this exhilarating activity provides a unique perspective of the park's natural beauty.

Unicoi has well-maintained campgrounds that cater to both tent campers and RVs. Each site is equipped with modern amenities like electrical hookups, picnic tables, and fire pits.

For those seeking a more comfortable stay, the lodge offers cozy accommodations with beautiful views of the surrounding mountains and lake.

The park also features rustic cabins, which provide a more secluded and peaceful retreat for families or groups.

Unicoi State Park is home to a diverse array of wildlife, including deer, wild turkeys, and various species of birds. Birdwatchers will enjoy spotting native species such as woodpeckers, hawks, and songbirds. The park's tranquil environment makes it ideal for wildlife observation.

Tips

- Plan ahead: Unicoi State Park is a popular destination, especially during weekends and holidays. Make reservations for camping or lodging well in advance to ensure availability.
- Dress appropriately: The weather in the mountains can be unpredictable. Bring layers and be prepared for cooler temperatures in the evenings, even in the summer.
- Bring a camera: With its stunning landscapes, wildlife, and lake views, Unicoi State Park offers plenty of photo-worthy moments.
- Pack for adventure: If you plan on hiking or engaging in outdoor activities, bring essentials like water, snacks, sunscreen, and insect repellent.

Nearby Attractions

- Helen, Georgia: Just a few miles from the park, the town of Helen is a Bavarian-themed village known for its unique architecture, shops, and restaurants. Stroll through the streets, enjoy German-inspired cuisine, or visit during one of the town's many festivals, including the famous Oktoberfest.

- Anna Ruby Falls: Located in the nearby Chattahoochee National Forest, Anna Ruby Falls is a must-visit attraction. The twin waterfalls cascade down from Tray Mountain, offering a picturesque spot for photography and relaxation. The easy, paved trail makes it accessible for visitors of all ages.

- Smithgall Woods State Park: Just a short drive away, this park offers more hiking, fishing, and nature exploration opportunities. It's especially known for its trout fishing in Dukes Creek, one of Georgia's premier trout streams.

VOGEL STATE PARK

93

COUNTY: UNION   CITY: BLAIRSVILLE

DATE VISITED: WHO I WENT WITH:

           RATING: ☆ ☆ ☆ ☆ ☆   WILL I RETURN?   YES / NO

405 Vogel State Park Road
Blairsville, GA 30512
706-745-2628

Vogel State Park is one of Georgia's oldest and most picturesque state parks. With its stunning natural landscapes, tranquil lake, and proximity to the Appalachian Trail, Vogel is a beloved destination for hikers, campers, and outdoor enthusiasts. The park offers a perfect combination of scenic beauty, rich history, and outdoor adventure, making it a must-visit for anyone looking to experience the best of Georgia's natural wonders.

Vogel State Park is situated at the base of Blood Mountain, Georgia's highest summit on the Appalachian Trail. It's located about 12 miles south of Blairsville and approximately 2 hours north of Atlanta, making it a convenient getaway for city dwellers looking for a refreshing escape into nature.

Vogel State Park is a hub for outdoor activities, with a variety of experiences to suit every kind of traveler. Whether you're an avid hiker, a fishing enthusiast, or simply looking for a peaceful retreat, the park has something to offer.

Vogel is renowned for its exceptional hiking opportunities, with several trails that wind through the park's forested landscape. Some of the most popular trails include:

- Bear Hair Gap Trail: This 4-mile loop is a moderately difficult hike that offers spectacular views of the surrounding mountains and Vogel Lake. It's perfect for hikers looking to experience both the beauty and challenge of the region.
- Trahlyta Lake Trail: An easy 1-mile loop that circles Lake Trahlyta, offering picturesque views of the lake and the mountains. The trail also leads to the Trahlyta Waterfall, a must-see feature that cascades down from the lake's dam.
- Coosa Backcountry Trail: For more seasoned hikers, this strenuous 12.9-mile trail loops through the rugged terrain of the Chattahoochee National Forest. It's a challenging hike that rewards visitors with serene wilderness and incredible mountain vistas.

One of the highlights of Vogel State Park is Lake Trahlyta, a 22-acre mountain lake that offers a peaceful setting for a variety of water activities.

The lake is stocked with trout and other fish, making it a popular spot for anglers. Whether you're fishing from the shore or a boat, the lake provides excellent opportunities for catching a variety of fish.

Rentals for kayaks and paddleboards are available, allowing visitors to explore the calm waters while taking in the breathtaking views of Blood Mountain.

In the summer months, there is a designated swimming area for those who want to cool off in the clear mountain waters. The beach area is perfect for families and children.

Vogel offers a range of accommodations to suit all types of campers, from rustic tent sites to cozy cabins.

The park features more than 90 campsites for tents and RVs, complete with water, electricity, picnic tables, and fire rings. The campgrounds are nestled among the trees, providing a peaceful and natural setting.

For a more comfortable stay, the park has 35 charming cottages that range from one to three bedrooms. These fully equipped cottages provide a cozy and private retreat, with some offering beautiful views of the lake.

For group camping or those seeking a more rugged experience, the park also has pioneer campgrounds, which are more secluded and perfect for scout groups or large gatherings.

Vogel State Park is home to a wide array of wildlife. Visitors might spot deer, wild turkeys, and various bird species, including hawks and woodpeckers. The park's quiet and natural surroundings make it an excellent spot for birdwatching and wildlife photography.

With several scenic picnic areas scattered throughout the park, Vogel is an ideal spot for a relaxing picnic. There are both lakeside and forested spots to choose from, many of which offer grills and tables for a convenient outdoor meal.

Tips

- Visit in fall: Vogel State Park is particularly beautiful in the fall, when the forest explodes with vibrant hues of red, orange, and yellow. The park's scenic trails and

lake offer incredible opportunities for fall foliage photography.
- Pack for hiking: If you plan on hiking, especially on more challenging trails like Coosa Backcountry Trail, be sure to bring plenty of water, snacks, and sturdy footwear.
- Check the weather: The weather in the mountains can change quickly, so it's a good idea to check the forecast before heading out, especially if you plan on camping or hiking longer trails.
- Plan for weekends: Vogel State Park is a popular destination, especially on weekends and holidays. Arrive early or consider visiting during the week if you prefer a quieter experience.

Nearby Attractions

- Blood Mountain: Just a short drive from Vogel, Blood Mountain is the highest peak on Georgia's section of the Appalachian Trail. The hike to the summit is challenging but rewards hikers with panoramic views of the surrounding mountains and valleys.

- Helton Creek Falls: Located just a few miles from the park, this beautiful double waterfall is easily accessible via a short hike. It's a perfect spot for photography or a peaceful break during your adventures.

- Brasstown Bald: Georgia's highest point, Brasstown Bald, is located about 30 minutes from Vogel. A short but steep trail leads to an observation tower at the summit, offering 360-degree views of the surrounding mountains. On clear days, you can see into four states.

94 WEBB MILITARY MUSEUM

COUNTY: CHATHAM **CITY:** SAVANNAH

DATE VISITED: **WHO I WENT WITH:**

RATING: ☆ ☆ ☆ ☆ ☆ **WILL I RETURN?** YES / NO

411 E. York Street
Savannah, GA 31401
912-663-0398

Webb Military Museum is a unique and captivating museum in the heart of Savannah, Georgia. This one-of-a-kind museum is dedicated to honoring the brave men and women who served in the armed forces. Featuring an extensive collection of military artifacts from the Civil War to modern-day conflicts, the Webb Military Museum offers a personal and insightful look into the history of warfare and the soldiers who fought in it. Whether you're a history enthusiast, a military veteran, or simply curious about military history, this museum is a must-see destination.

Founded by Gary Webb, a passionate collector of military memorabilia, the museum opened in 2015. Webb's interest in military history began as a child, inspired by family members who served in the armed forces. Over the years, his collection grew into a vast array of uniforms, medals, weapons, and personal items from various conflicts. Today, the Webb Military Museum stands as a tribute to the sacrifices made by soldiers throughout history, providing visitors with a personal connection to the individuals who served.

The museum showcases an extensive collection spanning several conflicts, including the Civil War, World Wars I and II, the Korean War, the Vietnam War, and the Gulf War. Each display offers a detailed look into the experiences of soldiers during these periods. What sets the Webb Military Museum apart is its focus on personal items from soldiers. Uniforms, letters, and photos give visitors a humanized view of war, offering a personal connection to the stories behind the artifacts.

The largest section of the museum is dedicated to World War II, featuring uniforms, helmets, and equipment from both Allied and Axis forces. You'll find items from the U.S., Germany, Britain, Russia, and Japan, making this section a fascinating insight into the global nature of the conflict. The Civil War section is particularly poignant, given Savannah's historical significance during the conflict. The museum features Confederate and Union uniforms, weapons, and personal letters, highlighting the personal toll of the war.

While many museums discourage touching artifacts, the Webb Military Museum allows visitors to interact with certain exhibits. You'll have the opportunity to hold replica items, like helmets and canteens, for a more immersive experience. Knowledgeable staff offer guided tours of the museum, sharing in-depth stories about the artifacts and the soldiers who owned them. The personal anecdotes provided during the tour make the visit even more enriching.

The museum frequently hosts events featuring local veterans who share their personal stories. These sessions provide visitors with a rare opportunity to hear firsthand accounts of military service. The Webb Military Museum also offers educational programs for school groups, focusing on the historical significance of the items in the museum and providing an engaging learning experience for students of all ages.

Photography is encouraged at the Webb Military Museum, allowing visitors to capture the remarkable artifacts on display. The museum's lighting and setup make it easy to take great photos of the exhibits, so be sure to bring your camera.

Tips

- Allow time to explore: Plan to spend at least an hour exploring the museum's detailed exhibits. If you're a military history enthusiast, you may want to allow more time to fully appreciate the collection.
- Comfortable shoes: The museum is housed in a historic building, so comfortable shoes are recommended for walking around the exhibits.
- Check for special events: Be sure to ask about any special events or talks happening during your visit. These can add an extra layer of enjoyment and education to your experience.

Nearby Attractions

- Forsyth Park: Just a short walk away, Forsyth Park is one of Savannah's most iconic landmarks. Its famous fountain and beautiful green spaces offer a peaceful retreat after your museum visit.

- Savannah History Museum: Learn more about Savannah's rich past at the Savannah History Museum, located nearby in the old Central of Georgia Railway Station.

- Colonial Park Cemetery: History buffs may also enjoy a visit to Colonial Park Cemetery, which dates back to 1750 and is the resting place of many notable figures from Savannah's early history.

95 WILD ADVENTURES THEME PARK

COUNTY: LOWNDES **CITY:** VALDOSTA

DATE VISITED: **WHO I WENT WITH:**

RATING: ☆ ☆ ☆ ☆ ☆ **WILL I RETURN?** YES / NO

3766 Old Clyattville Road
Valdosta, GA 31601
229-219-7080

Wild Adventures Theme Park is one of Georgia's premier family-friendly destinations. Located in Valdosta, this exciting theme park combines thrilling roller coasters, live animal exhibits, and a water park all in one location. Wild Adventures is perfect for visitors of all ages, offering a blend of high-energy rides, wildlife experiences, and seasonal events. Whether you're seeking adrenaline-pumping thrills, a refreshing splash in the water park, or a day of family fun, Wild Adventures has something for everyone.

Originally opened in 1996, Wild Adventures began as a small animal park but has since expanded into one of Georgia's most popular attractions, offering not just animals but also thrilling rides, water attractions, and live entertainment. Over the years, the park has grown to include more than 40 rides, hundreds of animals, and a host of events that draw visitors from across the Southeast.

Wild Adventures is home to several roller coasters that provide heart-pounding excitement. The park's standout attraction, the "Cheetah," is a wooden coaster that reaches speeds of up to 60 mph, offering a fast and wild ride through the trees. Other thrilling rides include the "Boomerang," a steel coaster that takes riders through multiple loops both forwards and backwards, and "Swamp Thing," a suspended coaster that lets your feet dangle as you twist and turn above the park.

For those looking for milder fun, Wild Adventures offers a range of rides suitable for families and younger children. "Safari Train" provides a relaxing tour around the park, and "Rattler" is a mini coaster perfect for little thrill-seekers. The Ferris Wheel, bumper cars, and carousel are also great options for family-friendly fun.

Splash Island, Wild Adventures' water park, is a perfect way to cool off during the hot Georgia summer. The park features thrilling water slides like the "Kona Cliffs," which sends riders speeding down twisting turns, and "Hakini Rapids," a high-speed multi-lane racer slide. For a more relaxing experience, visitors can float down the "Paradise River" or enjoy the waves in the massive "Catchawave Bay."

Splash Island also features several areas designed just for younger visitors, including "Wahee Cyclone," a splash-filled playground, and "Bongo Bay," which offers shallow pools and mini slides for little ones.

Wildlife Encounters

In addition to its rides, Wild Adventures is also a zoo. The park features a variety of animals from around the world, including giraffes, tigers, zebras, and exotic birds. The "Safari Train" ride takes visitors through the animal habitats, providing an up-close look at these amazing creatures. Wild Adventures offers hands-on experiences for animal lovers, including the opportunity to feed giraffes and visit the petting zoo, where kids can meet friendly goats, sheep, and other barnyard animals.

Wild Adventures features live entertainment throughout the park, with daily shows that include everything from animal demonstrations to high-energy musical performances. The "Tigers of India" show is a crowd favorite, showcasing the power and agility of Bengal tigers.

Throughout the year, Wild Adventures hosts a variety of special events and festivals, including the popular "Wild Adventures Christmas," with dazzling light displays and holiday performances, and the spooky "Terror in the Wild" during Halloween, which transforms the park into a haunted experience. Check the park's calendar for details on upcoming events during your visit.

For those looking to extend their visit, Wild Adventures offers onsite camping at the "Wild Adventures RV Park." Located just a short walk from the park entrance, the campground provides full RV hookups and tent sites, making it a convenient option for visitors who want to immerse themselves in the fun for more than just a day.

The park features a variety of dining options to satisfy any appetite, from quick snacks to full meals. Grab a burger or hot dog at "Safari Grill," enjoy pizza at "Dockside Café," or cool down with an ice cream cone from "Coolsville." There are also several picnic areas throughout the park where visitors can bring their own food and enjoy a meal in a relaxing setting.

Tips

- Wear comfortable clothing: You'll be walking a lot, so comfortable shoes are a must. If you're visiting during the summer, be sure to bring sunscreen, a hat, and a swimsuit if you plan to enjoy Splash Island.

- Stay hydrated: Georgia's heat can be intense, especially in the summer months, so drink plenty of water and take breaks in shaded areas.
- Check the event schedule: Be sure to check the park's event schedule online before your visit to make the most of your day. Some of the live shows and special events are can't-miss experiences!

Nearby Attractions

- Grand Bay Wildlife Management Area: Located just 20 minutes from Wild Adventures, the Grand Bay Wildlife Management Area is a vast natural preserve perfect for nature lovers. Visitors can explore the boardwalk through the wetlands, climb the observation tower for panoramic views, and enjoy birdwatching or spotting local wildlife. It's an excellent spot for a peaceful retreat into nature after a day of theme park excitement.

- Valdosta Wake Compound: For water sports enthusiasts, the Valdosta Wake Compound is a must-visit. This wakeboarding park, about 15 minutes from Wild Adventures, offers cable and boat wakeboarding for all skill levels. Whether you're a beginner or an experienced rider, it's a thrilling way to spend time on the water and try something new.

- Georgia Museum of Agriculture and Historic Village: A 40-minute drive north of Wild Adventures in Tifton, the Georgia Museum of Agriculture and Historic Village is a living history museum that transports visitors to the 19th century. You can explore the historic village, ride a steam train, and see demonstrations of traditional farming techniques. It's an educational and fun experience, perfect for families or history buffs.

96 WILD ANIMAL SAFARI

COUNTY: HARRIS **CITY:** PINE MOUNTAIN

DATE VISITED: **WHO I WENT WITH:**

RATING: ☆ ☆ ☆ ☆ ☆   **WILL I RETURN?** YES / NO

1300 Oak Grove Rd
Pine Mountain, GA 31822
706-663-8744

Wild Animal Safari, one of Georgia's most exciting and unique wildlife destinations! Located in Pine Mountain, this interactive drive-through safari park offers a rare chance to get up close and personal with animals from all over the world. Whether you choose to explore the park in your own vehicle or hop on a guided tour, Wild Animal Safari promises a memorable adventure for animal lovers of all ages. With over 75 species and hundreds of animals, it's an experience that combines the thrill of a safari with the fun of a family-friendly outing.

Established in 1991, Wild Animal Safari quickly became a beloved destination for both locals and tourists alike. The park offers a unique combination of a drive-through safari and walk-through exhibits, providing guests with a variety of ways to see animals up close. With its mission of conservation and education, the park not only entertains but also raises awareness about wildlife preservation and the importance of protecting animal habitats.

The main attraction at Wild Animal Safari is the 3.5-mile drive-through safari, where you can observe animals roaming freely in large, naturalistic enclosures. From the safety and comfort of your own car, you'll encounter giraffes, zebras, antelope, and many other fascinating creatures. For an even more immersive experience, the park also offers rental vehicles, known as "zebra vans," designed for the best possible animal viewing.

One of the most exciting aspects of the drive-through safari is the opportunity to feed the animals. Many of the park's residents, like giraffes, camels, and bison, are friendly and will come right up to your vehicle for a snack. Feeding bags are available for purchase at the entrance, so you can interact safely with the animals while keeping them well-fed and happy.

After your drive-through safari, you can continue your adventure in the Walk-About Adventure Zoo. This section of the park allows you to stroll along walking paths to view and interact with more animals in traditional enclosures. Here, you'll find a range of exotic species including lemurs, reptiles, and birds.

The walk-about area also includes special enclosures where you can get even closer to the animals. The petting zoo is a favorite among families, giving kids a chance to meet and feed friendly goats and sheep. Other highlights include the chance to see big cats like lions and tigers, as well as playful monkeys and colorful parrots.

Watch in awe as towering giraffes stretch their long necks to eat from your hand during the drive-through safari. See the majestic power of lions and tigers up close in specially designed habitats, giving you a safe but thrilling view of these incredible predators. From brightly colored macaws to charming peacocks, the Walk-About Adventure Zoo is home to a variety of beautiful birds that add vibrant color to your visit.

For a more educational experience, the park offers guided tours aboard safari buses. These tours are led by knowledgeable guides who share fascinating facts about the animals and their natural habitats. The guides are also experts at spotting animals that may be hiding, ensuring you don't miss any of the park's incredible wildlife.

Throughout the year, Wild Animal Safari offers special animal encounter programs where you can meet and learn about some of the park's most beloved animals. These encounters provide visitors with a chance to ask questions, take photos, and get up close to animals under the supervision of experienced handlers.

The drive-through safari and walk-about areas are filled with excellent photo opportunities. Whether you're snapping selfies with a curious zebra or capturing the regal stance of a lion, be sure to bring your camera to document your adventure. The best time for photos is typically in the early morning or late afternoon when the animals are most active.

Tips

- Bring water and snacks: While there are concessions available, bringing your own water and snacks can keep you refreshed during your safari. Picnic areas are available for a relaxing break.
- Prepare for the weather: Pine Mountain can get hot, especially in summer, so dress comfortably, wear sunscreen, and bring hats or sunglasses. The safari is a car-based activity, but the walk-about area is outdoors, so plan accordingly.
- Best times to visit: Early morning or late afternoon are the best times to visit if you want to see the animals at their most active. Avoid the midday heat for a more enjoyable experience.

Nearby Attractions

- Callaway Gardens: Located just 15 minutes away from Wild Animal Safari, Callaway Gardens is a stunning 2,500-acre resort that offers beautiful gardens, a butterfly conservatory, nature trails, and opportunities for outdoor recreation like biking, fishing, and zip-lining. It's a perfect place to relax and enjoy nature after a day of animal adventures. The gardens also feature seasonal events, including the famous Fantasy in Lights holiday display.

- F.D. Roosevelt State Park: Situated about 20 minutes from Wild Animal Safari, F.D. Roosevelt State Park is the largest state park in Georgia, covering 9,000 acres. Known for its scenic hiking trails, such as the Pine Mountain Trail, the park offers breathtaking views of the surrounding valleys and mountains. Visitors can enjoy activities like fishing, horseback riding, and picnicking, making it an ideal spot for outdoor enthusiasts.

- Little White House Historic Site: Approximately 25 minutes away in Warm Springs, Georgia, the Little White House is a historic site where President Franklin D. Roosevelt spent much of his time. This charming home-turned-museum offers a glimpse into the life of FDR and his time in Georgia, complete with exhibits detailing his presidency and personal life. The site also features the Warm Springs pools, known for their therapeutic mineral waters, which Roosevelt visited for his polio treatment.

97 WOLF MOUNTAIN VINEYARDS & WINERY

COUNTY: LUMPKIN   **CITY:** DAHLONEGA

DATE VISITED: **WHO I WENT WITH:**

RATING: ☆ ☆ ☆ ☆ ☆   **WILL I RETURN?** YES / NO

180 Wolf Mountain Trail
Dahlonega, GA 30533
706-867-9862

Wolf Mountain Vineyards & Winery is a hidden gem nestled in the foothills of the North Georgia Mountains. Known for its award-winning wines, breathtaking views, and elegant atmosphere, Wolf Mountain is a must-visit destination for wine enthusiasts and those seeking a serene, picturesque escape. Located in Dahlonega, Georgia, this family-owned winery offers visitors an unforgettable experience, from wine tastings to gourmet dining and vineyard tours. Whether you're a wine connoisseur or simply looking for a beautiful spot to relax, Wolf Mountain Vineyards has something special to offer.

Established in 1999 by the Boegner family, Wolf Mountain Vineyards quickly gained a reputation for producing exceptional wines and offering a sophisticated, European-style winery experience. The first vines were planted in 2000, and since then, the winery has received numerous awards for its handcrafted, estate-grown wines. With a focus on French-inspired winemaking techniques, the vineyard has become a leader in Georgia's emerging wine scene, blending tradition with innovation.

One of the highlights of visiting Wolf Mountain Vineyards is its breathtaking setting. Perched atop a hillside, the winery boasts panoramic views of the surrounding Blue Ridge Mountains and the rolling vineyards below. Visitors can enjoy these views from the expansive outdoor terrace or the cozy, rustic indoor tasting room, which features large windows and a welcoming fireplace. Whether you're sitting outside on a sunny day or warming up indoors in cooler weather, the beauty of the landscape is always on display.

Wolf Mountain offers a selection of red, white, and sparkling wines, many of which are made from grapes grown on the estate. Varietals include Chardonnay, Mourvèdre, and Touriga Nacional, among others. During a tasting, you'll have the opportunity to sample these expertly crafted wines and learn about the winemaking process, from vineyard to bottle. Knowledgeable staff are on hand to guide you through each tasting and provide insights into the unique characteristics of each wine.

Wolf Mountain is particularly well-known for its méthode champenoise sparkling wines, made in the traditional French style. These elegant, bubbly wines are perfect for special occasions or simply enjoying a relaxing afternoon at the vineyard.

One of the winery's most popular offerings is its gourmet Sunday brunch, served in the Vineyard Café. The brunch features a rotating seasonal menu inspired by regional and European flavors, with dishes crafted from fresh, local ingredients. Pair your meal with one of Wolf Mountain's wines for a truly decadent experience. Reservations are strongly recommended, as this event often sells out.

In addition to the brunch, the Vineyard Café offers a delicious seasonal lunch menu, available on select days. From farm-to-table salads to hearty sandwiches and artisanal cheeses, there's something for everyone to enjoy. Outdoor seating is available, allowing you to dine al fresco while taking in the vineyard views.

For those interested in learning more about the winemaking process, Wolf Mountain offers guided tours of the vineyard and production facilities. These tours provide a fascinating look at how the grapes are grown, harvested, and transformed into wine. You'll visit the vineyard's state-of-the-art winery, where the magic happens, and see firsthand the attention to detail that goes into every bottle. Tours are typically offered on weekends and are a great addition to any visit.

Wolf Mountain Vineyards is a popular venue for weddings, corporate events, and private parties. The stunning natural setting, combined with elegant indoor and outdoor spaces, makes it an ideal location for special occasions. The winery offers a variety of event packages that include catering, wine selections, and personalized service, ensuring that every detail is taken care of for a memorable event.

For those who can't get enough of Wolf Mountain's wines, the winery offers a Wine Club that provides exclusive access to limited-edition releases, discounts on purchases, and invitations to member-only events. Members receive quarterly shipments of the winery's best selections, making it a perfect way to enjoy Wolf Mountain wines year-round, even from afar.

Tips

- Make reservations: If you plan to visit on a weekend or attend the Sunday brunch, reservations are highly recommended. The winery is a popular

destination, and spots fill up quickly, especially during peak seasons.
- Dress comfortably: While the winery offers a sophisticated atmosphere, it's also located in the mountains, so be sure to wear comfortable shoes if you plan to walk around the vineyard or take a tour.
- Plan for weather: Check the forecast before your visit, especially if you're planning to spend time on the outdoor terrace or walking the grounds. Layered clothing is recommended, as temperatures in the mountains can vary throughout the day.

Nearby Attractions

- Dahlonega Gold Museum: Located in the historic town square of Dahlonega, the Gold Museum offers a fascinating glimpse into Georgia's gold rush history. It's a great spot to learn about the area's rich heritage before or after your visit to the vineyard.

- Dahlonega Wine Trail: Dahlonega is the heart of Georgia's wine country, and Wolf Mountain is just one of several excellent wineries in the area. Consider making a day of it by exploring the Dahlonega Wine Trail, which includes stops at other nearby wineries, all offering tastings and tours.

- Amicalola Falls State Park: Just a short drive away, Amicalola Falls is one of Georgia's most beautiful natural attractions. The 729-foot waterfall is the tallest in the Southeast, and the surrounding park offers hiking trails, scenic views, and picnic areas, making it a perfect outdoor destination.

----

98   WORMSLOE HISTORIC SITE

COUNTY: CHATHAM   **CITY:** SAVANNAH

DATE VISITED: **WHO I WENT WITH:**

       RATING: ☆ ☆ ☆ ☆ ☆   **WILL I RETURN?** YES / NO

7601 Skidaway Road
Savannah, GA 31406
912-353-3023

Located just outside Savannah, Wormsloe Historic Site is known for its stunning avenue of live oak trees, rich colonial history, and expansive grounds. This historic site offers visitors a unique opportunity to explore the remnants of Georgia's colonial past while walking through some of the most beautiful landscapes in the South. Whether you're a history enthusiast or simply looking for a peaceful outdoor experience, Wormsloe promises an unforgettable visit.

Established in 1736, Wormsloe was the estate of Noble Jones, one of the first English settlers in Georgia and a prominent figure in the colony's early history. Jones was a carpenter, surveyor, and soldier, and he built a fortified home on the property to defend against Spanish invasions. Today, the site preserves the ruins of his original tabby house, which is the oldest standing structure in Savannah. Wormsloe offers a glimpse into colonial life, providing a fascinating look at Georgia's founding and its early settlers.

One of the most famous features of Wormsloe is its Avenue of Oaks, a breathtaking mile-long driveway lined with over 400 live oak trees draped in Spanish moss. This enchanting tunnel of trees is one of the most photographed locations in Georgia and sets the tone for the historical and natural beauty that awaits inside the site. Visitors can walk or drive through the avenue, which offers a truly magical entrance into Wormsloe.

Noble Jones' Tabby House Ruins: The centerpiece of Wormsloe Historic Site is the remains of the original home built by Noble Jones in the 18th century. Made from tabby, a type of concrete created from oyster shells, the house is one of the few surviving colonial-era structures in the state. You can explore the ruins and learn about how the settlers used the local materials to build their homes and fortifications.

Colonial Life Museum: The site's museum offers informative exhibits about Georgia's early settlers, colonial life, and the role Noble Jones played in the colony's defense and development. You'll find artifacts from the colonial period, including tools, weapons, and household items, providing insight into the daily lives of Wormsloe's early inhabitants.

In addition to its historical attractions, Wormsloe is a haven for nature lovers. The site features several well-marked hiking trails that wind through the property's beautiful maritime forest and salt marshes. The trails vary in length and difficulty, making them accessible for all ages and fitness levels.

Battery Trail: This short trail leads visitors to a scenic overlook of the salt marshes, where you can observe wildlife such as wading birds and crabs. The peaceful surroundings make this a perfect spot for nature photography and quiet contemplation.

Jones' Narrows: This longer trail takes you deeper into the woods, where you'll encounter a variety of native plants and wildlife. The path also passes by several historical markers, giving you the chance to learn more about the land's significance.

Throughout the year, Wormsloe hosts living history demonstrations, where costumed interpreters recreate the daily activities of the 18th-century settlers. These programs include demonstrations of colonial crafts, blacksmithing, and musket firing, giving visitors a hands-on understanding of the challenges and skills required for survival in Georgia's early colonial days. These events are a great way to engage with the history of the site in a dynamic and interactive manner.

Wormsloe offers guided tours led by knowledgeable staff who provide in-depth information about the history of the site, the Jones family, and the significance of the ruins. These tours are a great way to gain a deeper understanding of the colonial era and Georgia's early days.

After exploring the site, visitors can relax and enjoy a meal at one of the designated picnic areas. These spots are scattered throughout the grounds, offering serene views of the surrounding woods and marshlands. It's an ideal way to end your visit, surrounded by nature and history.

With its scenic beauty and historic charm, Wormsloe is a popular spot for photography. Whether capturing the grandeur of the oak-lined avenue, the quiet ruins, or the coastal landscapes, there's no shortage of stunning backdrops for both amateur and professional photographers.

Tips

- Wear comfortable shoes: The site includes walking trails and paths over uneven terrain, so comfortable, sturdy footwear is recommended for exploring.
- Plan for weather: Georgia can be hot and humid, especially in the summer, so be sure to bring water and dress in layers. Rain can also affect trail conditions, so it's a good idea to check the weather forecast before your visit.
- Bring a camera: The oak-lined avenue and scenic trails provide fantastic photo opportunities. Be sure to capture the natural beauty of Wormsloe.

Nearby Attractions

- Skidaway Island State Park: Just a short drive away, this beautiful state park offers hiking trails, birdwatching, and camping. The park's marshland setting is perfect for spotting wildlife and enjoying outdoor activities.

- Isle of Hope Historic District: Located nearby, Isle of Hope is a charming historic neighborhood with picturesque waterfront views, old oak trees, and beautiful antebellum homes. A leisurely drive or walk through this area provides a glimpse into the region's more recent history.

- Savannah's Historic District: Only 20 minutes away, Savannah's Historic District is a must-see. Explore the cobblestone streets, elegant squares, and historic homes of one of America's most beautiful cities. Don't miss popular landmarks like Forsyth Park and River Street.

----

99 YOUR DEKALB FARMERS MARKET

COUNTY: DEKALB   CITY: DECATUR

DATE VISITED: WHO I WENT WITH:

            RATING: ☆ ☆ ☆ ☆ ☆   WILL I RETURN?   YES / NO

3000 East Ponce De Leon Avenue
Decatur, GA 30030
404-377-6400

Your DeKalb Farmers Marketis one of Georgia's most vibrant and diverse markets located in Decatur, just outside of Atlanta. Known for its wide array of fresh produce, international groceries, and specialty items, Your DeKalb Farmers Market is a unique shopping destination for food lovers, chefs, and anyone seeking high-quality ingredients from around the world. Whether you're shopping for fresh seafood, exotic spices, or organic fruits and vegetables, this bustling market offers an unparalleled selection that reflects the diverse communities of the Atlanta area.

Founded in 1977 by Robert Blazer, Your DeKalb Farmers Market started as a small produce stand and has since grown into a 140,000 square-foot international market serving millions of customers each year. The market's philosophy is centered around offering fresh, sustainably sourced foods at affordable prices, all while supporting local farmers and communities. Over the years, it has become a go-to destination for people looking to experience flavors and products from across the globe.

At Your DeKalb Farmers Market, you'll find products from over 180 countries, making it one of the most culturally diverse markets in the Southeast. Whether you're looking for unique ingredients from Asia, Africa, Latin America, or Europe, this market has it all. The variety of products includes fresh fruits and vegetables, meats, seafood, cheeses, baked goods, spices, and much more.

The produce section is a highlight, offering a vast selection of organic and conventional fruits and vegetables. From exotic fruits like dragon fruit and rambutan to locally grown greens and herbs, you'll find fresh, high-quality options for every type of dish.

Your DeKalb Farmers Market is well-known for its extensive seafood and meat departments. The seafood section offers everything from fresh salmon and shrimp to more unique options like octopus and whole fish, all sourced from sustainable fisheries. The meat section features organic and grass-fed options, including beef, lamb, chicken, and even specialty meats like goat and rabbit.

The international section is a treasure trove of spices, sauces, grains, and snacks from around the world. You can find items like curry powders from India, olive oils from Greece, dried mushrooms from Asia, and countless other specialty products that make international cooking easy and accessible.

The market's in-house bakery is a must-visit, offering freshly baked breads, pastries, cakes, and cookies made from scratch daily. You'll find artisanal breads like sourdough and French baguettes, as well as international specialties like Italian focaccia and Middle Eastern flatbreads.

The deli section offers a variety of prepared foods, including soups, salads, and hot dishes that are perfect for a quick lunch or take-home meal. The variety reflects the market's global focus, with dishes ranging from Mediterranean salads to Indian curries and American classics.

One of the standout features of Your DeKalb Farmers Market is its extensive bulk section. Here, you can buy grains, beans, nuts, dried fruits, and spices in bulk, which not only reduces packaging waste but also allows you to purchase just the amount you need. The spice section is particularly impressive, offering hard-to-find international spices at competitive prices. From cumin and coriander to saffron and cardamom, this is a paradise for home cooks and professional chefs alike.

Your DeKalb Farmers Market is an experience in itself, with aisles filled with fresh and exotic goods. Take your time to explore each section, from the vibrant produce displays to the aromatic spice shelves.

While shopping, be on the lookout for samples. The market occasionally offers tastings of their fresh products, including cheeses, baked goods, and deli items. This is a great way to discover new flavors or try before you buy.

Tips

- Bring your own bags: The market does not provide plastic bags, so be sure to bring reusable shopping bags or baskets for your groceries.
- Wear comfortable shoes: The market is large and you'll likely be doing a lot of walking, so comfortable footwear is recommended.
- Shop early: If you're looking for the freshest produce and seafood, try to arrive early in the day. The market is often busiest in the afternoon, especially on

weekends.

- Plan to explore: With such a wide variety of products, take your time to explore the market fully. You may discover new and unique items you hadn't planned to buy.

Nearby Attractions

- Decatur Square: Just a short drive away, Decatur Square is a charming area filled with boutique shops, cafes, and restaurants. It's the perfect place to grab a coffee or relax after a day of shopping at the market.

- Fernbank Museum of Natural History: Located about 10 minutes from the market, Fernbank Museum offers fascinating exhibits on dinosaurs, Georgia's natural history, and cultural artifacts. The museum also features an outdoor adventure area for kids and an IMAX theater.

- Stone Mountain Park: About 20 minutes from the market, Stone Mountain Park offers hiking trails, a scenic mountain climb, and seasonal attractions like the laser show and holiday events. It's a great destination for outdoor enthusiasts looking to enjoy Georgia's natural beauty.

ZOO ATLANTA

100

COUNTY: FULTON   **CITY:** ATLANTA

DATE VISITED: **WHO I WENT WITH:**

RATING: ☆ ☆ ☆ ☆ ☆   **WILL I RETURN?** YES / NO

800 Cherokee Avenue SE
Atlanta GA 30315
404-624-9453

Zoo Atlanta is one of the oldest and most respected zoos in the United States. Nestled in the heart of Atlanta, Georgia, this 40-acre zoo is home to more than 1,000 animals representing over 200 species. Zoo Atlanta is dedicated to conservation, education, and recreation, making it an ideal destination for families, animal lovers, and anyone interested in learning more about the natural world. With its engaging exhibits, interactive experiences, and commitment to wildlife conservation, Zoo Atlanta promises a fun and educational outing for visitors of all ages.

Founded in 1889, Zoo Atlanta has a rich history as one of the first zoos in the Southeast. Originally a small collection of animals, the zoo has grown significantly over the years. Today, it plays a crucial role in wildlife conservation and research, housing endangered species and supporting global conservation efforts. Zoo Atlanta is also known for its innovative exhibits that prioritize animal welfare and naturalistic habitats.

Zoo Atlanta features a diverse array of exhibits that showcase animals from around the globe. Some of the must-see exhibits include:

Gorilla Valley: This impressive habitat allows visitors to observe the majestic western lowland gorillas in a lush, naturalistic environment. The exhibit includes a viewing area where guests can see these incredible animals up close and learn about their behavior and conservation efforts.

African Savanna: Experience the sights and sounds of the African plains in this expansive exhibit, which features African elephants, zebras, ostriches, and more. The immersive environment mimics the savanna landscape, providing a great opportunity for photography and observation.

Tropical Rainforest: Step into the vibrant world of the tropical rainforest, where you'll find species such as orangutans, lemurs, and various reptiles and amphibians. The exhibit highlights the importance of rainforest conservation and the biodiversity of these ecosystems.

Scaly Slimy Spectacular: This exciting exhibit showcases reptiles, amphibians, and other creatures that slither and crawl. With interactive displays and fascinating educational information, visitors will gain a deeper understanding of these often-overlooked animals.

Zoo Atlanta offers numerous interactive experiences that engage visitors and deepen their understanding of wildlife conservation:

Keeper Talks: Throughout the day, zookeepers give informative talks about various animals, their habitats, and conservation efforts. These talks often include live demonstrations and provide a unique opportunity to ask questions.

Animal Encounters: Guests can participate in up-close animal encounters, where they can learn more about specific species and even touch certain animals under the guidance of zookeepers. This hands-on experience is both educational and memorable.

Children's Zoo: Designed especially for younger visitors, the Children's Zoo features a petting area with friendly animals, interactive exhibits, and educational programs that inspire a love for wildlife in children. It's a fantastic spot for families to spend quality time together.

Zoo Atlanta is committed to conservation both locally and globally. The zoo participates in various breeding programs for endangered species and supports numerous conservation initiatives worldwide. Visitors can learn about these efforts through educational signage throughout the zoo and during keeper talks. Additionally, Zoo Atlanta collaborates with organizations to protect wildlife habitats and promote sustainable practices.

The zoo offers several dining options for visitors looking to grab a bite to eat. From casual snack stands to sit-down restaurants, there are plenty of choices to satisfy your hunger. Try the African-themed dishes at the Savannah Grill or enjoy classic zoo fare at the Zoo Café. Outdoor seating is available, allowing you to relax and enjoy your meal amidst the beautiful surroundings.

Don't forget to stop by the zoo's gift shop, where you can find a wide variety of souvenirs, including plush animals, educational books, and eco-friendly products. Purchasing items from the gift shop supports the zoo's conservation programs and initiatives.

Tips

- Arrive early: To make the most of your day, arrive early to avoid crowds and enjoy a quieter experience.
- Bring a camera: With so many amazing animals and exhibits, be sure to capture your memories with photos throughout the zoo.
- Plan your route: The zoo is large, so consider reviewing the map upon arrival to prioritize the exhibits you want to see and plan your route accordingly.
- Stay hydrated: With all the walking and outdoor activities, be sure to bring water or purchase drinks at the zoo to stay hydrated.

Nearby Attractions

- Grant Park: Located adjacent to the zoo, Grant Park is a beautiful urban park with walking trails, playgrounds, and picnic areas. It's a great place to relax and enjoy nature after your visit to the zoo.

- Atlanta Botanical Garden: Just a short drive away, the Atlanta Botanical Garden features stunning plant collections, seasonal displays, and beautiful landscapes. The garden also offers special events and educational programs throughout the year.

- Martin Luther King Jr. National Historical Park: A short distance from the zoo, this historical site honors the legacy of Dr. Martin Luther King Jr. Visitors can explore his childhood home, the Ebenezer Baptist Church, and the King Center, providing a meaningful and educational experience.

PHOTOS   PARK NAME..

PHOTOS   PARK NAME……………………………………………………………………………..

PHOTOS   PARK NAME..

PHOTOS   PARK NAME..

PHOTOS   PARK NAME..

Thank you for buying my book!
I hope you like it.

Your feedback is important to me, and I would greatly appreciate it if you could take a moment to share your thoughts by leaving an online review.

Your review will not only help me improve as an author but also assist other potential readers in making informed decisions.

Warm regards,

Max Kukis Galgan

Write to me if you think I should improve anything in my book:

maxkukisgalgan@gmail.com

ALABAMA STATE PARKS BUCKET LIST	**ARIZONA** STATE PARKS BUCKET LIST	**ARKANSAS** STATE PARKS BUCKET LIST
CALIFORNIA STATE PARKS BUCKET LIST	**COLORADO** STATE PARKS BUCKET LIST	**FLORIDA** STATE PARKS BUCKET LIST
GEORGIA STATE PARKS BUCKET LIST	**IDAHO** STATE PARKS BUCKET LIST	**ILLINOIS** STATE PARKS BUCKET LIST

INDIANA STATE PARKS BUCKET LIST	**IOWA** STATE PARKS BUCKET LIST	**KANSAS** STATE PARKS BUCKET LIST
KENTUCKY STATE PARKS BUCKET LIST	**MAINE** STATE PARKS BUCKET LIST	**MARYLAND** STATE PARKS BUCKET LIST
MICHIGAN STATE PARKS BUCKET LIST	**MINNESOTA** STATE PARKS BUCKET LIST	**MISSOURI** STATE PARKS BUCKET LIST

NEBRASKA STATE PARKS	NEW YORK STATE PARKS	OHIO STATE PARKS
OREGON STATE PARKS	PENNSYLVANIA STATE PARKS	TENNESSEE STATE PARKS
TEXAS STATE PARKS	UTAH STATE PARKS	VIRGINIA STATE PARKS

WASHINGTON
STATE PARKS
BUCKET LIST

WISCONSIN
STATE PARKS
BUCKET LIST

WEST VIRGINIA
STATE PARKS
BUCKET LIST

ARIZONA
BUCKET LIST
100 BEST PLACES TO VISIT

FLORIDA
BUCKET LIST
100 BEST PLACES TO VISIT

MINNESOTA
BUCKET LIST
100 BEST PLACES TO VISIT

TENNESSEE
BUCKET LIST
100 BEST PLACES TO VISIT

TEXAS
BUCKET LIST
100 BEST PLACES TO VISIT

NATIONAL PARKS
BUCKET LIST